Leveraged Finance

The Frank J. Fabozzi Series

Leveraged Finance

*Concepts, Methods, and
Trading of High-Yield Bonds,
Loans, and Derivatives*

STEPHEN J. ANTCZAK
DOUGLAS J. LUCAS
FRANK J. FABOZZI

WILEY

John Wiley & Sons, Inc.

Library of Congress Cataloging-in-Publication Data

Antczak, Stephen J., 1968-
    Leveraged finance : concepts, methods, and trading of high-yield bonds, loans and derivatives / Stephen J. Antczak, Douglas J. Lucas, Frank J. Fabozzi.
    p. cm.—(The Frank J. Fabozzi series)
    Includes index.
    ISBN 978-0-470-50370-6 (cloth)
    1. Financial leverage. 2. Securities. I. Lucas, Douglas J. II. Fabozzi, Frank J. III. Title.
HG4521.A6195 2009
332.63–dc22
                        2009014329

10 9 8 7 6 5 4 3 2 1

Contents

Preface

Over 80% of my portfolio is sitting in T-bills. This cannot continue. I know that the economy is under extreme pressure and the fundamental backdrop is terrible for almost all asset valuations, but I cannot justify holding government securities paying 0% to my investors. They can do that on their own. I do not need an asset that is perfectly safe, what I am looking for is something that offers attractive risk-adjusted return potential. What in your market fits this profile? Leveraged loans? Triple-A CLO tranches? Anything?

—A portfolio manager of a large equity fund, January 2009

This book was written during one of the most trying times in the history of the global financial markets. The financial crisis that began in 2007 has prompted unprecedented volatility in asset valuations and has left many economies across the world in recession. Given such an extreme investment environment, market participants may have to employ nontraditional approaches when making investment decisions in order to maintain an appropriate risk–return profile. We believe that the leveraged finance market can be a very important tool in this regard.

This book will not attempt to predict the future of the financial markets or the ultimate outcome of the financial crisis. Rather, the purpose of this book is to help readers understand the principles of the leveraged finance market. In this book, readers can learn about the tools available in the leveraged finance market, how they are related to assets and investment opportunities in other markets (such as the equity market), and how to apply these concepts in the real world.

As can be seen from the quotation above, many nontraditional leveraged finance investors have questions about the technicals and the opportunities in this market. This book provides both, and can be of assistance to those participants as they come up the learning curve of a new market. This book can also help existing leveraged finance market investors looking for a refresher on the basic principles or as a desk reference for putting ideas into action. This book can also be useful for anyone outside the financial industry looking for an understanding of these dynamic markets.

As this book goes to print, the financial markets remain under extreme pressure. However, we are confident that it will not last forever. Those investors with the knowledge and skill to participate in the leverage finance space stand to benefit from the many opportunities that the current environment is creating. It is our hope that the contents of this book will help investors identify and take advantage of these opportunities.

ACKNOWLEDGMENTS

We would like to thank a number of people within UBS for their contributions to this book, including Jung Lee and Chris Hazelton, analysts who provided critically important analytical work throughout the book. In addition, we would like to thank Sean Dowd, Brendan Dillon, George Bory, Laurie Goodman, Jim Stehli, and Keith Grimaldi for their support. David Kim and George Attokkaran coauthored with us parts of Chapters 7, 8, and 11, Siddharth Mathur coauthored with us Chapters 5 and 6, and Brian Kim, Tommy Leung, David Havens, and Robert Hopper made important contributions to various chapters. The core of Chapter 10 draws from previous writings with Jane Howe Tripp.

Stephen J. Antczak
Douglas J. Lucas
Frank J. Fabozzi

About the Authors

Stephen J. Antczak is an Executive Director within the UBS Fixed Income Research Department, and currently heads the Leveraged Finance Strategy team. He has worked in a strategy capacity for over 14 years across a broad range of markets, including the cash and synthetic government markets, the investment-grade corporate market, and the high-yield bond, loan, and derivative markets. His research is widely followed by both institutional and retail investors, and is often cited by various media outlets and in academic forums. In addition to providing commentary on leverage finance, he has developed proprietary models for identifying and taking advantage of dislocations within and across various asset classes. Mr. Antczak also has extensive experience in portfolio creation, optimization, and hedging. Prior to joining UBS in 2001, Mr. Antczak was a senior strategist at Merrill Lynch, and has also worked at the Bureau of Labor Statistics as an economist. Stephen graduated from the University of Michigan with a B.A. in economics, and an M.B.A. in business economics. He was awarded Chartered Financial Analyst status in 1999.

Douglas J. Lucas is the Group Managing Director and Manager of Ratings Research at Moody's Investor Service since November 2008. Prior to that, he was an Executive Director at UBS and head of CDO Research. His CDO team was ranked #1, #2, and #3 from 2005 through 2008 by Institutional Investor. His prior positions include head of CDO research at JPMorgan, co-CEO of Salomon Swapco, and analyst at Moody's Investors Service. While at Moody's, he authored the rating agency's first default and rating transition studies, quantified the expected loss rating approach, and developed the rating methodologies for collateralized debt obligations and triple-A special purpose derivatives dealers. He is known for doing some of the first quantitative work in default correlation. Mr. Lucas, the coauthor of several books in structured finance, served two terms as Chairman of the Bond Market Association's CDO Research Committee and has a B.A. magna cum laude in Economics from UCLA and an M.B.A. with Honors from the University of Chicago.

Frank J. Fabozzi is Professor in the Practice of Finance and Becton Fellow at the Yale School of Management. Prior to joining the Yale faculty, he was a Visiting Professor of Finance in the Sloan School at MIT. Professor Fabozzi is a Fellow of the International Center for Finance at Yale University and on the Advisory Council for the Department of Operations Research and Financial Engineering at Princeton University. He is the editor of the *Journal of Portfolio Management* and an associate editor of the *Journal of Fixed Income* and *Journal of Structured Finance*. He earned a doctorate in economics from the City University of New York in 1972. In 2002, Professor Fabozzi was inducted into the Fixed Income Analysts Society's Hall of Fame and is the 2007 recipient of the C. Stewart Sheppard Award given by the CFA Institute. He earned the designation of Chartered Financial Analyst and Certified Public Accountant. He has authored and edited numerous books on finance.

1

Introduction

In the credit market, banks, and brokers raise debt capital for corporate entities that need funds for a variety of reasons such as working capital needs, merger and acquisition activities, share buybacks, and capital expenditures. Capital can be raised via various debt instruments, but primarily through bonds and loans.

One segment of the overall credit market, the leveraged finance market, is comprised of market participants (i.e., issuers and investors) with somewhat unique needs. With regard to issuers, these unique needs result from the fact that they have, or desire to have, a proportionally large amount of debt relative to a "normal" corporate capital structure. An issuer in the leveraged finance market is usually considered more risky than a company with a more balanced capital structure and, as a result, has a relatively low credit rating. Issuers in the leveraged finance market are companies that issue debt and have a credit rating below investment-grade (below BBB–/Baa3).

Of course, investors in the leveraged finance market expect that with more risk comes more return potential. Investors range from hedge funds to insurance companies, but the one common thread shared by all leveraged finance investors is that they all have relatively high return objectives. In the past, the assets within the leveraged finance market fell into one of two categories: cash bonds or cash loans. But this has changed. With the introduction of products such as credit default swaps, synthetic indexes, and tranching of the indexes, leveraged finance investors have many tools to work with and assets to consider.

This book attempts to tie the various pieces that comprise the leveraged finance market together. Its 14 chapters are divided into five parts:

Part One: The Cash Market
Part Two: The Structured Market
Part Three: The Synthetic Market
Part Four: How to Trade the Leveraged Finance Market
Part Five: Default Correlation

PART ONE: THE CASH MARKET

Part One addresses the cash markets, which include high-yield bonds (also referred to as speculative-grade or junk bonds), and leveraged loans.

Chapter 2 focuses specifically on the *high-yield bond market*. This market segment has been evolving dramatically, which makes understanding the basics of this space so important. This chapter provides an overview of the high-yield space, details some specific changes in the landscape, such as bond structures and the size and growth of the market. It also addresses topics such as ratings transitions, risk and returns, and recovery prospects in the event of default.

Chapter 3 focuses on the *leveraged loan market*. A leveraged loan is one extended to a speculative-grade borrower (i.e., a borrower rated below investment-grade, or below BBB–/Baa3). When market participants refer to "loans," they generally mean broadly syndicated (to 10 or more bank and nonbank investors) leveraged loans. They also typically mean senior secured loans, which sit at the topmost rank in the borrower's capital structure, and generally, they mean larger loans to larger companies.

Loans are a key part of financing packages by companies rated below investment-grade. Debt capitalization for a typical credit in the leveraged finance space is about 65% to 70% loans and 30% to 35% bonds, although variations can be significant. The investor base in the leveraged loan market has been in flux since the end of 2007, with a number of nontraditional investors looking to get in (e.g., equity funds, distressed investors, private equity) and others trying to trim exposure (e.g., select hedge funds). In Chapter 3, we provide an overview of the loan market, with topics including a description of a typical loan, changes in market dynamics, and a discussion of emerging trading strategies.

PART TWO: THE STRUCTURED MARKETS

Part Two takes a look into the structured market, focusing on one type of collateralized debt obligation—*collateralized loan obligations* (CLOs). *Collateralized loan obligations* (CLOs) have been around for over 20 years and until September 2007 bought two-thirds of all U.S. leveraged loans. A CLO issues debt and equity and uses the money it raises to invest in a portfolio of leveraged loans. It distributes the cash flows from its asset portfolio to the holders of its various liabilities in prescribed ways that take into account the relative seniority of those liabilities.

In Chapter 4, we look at the general CLO market characteristics and their relationship with leveraged loans. A CLO can be well described by focusing on its four important attributes: assets, liabilities, purposes, and credit structures. Like any company, a CLO has assets. With a CLO, these are usually corporate loans. And like any company, a CLO has liabilities. With a CLO, these run the gamut of equity to AAA rated senior debt. Beyond the seniority and subordination of CLO liabilities, CLOs have additional structural credit protections, which fall into the category of either cash flow or market value protections. Finally, every CLO has a purpose that it was created to fulfill, and these fall into the categories of arbitrage or balance sheet. In this chapter, we look in detail at the different types of assets CLOs hold, the different liabilities they issue, the two different credit structures they employ, and, finally, at the two purposes for which CLOs are created.

Chapter 5 runs through collateral overlap among CLOs. If you are an investor in the leveraged finance market and have the feeling that you've seen a CLO's collateral portfolio before, it's because you probably have. CLO portfolios, even from CLOs issued in different years, tend to have a lot of underlying loan borrowers in common. This is in part the result of loan repayments causing CLO managers to continually be in the market buying loans for their CLOs. Also in this chapter, we look at collateral vintage, and find that different vintage CLOs have similar collateral. In this chapter, we first present several measurements related to collateral overlap and single-name concentration. We look at collateral overlap between individual CLOs, between CLO managers, and between CLO vintages. Next, we look at the most common credits across CLOs and across CLO managers. Finally, we look at the relative risks of collateral overlap and single-name concentration.

Chapter 6 addresses the resiliency of CLO returns to defaults and recoveries. With the help of Moody's Wall Street Analytics, we analyze 340 CLOs issued from 2003 to 2007. We tested CLOs in the worst default and recovery environment U.S. leverage loans have experienced since the inception of the market in 1995. On average, every vintage and rating down to Ba2 returns more than LIBOR, even if purchased at par. We also tested CLO debt tranches in a "Great Depression" high-yield bond default and recovery scenario. On average, Aaa, Aa2, and most A2 tranches still return more than LIBOR, even if purchased at par.

We also discuss distressed loan prices, overflowing triple-C buckets and CLO returns. When market participants model CLO returns, they focus primarily on defaults and recoveries. But since the recent dislocation in the credit markets, two other factors demand attention: the size of the CLO's triple-C asset bucket and the price at which the CLO reinvests in new collateral loans. This chapter looks at the separate and joint effects of reinvestment prices and triple-C buckets on different CLO tranches. Then, it goes through each CLO tranche and looks at the joint effects.

PART THREE: THE SYNTHETIC MARKETS

Part Three introduces the relatively young *synthetic markets*, which include *credit default swaps* (CDS), the traded credit indexes, and index tranches. Credit default swaps enable the isolation and transfer of credit risk between two parties. They are bilateral financial contracts which allow credit risk to be isolated from the other risks of an instrument, such as interest rate risk, and passed from one party to another party. Aside from the ability to isolate credit risk, other reasons for the use of credit derivatives include asset replication/diversification, leverage, yield enhancement, hedging needs, and relative value opportunities. Like Part One, we start with the basics.

Chapter 7 discusses credit default swaps. The CDS market has grown tremendously since 1996 in terms of both trading volume and product evolution. The notional amount of outstanding CDS rose from $20 billion in 1996 to over $54 trillion through the first half of 2008. In terms of product evolution, the market has developed from one that was characterized by highly idiosyncratic contracts taking a great deal of time to negotiate into a standardized product traded in a liquid market offering competitive quotations on single-name instruments and indexes of credits. We begin the chapter with a brief introduction to credit default swaps on specific corporate issuers, including how they work, who uses them, and what are they used for.

Also in Chapter 7, we discuss the *credit indexes*. Predefined, single-name CDS contracts are grouped by market segment, specifically the high-yield bond segment (the high-yield index is denoted CDX. HY) and the loan segment (index denoted LCDX). The core buyers and sellers of the indexes have been index arbitrager players, correlation desks, bank portfolios and proprietary trading desks, and credit hedge funds. Increasingly, greater participation by equity and macrohedge funds has been observed. These investors are looking for the following from the indexes: a barometer of market sentiment, a hedging tool, arbitrage and relative value positioning, and capital structure positioning.

Understanding the credit indexes is critical for Chapter 8, which covers *index tranches*. Similar to the proceeding chapters in Part Three, we walk through the basics of the market, and how and why it came into existence.

PART FOUR: HOW TO TRADE THE LEVERAGED FINANCE MARKET

Part Four reviews how investors can trade within the leveraged finance market.

In Chapter 9, we assess return prospects in the high-yield market during economic downtowns. In order to do so, we examine the relationship between economic growth and valuations during the five most recent recessions prior to the current downturn. In particular, we evaluate the performance of each heading into, during, and following the official recessionary period. In addition to looking at the performance at the broad market level, we review the performance at the sector level and across rating categories.

Chapter 10 provides a framework for credit analysis of corporate debt and explains how credit analysis is more than just the traditional analysis of financial ratios. This is particularly true when evaluating high-yield borrowers.

Chapter 11 introduces "the basis," that link between the cash markets (bonds and loans) and the synthetic markets (CDS and indexes). Understanding the basis is important for many reasons. For one, it serves as a simple reference point between the valuations of each market. As such, it can guide an investor as to where to find attractive value when looking to add or reduce exposure to a particular issuer. Also in this chapter, we walk readers through gauging the basis and how to construct basis packages to take advantage of dislocations between the cash and synthetic markets.

Chapter 12 takes a look at how much investors should be paid to take risk. In this chapter, we present four types of risk: single-name credit risk (i.e., compensation for exposure to a particular issuer); curve risk (i.e., compensation for long/short positions on the same issuer's credit curve); basis risk (i.e., compensation for long/short combinations expressed in the cash and synthetic markets, expanding on the topic addressed in Chapter 11); and capital structure risk (i.e., compensation for long/short combinations among different liabilities of the same issuer).

PART FIVE: DEFAULT CORRELATION

Part Five addresses *default correlation*. Default correlation is the phenomenon that the likelihood of one obligor defaulting on its debt is affected by whether or not another obligor has defaulted on its debts. A simple example of this is if one firm is the creditor of another—if Credit A defaults on its obligations to Credit B, we think it is more likely that Credit B will be unable to pay its own obligations.

Chapter 13 covers the basics of default correlation. In this chapter, we provide a not overly mathematical guide to default correlation. We define default correlation and discuss its causes in the context of systematic and unsystematic drivers of default. We use Venn diagrams to picture default probability and default correlation, and provide mathematical formulas for default correlation, joint probability of default, and the calculation of empirical default correlation. We emphasize higher orders of default correlation and the insufficiency of pair-wise default correlation to define default probabilities in a portfolio comprised of more than two credits.

Chapter 14 looks at empirical default correlations using company- and industry-specific issues that could lead to default. In this chapter, we explain the calculation and results of historic default correlation. We show that default correlations among well-diversified portfolios vary by the ratings of the credits and also by the time period over which defaults are examined. We describe two major problems in measuring default correlation and therefore implementing a default correlation solution: (1) There is no way to distinguish changing default probability from default correlation; and (2) the way default correlation is commonly looked at ignores time series correlation of default probability. We discuss the various ways analysts have attempted to incorporate default correlation into their analysis of credit risky portfolios, such as the (in our view) antiquated method of industry and single-name exposure limits, Moody's ad hoc method of assessing the trade-off between industry and single-name diversity in their Diversity Score, the changing-default probability approach of Credit Suisse, and the historical market value approach of KMV. Also in this chapter, we question whether any default correlation modeling is necessary when comparing well-diversified portfolios. Given a certain level of single-name and industry diversity, we doubt that typical portfolios have very different default correlations and we are skeptical of any measurement showing that they do. However, we do see value in creating default probability distributions.

The Cash Market

2

The High-Yield Bond Market

The high-yield bond market is a fairly dynamic asset class that has had an evolving investment universe, with assets such as credit default swaps (CDS), synthetic indexes, and tranches of synthetic indexes—instruments described in later chapters of this book—being added to the mix. The market also has had a changing buy-side, with a trend of greater participation by hedge funds and equity investors and a decline in participation by mutual funds. In terms of the sell-side, the number of market participants is shrinking, in part due to both near-term (credit crunch, bankruptcies, mergers) and longer-term factors (increased transparency). Transparency was added to the market when the National Association of Securities Dealers (NASD) and the U.S. Securities and Exchange Commission (SEC) developed a program in 2002 requiring all members to report their transactions to the Trade Reporting and Compliance Engine (TRACE).

In this chapter, we provide an overview of the high-yield bond market and detail specific changes in the landscape.

THE REASONS COMPANIES ARE CLASSIFIED AS HIGH-YIELD ISSUERS

Why are companies rated double-B or below? There tend to be three reasons, which we detail here.

Original Issuers

"New" companies can have many positive characteristics—wonderful growth prospects, no burdensome legacy costs, and so on. That said, growing corporations can lack the stronger balance sheet and better income statement profile of more established corporations. High-yield debt issued by such credits, referred to as *original-issue high-yield debt*, is often sold with a story projecting future financial strength (for example, "They'll grow into the capital structure!"). And there are also older, established firms with financials that do not quite meet the requirements to be rated investment-grade. Also worth noting is that subordinated debt of investment-grade issuers can often fall into the high-yield universe.

Fallen Angels

Fallen angels are companies that formerly had investment-grade-rated debt, but have since come upon hard times resulting in deteriorating balance sheets, weakening coverage metrics, and so on. Two of the most notable fallen angels are General Motors and Ford Motor Company. From 1975 to 1981, GM was rated triple-A by Standard & Poor's (S&P); Ford was rated double-A by S&P from 1971 to 1980. Figure 2.1 shows that the ratings for both began slipping in the 1980s, and in 2005, Moody's lowered the rating on both automakers

FIGURE 2.1   Rating Progression of Ford and GM since the Mid-1980s

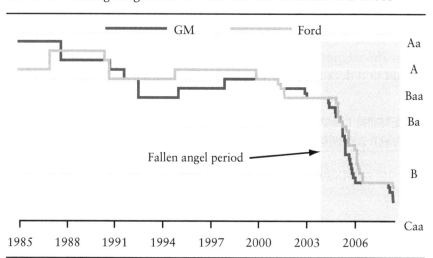

Data for this figure obtained from UBS, Bloomberg, and Moody's.

to high-yield bond status. As of the third quarter of 2008, GM and Ford were rated Caa2/B– and Caa1/B–, respectively.

Some fallen angels recover, such as Electronic Data Systems, which was downgraded by Moody's to Ba1 in July 2004 and then was restored to investment-grade status in March 2008, although most do not. Investors in fallen angels are typically interested in the workout value of the debt in a reorganization or liquidation, whether within or outside the bankruptcy courts.

Names Engaged in Shareholder-Friendly Activity

Companies involved in shareholder-friendly activity deliberately increase their debt burden with a view toward maximizing shareholder value. Specifically, cash is paid out, net worth decreased, leverage increased, but return on equity rises. In Table 2.1, we present the 10 largest leveraged buyout (LBO) deals that were done in recent years.

SIZE AND GROWTH OF THE CASH MARKET

As of September 30, 2008, the total notional amount of speculative grade bonds outstanding stood at about $800 billion. This number

TABLE 2.1 Shareholder-Friendly Activity: 10 Largest LBO Deals since 2006

Date	Target Name	Value of Deal ($m)
6/30/07	BCE Inc	46,836
11/19/06	Equity Office Properties	37,712
7/24/06	HCA Inc	32,147
10/2/06	Kinder Morgan Inc	27,592
11/16/06	Clear Channel Comm	27,490
5/29/06	Harrah's Entertainment	27,389
4/2/07	First Data Corp	27,032
5/20/07	Alltel Corp	26,902
7/3/07	Hilton Hotels Corp	26,702
5/29/07	Archstone-Smith Trust	21,713

Data for this table obtained from UBS.

FIGURE 2.2   High-Yield Bonds Outstanding since 1997

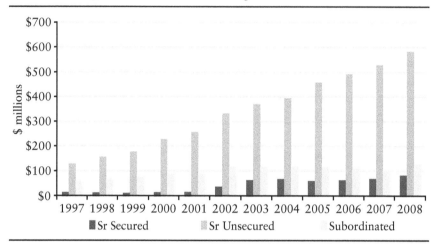

includes floating rate bonds and other nonindex eligible securities.
Figure 2.2 shows the growth since 1997. The high-yield bond market
has expanded an average 17% per year since 1997. The size of both
the *senior-secured* and *unsecured* segments of the market have more
than tripled in size to $86 billion and $586 billion, respectively. *Subordinate* bonds have also grown significantly, almost doubling in size
since 1997 to $129 billion.

The total outstanding amount of "index-eligible" securities stood
at about $550 billion at the end of October 2008, a significantly larger
market compared to only $183 billion outstanding at the beginning of
1997. There is no absolute criteria for index-eligibility, but the index-eligible universe typically includes bonds with more than one year to
maturity, a fixed rate coupon, and a minimum amount outstanding
(for example, $250 million), among other constraints. Most investors care about index-eligible assets, as this is typically the reference
point by which their portfolio performance is measured. In market
value terms, we estimate that the size of the index-eligible high-yield
market is about $360 billion as of October 30, 2008 (average dollar
price of $65 × approximately $550 billion = $358 billion).

TABLE 2.2   Ten Largest Sectors by Par Value as of November 6, 2008

Sector	Percent
Cable/Media	11.8%
Energy	9.7%
Autos	9.6%
Utilities	7.6%
Gaming/Leisure/Lodging	6.2%
Health Care	5.5%
Telecom/Wireless	5.2%
Services	5.2%
Technology	4.4%
Home Builders	3.7%

Data for this table obtained from UBS and *Yield Book*.

Size by Sector and Rating

Table 2.2 shows the size of the high-yield market by sector as of November 6, 2008. According to *Yield Book*[1] and based on par amount outstanding, the largest sector is Cable/Media (11.8%), followed by Energy (9.7%) and Autos (9.6%). In terms of rating, the single-B space has the largest par value ($259 billion, or 48% of the market), followed by double-Bs ($176 billion, 33%), and triple-Cs ($103 billion, 19%).

Interestingly, the relative size of sectors can shift dramatically if we look at the market value rather than the par value, particularly if one is looking at deep cyclicals or defensive sectors (see Table 2.3). For example, the auto sector is a huge part of the market in par terms (9.6%), but in market value terms not quite so large (6.9%). Conversely, noncyclical sectors such as Energy (9.7% by par value, 11.0% by market value) and Health Care (5.5% by par value, 8.1% by market value) are much more dominant in market value terms.

---

[1] The Yield Book Inc. is a company that provides *The Yield Book*®, a fixed income analytics system, which, among other services, provides historical data on corporate bond yields, spreads, prices and returns. Information is available on www.yieldbook.com.

TABLE 2.3 Five Largest Changes Between Market Value and Par Value

Sector	Percent of Market		
	Par	Market	Difference
Health Care	5.5%	8.1%	2.7%
Utilities	7.6%	9.3%	1.7%
Energy	9.7%	11.0%	1.3%
Gaming/Leisure/ Lodging	6.2%	4.8%	−1.4%
Autos	9.6%	6.9%	−2.7%

Note: As of November 6, 2008.
Data for this table obtained from UBS and *Yield Book*.

New Issuance Supply

For corporations with diverse capital structures, access to the debt
capital markets is a key component of their business models, whether
it is to fund existing operations, expand their business, or replace
existing borrowing obligations. In terms of new issuance supply, the
high-yield market fell materially in 2008 from 2006 and 2007 levels.
As of November 2008, total new issuance had amounted to a little
over $64 billion. That compares to $136 billion in total new issuance through November 2007 (see Figure 2.3). This is not to say that
companies' need for new funding had fallen so dramatically from the
2006 and 2007 levels, but that they were not willing to issue new
bonds at levels (spread to Treasury plus concession to comparable
debt trading in the secondary market) required to be absorbed by
the market. Figure 2.3 also shows the extent of negative correlation
between new issue supply and spread levels.

Secondary market spreads, when combined with a commensurate
new issue concession, can offer a respectable proxy for how expensive new issuance can be. In Figure 2.4, we show the historical spread
levels of the High-Yield Corporate Cash Index and the double-B Corporate Cash Index. Also included is the triple-B (lowest level of the
investment-grade rating spectrum) spread level, which shows the dramatic cost of funding for high-yield credits, both absolutely and relative to their investment-grade peers. As of November 28, 2008, the
gap between the High-Yield Corporate Cash Index and the triple-B
Investment Grade Index stood at 1,224 basis points.

FIGURE 2.3 Speculative-Grade Bond Issuance versus Spread from 1998 to November 2008

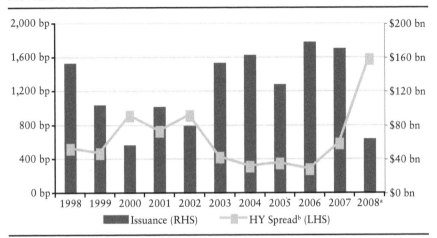

ᵃ As of November 6, 2008.
ᵇ Year-end levels for 1998–2007.
Data for this table obtained from UBS and Dealogic.

FIGURE 2.4 Historical Spread Level of the High-Yield Corporate Cash Index Plotted Against Double- and Triple-B Rated Corporates

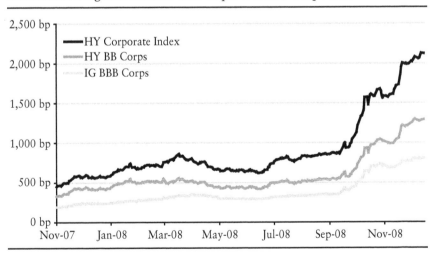

Note: As of November 28, 2008.
Data for this table obtained from UBS and *Yield Book*.

To show how dramatic and quickly the funding environment can change for individual corporates, consider the deals done by gaming and leisure company MGM Mirage in 2008. The company, facing both funding and profitability pressure due to deteriorating credit markets and economic conditions, issued $750 million in bonds (five-year maturity, 13% coupon) that was priced at a spread of 1,225 basis points over Treasuries in November 2008. By comparison, this company issued a similar sized deal (10-year, 7.5% coupon), only eight months earlier at 287 basis points over Treasuries.

Sensitivity of the "Typical" Bond Issuer to Funding Costs

Using data gathered from Bloomberg (including cash on hand, interest expense, earnings before interest, taxes, depreciation, and amortization (EBITDA), debt outstanding, and market cap), we present the key characteristics of 283 high-yield issuers. Data presented below reflects median values rather than averages, and are as of the second quarter of 2008.

Cash:	$96.5 million
Interest expense:	$69.2 million
Last 12 months (LTM) EBITDA:	$321.4 million
Debt outstanding:	$1,144.4 million
Cost of financing:	6% (= $69.2 million/ $1,144.4 million)

Given this information, we examined how vulnerable the typical company's leverage profile can be to operational and financial challenges. In particular, we focus on how sensitive the debt/LTM (last 12 months) EBTDA ratio (earnings before taxes, depreciation, amortization) is to changes in earnings prospects and funding costs. Note that we use EBTDA rather than net income for simplicity.

In Table 2.4, we present a matrix that highlights EBTDA of a typical company given assumed changes in EBITDA and interest expense. For example, if we assume debt costs rise another 10 percentage points (from 19.4% to 30%), the decline in profits for the typical company would only be $7 million. The reason is because a relative modest amount of debt is exposed to higher refinancing costs

TABLE 2.4   EBTDA Given Changes in Cost of Debt and EBITDA ($ mm)

		Cost of Debt in Percentage Points				
		10.0%	15.0%	19.4%	25.0%	30.0%
Percent Change in EBITDA	5%	$264	$261	$258	$254	$251
	0%	$248	$245	$242	$238	$235
	−5%	$232	$229	$226	$222	$219
	−10%	$216	$213	$210	$206	$203
	−15%	$200	$197	$194	$190	$186
	−20%	$184	$181	$178	$174	$170

Note: We do not take into account tax implications of higher interest payments.
Data for this table obtained from UBS and Bloomberg.

in the near term. Declines in EBITDA clearly have a more dramatic impact, at least at the time this book goes to print.

What Is Supply Used For?

Let's look at what companies have used capital raised in the bond market for in recent years. We looked at the use of proceeds of deals issued from 2005 to the third quarter of 2008, and found that they fell within five general categories:

- Merger and acquisitions (M&A) activity
- Shareholder-friendly activities
- General corporate purposes/working cap
- Project finance
- Refinancings

Figures 2.5 and 2.6 show the historical use of bond proceeds by year from 2005 to the third quarter of 2008. Figure 2.5 shows the use in dollar amount while Figure 2.6 shows it as a percentage of annual issuance. As can be seen from these two figures, by and large, proceeds raised in recent years were used for two reasons, shareholder-friendly activities and refinancing. During the period investigated, a total of $164 billion and $165 billion have been raised for shareholder-friendly activities and refinancing, respectively. Compared to the total

FIGURE 2.5 Dollar Amount of Historical Use of Bond Proceeds, 2005–3Q-2008

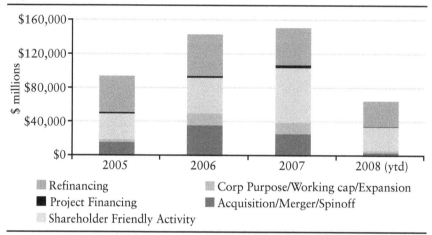

Note: As of November 20, 2008.
Data for this figure obtained from UBS and S&P. Copyright © 2009 Standard & Poor's Financial Services LLC ("S&P"). Reproduction in any form is prohibited without S&P's prior written permission.

FIGURE 2.6 Percentage of Historical Use of Bond Proceeds, 2005–3Q-2008

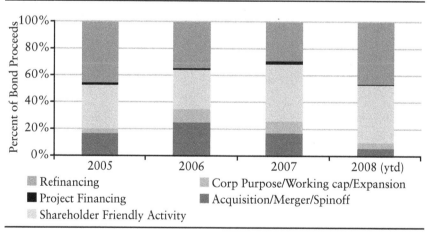

Note: As of November 20, 2008.
Data for this figure obtained from UBS and S&P. Copyright © 2009 Standard & Poor's Financial Services LLC ("S&P"). Reproduction in any form is prohibited without S&P's prior written permission.

capital raised in the high-yield bond market ($452 billion total over the four years investigated), these two purposes together consist of over 70% of the proceeds used. However, the distribution of the use of the proceeds is highly volatile over time, and in large part, influenced by market tone. For example, almost $65 billion was raised for shareholder-friendly purposes in 2007 (the end of the bull market period, beginning of the bear period), but only $28 billion in 2008 (most of which were a result of deals agreed to in the bull period).

TYPES OF STRUCTURES

When the high-yield market began, most issues employed a conventional bond structure. That is, they paid a fixed coupon rate and were term bonds, and the proportion of bonds to loans was more or less "balanced." Bonds issued in recent years, however, have evolved somewhat. In particular, structures have features that are more attractive to issuers. For example, to avoid using cash to make near-term coupon payments, issuers have developed "cash hoarding" coupon structures. These structures include deferred interest bonds, step-up bonds, and payment-in-kind bonds.

Deferred-interest bonds are one type of cash hoarding coupon structure. They sell at a deep discount in the primary market and do not pay interest for an initial period, typically from three to seven years. For example, in June 2008, Intelsat issued a deferred-interest bond due in February 2015. This bond is zero coupon through February 2010, after which the coupon changes to 9.5%, which is good through February 2015, the final maturity date.

Step-up bonds do pay cash coupon interest, but the coupon rate is low for an initial period and then increases ("steps up") to a higher coupon rate. The coupon step up can also be triggered by factors such as a ratings downgrade. The AES bonds maturing on November 14, 2011, provide an example of such a step feature. The coupon for this issue began at 7.625% (its first coupon payment was on November 15, 2002), but by the last coupon date (November 14, 2011) this bond is scheduled to pay a coupon of 8.625%.

Payment-in-kind (PIK) bonds give the issuer an option to pay cash at a coupon payment date or give the bondholder a similar bond (i.e., a bond with the same coupon rate and a par value equal to the amount of the coupon payment that would have been paid). The period during which the issuer can make this choice varies, often from 5 to 10 years. Given how limited access to funding had become in 2008, a number of companies that had issued PIKs decided to pay coupons in kind in order to conserve liquidity. For example, Realogy Corp., the owner of real-estate brokerage businesses Century 21 and Coldwell Banker, facing a deteriorating housing market environment, decided to preserve their cash and to take advantage of the PIK feature in their 11% notes due in April of 2014. The company issued $32 million in debt in place of a cash interest payment in March 2008. According to Bloomberg, there are many other corporates that have issued debt securities with the PIK feature, including First Data, HCA, and Univision.

A LOOK AT RATINGS

A company's credit rating has a number of important functions. From an issuer's perspective, a rating can influence who can invest in its bond. For example, many asset managers have limits on how much triple-C paper they can hold in their portfolios. A credit rating also influences how much interest an issuer has to pay. For example, if triple-Cs trade tight to double-As on average, investors will tend to avoid triple-C exposure in general. From an investor's perspective, ratings can be an important barometer of credit risk.

Below we highlight two key factors with regard to company ratings. Specifically, we address:

- What is the profile of a typical company with a particular rating?
- How is the average company with a particular rating likely to move across the ratings spectrum over time?

What Does a High-Yield Company Look Like?

With regard to the business and financial profile of high-yield companies, in Table 2.5 we present a business–financial risk matrix. First, we define (based on S&P criteria) how risky a company's financial status is. For example, the typical company with an intermediate

TABLE 2.5 Rating Matrix Guide: A Rule of Thumb About How Ratings Are Determined

What do the financial ratios indicate about the risks?

	Financial Risk Profile				
	Minimal	Modest	Intermediate	Aggressive	Highly Leveraged
Cash flow (Funds from operations/Debt)[a]	over 60%	45%–60%	30%–45%	15%–30%	< 15%
Debt leverage (Total debt/Capital)	< 25%	25%–35%	35%–45%	45%–55%	over 55%
Debt/EBITDA	< 1.4x	1.4x–2.0x	2.0x–3.0x	3.0x–4.5x	over 4.5x

Match the financial risk with an issuer's business risk for a rating

	Financial Risk Profile				
	Minimal	Modest	Intermediate	Aggressive	Highly Leveraged
Excellent business risk					BB
Strong business risk					BB–
Satisfactory business risk				BB+	B+
Weak business risk			BB+	BB–	B
Vulnerable business risk	BB	B+	B+	B	B–

[a] Fully adjusted, historically demonstrated, and expected to continue consistently.
Data for this table obtained from UBS and S&P. Copyright © 2009 Standard & Poor's Financial Services LLC ("S&P").
Reproduction in any form is prohibited without S&P's prior written permission.

financial risk profile will tend to have a cash flow ratio[2] of 30% to 45%, leverage ratios[3] in the 35% to 45% range, and debt multiples[4] in the 2x to 3x range. We also present an assessment of business risk (again, based on S&P criteria), which tends to be a bit more qualitative.

When overlying these two elements of risk, we see that companies with more aggressive financial profiles tend to be high-yield, even if business risk is modest. Conversely, companies with weaker business models may still be classified as high-grade issuers if financial policies are conservative.

Note that the rating matrix in Table 2.5 is meant to be used only as a guide, not as a rule, and there will always be exceptions.

Historical Rating Transition Matrix

To see how ratings change over time, the rating agencies publish periodically this information in the form of a table. This table is called a *rating transition table* or *rating migration table*. The table is useful for investors in assessing potential downgrades and upgrades. A rating transition matrix is available for different transition periods.

Table 2.6 presents the average one-year rating migration rates based on data from 1970 to 2007. The first column shows the ratings at the start of the year. In the table, we start with four high-yield ratings and for each column the top row shows the rating at the end of the year. Let's interpret two of the numbers. Look at the cell where the rating at the beginning of the year is single-B and the rating at the end of the year is single-B. This cell represents the percentage of issues rated single-B at the beginning of the year that did not change their rating over the year. That is, there were no downgrades or upgrades. As can be seen, 73.44% of the issues rated single-B at the start of the year were rated single-B at the end of the year. Now look at the cell where the rating at the beginning of the year is single-B and at the end of the year is double-B. This shows the percentage of issues rated single-B at the beginning of the year that were upgraded to double-B by the end of the year. According to the table, this percentage is

---

[2] This ratio is calculated by dividing funds from operation by total debt.
[3] This ratio is calculated by dividing total debt by total capital.
[4] Calculated by dividing total debt by EBITDA.

TABLE 2.6 Average One-Year Letter Rating Migration Rates (monthly rating frequency), 1970–2007

From	Ratings	Aaa	Aa	A	Baa	Ba	B	Caa	Ca-C	Default	WR[a]
	Ba	0.01	0.06	0.38	5.7	75.65	7.74	0.53	0.05	1.1	8.8
	B	0.01	0.04	0.16	0.35	5.57	73.44	4.95	0.64	4.48	10.36
	Caa	0	0.03	0.03	0.19	0.66	10.73	57.24	3.62	14.67	12.82
	Ca-C	0	0	0	0	0.4	2.59	9.44	38.27	29.78	19.53

[a] WR = Withdrawn Rating

Data for this table obtained from UBS and Moody's.

5.57%. One can view this figure as a probability. It is the probability that an issue rated single-B will be upgraded to double-B by the end of the year. The rating transition matrix can be used to assess the probability of an upgrade, downgrade, and no change in rating.

There are three key points to note regarding rating transitions for high-yield bonds:

1. *Down more likely than up.* High-yield companies are more likely to edge down the ratings spectrum than up. For example, double-B issuers are likely to be upgraded 6.1% of the time over one year, but have a 9.4% chance of being downgraded or defaulting (6.1% vs. 10% for single-Bs, 11.6% vs. 18.3% for triple-Cs).
2. *Small moves are fairly balanced.* The migration up or down one rating notch by an issuer is fairly balanced. For example, a single-B has a 5.6% chance of becoming a double-B and a 5% chance of becoming a triple-C over one year.
3. *Tail risk is decidedly negative.* Looking at the triple-C rated issuers, the chance that an issuer moves to default is almost 15%, verse the chance of moving to triple-A or double-A (or even double-B!) is virtually zero.

RISK AND RETURN FOR BONDS

Credit conditions in 2008 resulted in a dramatic widening of bond spreads in the cash market, surpassing the previous cycle highs of over 1,000 basis points at the end of 2002 (see Figure 2.7). Although 12-month trailing default rates for bonds are nowhere near the historical highs (about 15% in the 1930s, according to Moody's), they have exhibited an upward trend as can be seen in Figure 2.7. However, it is not just default rates and spreads that should be used in assessing whether one should investor in high-yield bonds.

There is a good deal of research published on default rates by both rating agencies, academics, and investment banks.[5] From an

---

[5] See, for example, Edward I. Altman, "Measuring Corporate Bond Mortality and Performance," *Journal of Finance* 44 (September 1989): 909–922; Edward I. Altman, "Research Update: Mortality Rates and Losses, Bond Rating Drift," unpublished study prepared for a workshop sponsored by Merrill Lynch Merchant Banking Group, High Yield Sales and Trading,

FIGURE 2.7 Historical Bond Spreads and Default Rates: Correlation of 0.67

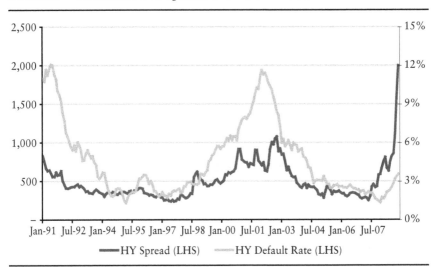

Note: As of November 6, 2008 for spread, September 30, 2008 for default rate.
Data for this figure obtained from UBS, Moody's and *Yield Book*.

1989; Edward I. Altman and Scott A. Nammacher, *Investing in Junk Bonds* (New York: John Wiley & Sons, Inc., 1987); Paul Asquith, David W. Mullins, Jr., and Eric D. Wolff, "Original Issue High Yield Bonds: Aging Analysis of Defaults, Exchanges, and Calls," *Journal of Finance* 44 (September 1989): 923–952; Marshall Blume and Donald Keim, "Risk and Return Characteristics of Lower-Grade Bonds 1977–1987," Working Paper (8-89), Rodney L. White Center for Financial Research, Wharton School, University of Pennsylvania, 1989; Marshall Blume and Donald Keim, "Realized Returns and Defaults on Lower-Grade Bonds," Rodney L. White Center for Financial Research, Wharton School, University of Pennsylvania, 1989; Bond Investors Association, "Bond Investors Association Issues Definitive Corporate Default Statistics," press release, August 15, 1989; Gregory T. Hradsky and Robert D. Long, "High Yield Default Losses and the Return Performance of Bankrupt Debt," *Financial Analysts Journal* (July–August 1989): 38–49; "Historical Default Rates of Corporate Bond Issuers 1970–1988," *Moody's Special Report*, July 1989 (New York: Moody's Investors Service); "High-Yield Bond Default Rates," *Standard & Poor's Creditweek* (August 7, 1989): 21–23; David Wyss, Christopher Probyn, and Robert de Angelis, "The Impact of Recession on High-

investor's perspective, default rates by themselves are not of para-
mount significance; it is perfectly possible for a portfolio of corporate
high-yield bonds to suffer defaults and to outperform Treasuries at
the same time, provided the yield spread of the portfolio is sufficiently high to offset the losses from default. Furthermore, because
holders of defaulted bonds typically recover a percentage of the face
amount of their investment, the default loss rate can be substantially
lower than the default rate. Assuming a bond is trading at par, the
default loss rate is defined as follows:

Default loss rate = Default rate × (100% − Recovery rate)

For instance, a default rate of 5% and a recovery rate of 30% means
a default loss rate of only 3.5% (= 5% × 70%). Therefore, focusing exclusively on default rates merely highlights the worst possible
outcome that a diversified portfolio of corporate bonds would suffer,
assuming all defaulted bonds would be totally worthless. Instead, the
focus in deciding as to whether to invest in high-yield bonds should
be based on return (i.e., the total return) and risk relative to investment objectives and other asset classes.

In Figure 2.8 and Table 2.7, we present the long-term profiles of
various asset classes relative to a high-yield bond portfolio by looking
back to the previous cycle. We use March 1997 through November
2005 as our reference period as it marks the most recent, complete
business cycle, which included the expansion of the economy during
the technology bubble, as well as the subsequent contraction and
recession following its burst. During this time period, the average
high-yield bond market return was about in line with the returns of
the other risk assets, including equities, albeit at a much lower risk
level than the equity market. An investor with a total return target of
10% could employ stocks, but a more efficient way to achieve this
return when taking into account risk appears to be a high-yield bond
portfolio with two to three times leverage.

Yield Bonds," DRI-McGraw-Hill (Washington, D.C.: Alliance for Capital
Access, 1989); and 1984–1989 issues of *High Yield Market Report: Fi-
nancing America's Futures* (New York and Beverly Hills: Drexel Burnham
Lambert, Incorporated).

FIGURE 2.8 Historical Risk and Return Across Asset Classes

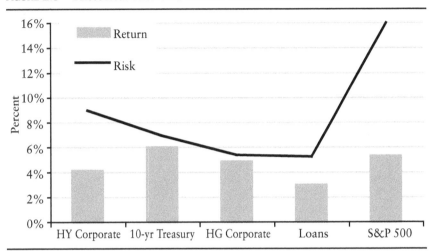

Note: As of October 2008.
Data for this figure obtained from UBS and S&P LCD.

TABLE 2.7 Return Potential of the High-Yield Corporate Market Relative to Other Asset Classes

Asset Class	Leverage	Annual Return	Net Return[a]	Standard Deviation	Sharpe Ratio[b]
HY Corporate	1×	6.46	6.46	7.92	0.38
	2×	12.92	8.96	15.84	0.60
	3×	19.38	11.45	23.75	0.67
10-yr Treasury		6.25		7.40	0.38
IG Corporate		6.84		4.74	0.71
Loans		5.11		1.99	−0.83
S&P 500		8.11		16.20	0.29

[a] Less cost of financing, assumed to be the 10-year average annual return for 3-month Treasury bill rate plus 50 basis points.
[b] Based on net return and standard deviation (of net return).
Data for this table obtained from UBS and S&P LCD. Copyright © 2009 Standard & Poor's Financial Services LLC ("S&P"). Reproduction in any form is prohibited without S&P's prior written permission.

FIGURE 2.9   Total Return by Asset Class in 2008

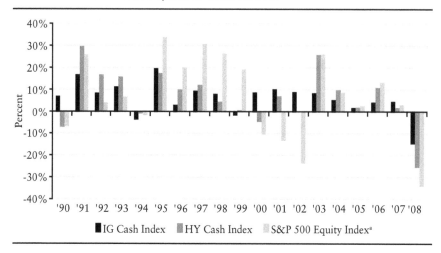

■ IG Cash Index   ■ HY Cash Index   ▨ S&P 500 Equity Index[a]

Note: As of November 17, 2008.
[a] S&P 500 return calculated on year-over-year price basis. 2008 is year-to-date.
Data for this figure obtained from UBS and *Yield Book.*

Not surprisingly, total returns in the high-yield bond sector suffered in 2008 with total returns down 25%. This is obviously abysmal performance in an absolute sense. But aside from Treasuries, all asset classes were under pressure. How did 2008 high-yield performance stack up relative to other assets? As Figure 2.9 shows, as of November 17, 2008, the total return of the high-yield cash market was down 25%, underperformed the investment-grade cash index (down approximately 14%) in 2008, but outperforming the equity market (down approximately 34%). High-yield performed pretty much as expected in a bear market—better than equities, but worse than investment-grade.

To see if this relative performance is consistent over time, we looked at the total return of the investment-grade, high-yield, and equity markets for the 18-year period ending in 2008. We defined bull markets as those years which had positive price returns, and bear markets as years with negative price returns. Here is what we found:

- *Bear market.* We observed eight "bear" years, in which the high-yield market generated an average return of –2.5%. Did high-yield tend to outperform equities and underperform investment-grade during these years? Not really—in only three of the eight observations did performance actually fit this script. For example, in 1999 the high-yield market generated a return of only 0.9% while equities returned almost 20%! The reason is in part because companies were levering up with shareholders benefiting at the expense of bondholders.

- *Bull market.* We observed 10 "bull" years, periods in which one would expect to see high-yield lag equities but outperform the investment-grade market. Once again, actual performance did not fit the script. For example, in 1991 high-yield returned more than 35%, while the S&P 500 was up 26%. The reason is in part because technical pressure unduly weighed on the high-yield market relative to fundamental prospects in prior years, which left high-yield with more room-to-run.

The key point is that when making asset allocation decisions across asset classes, understanding the technical conditions within the various markets is critically important, particularly over fairly short-term investment horizons.

WHAT'S PRICED IN?

All markets have had, to some extent, dislocations between fundamentals and valuations emerge during volatile market times, as demonstrated most clearly in 2008. The leveraged finance market in general has seen some of the most severe distortions. With the cash bond market trading near all-time wide spread levels at press time, what does it imply for default rates?

In this regard, we examined the implied default rate for the high-yield cash market as of October 30, 2008. Our analysis, presented in Table 2.8, shows that the implied default rate is over 21%, a significantly higher rate than the most recent historical peak of about 12% in the early 1990s (see Figure 2.10). We "backed out" how much default risk the market was braced for via an excess spread calculation. We assumed that the nominal spread that investors receive for holding high-yield bonds was compensation for two types of risk, credit risk and other risk (illiquidity, mark-to-market, etc.). The

TABLE 2.8 Calculation of Implied Default Rate in the Cash Bond Market on October 30, 2008

	Cash Bond Spread[a] (bp)	−	Default Rate (%)	×	Loss Given Default (%)	=	Excess Spread (bp)
Where are we now?							
Current	1483		3.43		60		1,277
Long-term average							200
Difference from average							+1,077
What are we braced for?							
Default rate needed to equate excess spread with historical norms							
Current	1483		21.39		60		200
Long-term average							200
Difference from average							+0

[a] Option-adjusted spread over LIBOR.
Data for this table obtained from UBS, Moody's and *Yield Book*.

FIGURE 2.10 Implied Default Rate in the Cash Bond Market, March 1970–September 2008

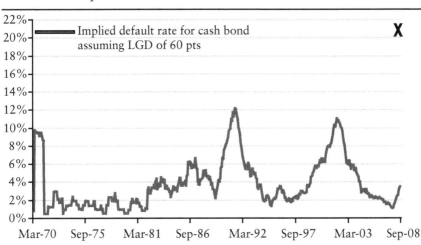

Note: As of October 30, 2008.
Data for this figure obtained from UBS and Moody's.

difference between the market's nominal spread for the market and compensation for credit risk (default rate multiplied by loss in the event of default) can be considered excess spread. Historically, excess spread has averaged about 200 bp, while the excess spread was 1,277 bp as of October 30, 2008. In order to get this level in line with historical norms, the default rate would have to rise to 21.39%. Note that in this calculation we assumed that loss in the event of default is in line with historical levels (60%).

We took our investigation a step further and put together an aggressive scenario analysis looking at the default potential in the high-yield cash market (see Table 2.9). We selected sectors that were thought to be particularly vulnerable to defaults at the end of 2008 (Finance, Home Builders, Retail Stores, Building Products, Publishing, and Autos). The par value outstanding in these sectors was $165.9 billion as of October 24, 2008. Using an assumption that 50% of the par value of these sectors would default in one year ($82.9 billion), and given that the total size of the high-yield cash market was $549.8 billion as of October 2008, the *incremental* impact on the default

TABLE 2.9 Incremental Impact on Default Rates Assuming an Aggressive Scenario

Select Vulnerable Sectors	Par Value ($bn)	Market Value ($bn)	Number of Issuers
Finance	70.3	37.6	27
Home Builders	19.8	13.3	13
Retail Stores	21.5	14.5	32
Auto	31.1	12.0	18
Publishing	17.4	7.3	18
Building Product	5.9	3.9	11
Total	$165.9	$88.6	116

What if 50% of these sectors defaulted?			What if 50% of these issuers defaulted?	
Par amount defaulted ($bn)	$82.9	$44.3	Number of defaults	58
Yield Book HY Index ($bn)	$549.8	$363.8	Total Number of Issuers	524
Impact on Default Rate	+15.1%	+12.2%	Impact on Default Rate	+11.1%

Note: As of October 24, 2008. Finance includes all Ford Motor Credit, GMAC and ResCap bonds. Data for this table obtained from UBS and *Yield Book.*

rate is about 15%. Although high, this scenario seems to be priced in to the spread levels at that time.

One important assumption that this figure takes into account is that all the issues are trading at par. Since nothing is trading at par in the environment analyzed, we reevaluated our scenario using the market value of the issues outstanding. The market value of these sectors totaled $88.6 billion; if we assume 50% default in one year ($44.3 billion), the *incremental* impact on the default rate is about 12%. Once again, although it is high, the market appears to have priced it in.

For those that care about issuer defaults rather than the dollar value of defaults, we counted 116 issuers within these "at risk" sectors as of October 24, 2008. Again, assuming 50% default in one year, the *incremental* impact on the default rate is about 11%.

HOW ABOUT RECOVERIES?

Market participants often assume an average recovery of 40% for bonds and 70% for loans. However, when trying to compare a bond versus a loan for the same company, these averages may not mean all that much. The companies that comprise the average bond market recovery are not the same as those that reflect the average experience in the loan market. Then what does an apples-to-apples comparison show?

We looked at bond and loan recovery experiences for 60 select names with both loans and bonds outstanding which defaulted in the 1985–2006 period. We divided the recoveries into five different buckets for both loans and bonds and counted how many of these 60 names fell into each recovery rate bucket. Note that the recovery rates are based on the average trading prices within 30-days after the default.

Our results are shown in Figures 2.11 and 2.12 for term loans and senior unsecured bonds, respectively. One consistency that we saw in our examination of defaults among companies with both bonds and loans outstanding is the distribution of recoveries around the average. Specifically, both bond and loan distributions were skewed, but loan recoveries exhibited a positive skew, while bond recoveries exhibited a negative skew.

Of the 60 names that we reviewed, 45% had over 80% of par recovered in the loan market. In contrast, 45% of bonds observed had recovery rates of less than 20%.

FIGURE 2.11   Recovery Rates for Term Loans: Defaults, 1986–2006

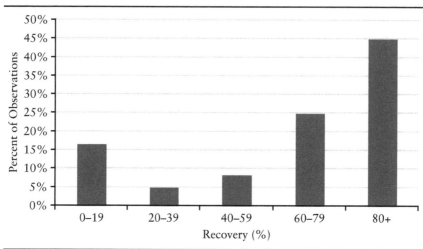

Note: Recovery rates are based on average of 30-days postdefault trading prices. Data for this figure obtained from UBS and Moody's.

FIGURE 2.12   Recovery Rates for Senior Unsecured Bonds: Defaults, 1985–2006

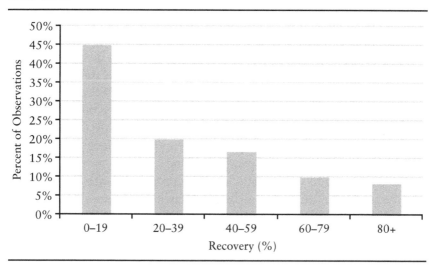

Note: Recovery rates are based on average of 30-days postdefault trading prices.
Data for this figure obtained from UBS and Moody's.

An important take away from this analysis is that when assessing recovery prospects, the distribution around the average may be more important than the average itself.

SUMMARY

The high-yield bond market continues to evolve, which makes understanding the basics of the market so important. This chapter provided an overview of the market and detailed specific changes in the landscape. This included a look at why companies are classified as high-yield in the first place, bond structures, and the size and growth of the market. It also addressed some of the key determinants of value in the market, included ratings transition, risk and returns, and recoveries.

After completing this chapter, investors should be prepared to delve into the next chapters, including the products in the synthetic markets and the indexes.

3

Leveraged Loans

The investor base in the leveraged loan market has been in flux since the end of 2007, with a number of nontraditional investors looking to get in (e.g., equity funds, distressed investors, private equity) and others trying to trim exposure (e.g., select hedge funds). In this chapter, we provide an overview of the loan market, with topics ranging from a description of a typical loan to changes in market dynamics.

A TALE OF TWO LOANS

Lessons sometimes have to be relearned in the financial markets, particularly when new participants enter a market. Consider the loan market—the fact that a senior loan is "secured" does not in itself guarantee the loan's credit quality or profit potential. To illustrate in more detail, consider two loans in the retail space issued by fictitious companies Northern and Southern, respectively. Key considerations for each company are outlined in Table 3.1.

Northern is a retail store chain with a terrific market share in its home base. That ends its good points. The stores and their equipment were old, and they were in bad locations. A larger, well-capitalized store chain had saturated a neighbouring market and was poised to invade Northern's territory.

If anyone knew these facts, they kept quiet about them. Northern's equity buyout firm was simultaneously doing another deal in a different part of the country. It did not, to put it gently, volunteer a lot of negative facts about Northern. The arranger of the loan was looking forward to a very lucrative fee from underwriting a public bond for Northern that was structured to be *pari passu* to the loan.

It later became public that the arranger retained only a few hundred thousand dollars of the loan.

The *coup de grace* of this disaster was that the loan was made to the holding company without any guarantees from the firm's operating subsidiaries. As the holding company had only one asset—common stock in its subsidiaries—lenders at the holding company level were structurally subordinate to the debt holders of those subsidiaries. The only source of funds to pay the holding company level loan was common stock dividends from operating subsidiaries. Those dividends could be paid to the holding company only after the subsidiaries had satisfied their own debt holders.

When Northern's senior secured debt traded down into the mid-teens, a vulture fund swooped in to buy it up. After amassing a large position, they visited the stores. This is the wrong sequence. The bargain they thought they had found turned out to be no such bargain at all. The final distribution to lenders, including the vulture fund, was a nickel on the dollar.

TABLE 3.1   A Comparison of Northern and Southern

	Northern	Southern
Business Backdrop		
Description	Retail store chain	Retail store chain
Strategic plan	Increase leverage	Sell off divisions
Financing Backdrop		
Loan	Senior Secured at HoldCo	Senior Secured at OpCo
Additional debt	Public bond at OpCo	Public bond at OpCo
Key Issues		
Business concerns	Aging PP&E Poor locations Encroaching competition	Other firms engaged in similar strategy to sell off divisions
Financing concerns	HoldCo's only asset was common stock in subsidiaries Arranger held minimal portion of loan	Over-leveraged

Data for this table obtained from UBS.

Several years later, another case showed how market expertise had evolved. Southern was a good retail store chain that was horribly overleveraged. On the day their loan closed, it was obvious to some observers that the chain stood a good chance of heading into trouble. The company's business plan depended on selling off divisions of the company to pay off debt (both bonds and the loan) and provide a liquidating dividend to equity holders. The problem was that at the time the loan was made a number of retailers were already engaged in the same strategy. As more retail chains went on the auction block, bids for these businesses became thinner and shorter.

Yet some of the pessimistic observers who felt the company was shaky still participated in the senior secured loan to Southern. Why? Several predicted that even if the company spiralled into bankruptcy, lenders would still receive principal and interest. In addition, they felt that there were more tools available to protect downside risk; shortly after closing, loan holders purchased CDS (credit default swap) protection.

As Southern sold divisions for prices far below their projections, the company began to fail on specific loan terms. The friendly, happy bankers who took Southern executives on golf outings were replaced by unfriendly, unhappy bankers who approached the workout specialist with a Simon Cowell–like temperament, if not finesse.

Secured lenders took advantage of every breach Southern made in the terms of its loan agreement to extract cash out of the company's operations to pay down loan balances. Bondholders, however, did not have similar protection in their covenants; and bond prices plummeted in secondary trading and CDS spread ballooned.

When the company eventually filed for bankruptcy, less than 40% of the original loan balance was still outstanding. Senior secured lenders received all principal and accrued interest, and to a large extent this recovery came at the expense of unsecured bondholders. As such, the CDS "hedge" was deep in-the-money as well. Thus, good loan structuring and hedging overcame a bad financing plan.

The key point to remember from this story is that investing in the "loan market" has always been credit-intensive, requiring a solid understanding of a company's business fundamentals, corporate management, stability of financing, and the like. That said, successful participation is not just about a deep understanding of credit fundamentals. The structure of a loan and trading/hedging strategies now play a critical role in determining the ultimate profitability of exposure to a particular credit.

INTRODUCTION TO LEVERAGED LOANS

The leveraged finance market was under extreme pressure in 2008. The overall cash loan market dropped more than 15 points from September to November 2008. Bids-wanted-in-competition (BWICs) continually circulated the market, liquidity was limited, bid-ask spreads ballooned, and by many measures volatility, had never been higher.

While traditional investors were hesitant to return to credit markets, nontraditional investors such as equity funds were assessing opportunities, looking to answer questions such as: How can a low-dollar, high-yielding loan benefit my stock portfolio? At current valuations, can my portfolio benefit from collateralized loan obligation (CLO) features such as collateral management, diversification, and historically low correlation with other asset classes? (To help answer the last question, Table 3.2 shows the correlation of cash loan returns with high-yield cash bond returns and the return on various equity indexes.) Moreover, many market participants—both traditional and nontraditional—wonder whether valuations in the loan and CLO markets may have moved a bit too far out of line with fundamentals.

To help investors evaluate these questions, in this section, we provide an in-depth look at the loan market. Specifically, we answer the following questions:

TABLE 3.2 Correlation of Cash Loan Returns with High-Yield Cash Bond, Various Equity Indexes, and the 30-Year Treasury Returns, January 1997–October 2008

	S&P Loan Index
High-Yield Cash Bonds	0.514
S&P 500 Equity Index	0.256
Dow Jones Industrial Equity Index	0.234
Russell 3000 Equity Index	0.279
Russell 2000 Equity Index	0.380
30-Year Treasury	−0.230

Data for this table obtained from Bloomberg and *Yield Book*.

▪ What exactly is a loan?
▪ Who issues loans and who invests in them, and why?
▪ How does the syndication process and secondary market trading work?
▪ How do lenders maintain their senior interest in borrower assets?
▪ What are the trends in loan market size, spreads, and terms, including protective covenants?
▪ What are some of the less conventional trading strategies that have emerged, and how investors can take advantage? (Also discussed in detail in Chapter 12.)

A Look at Issuers

A *syndicated loan* is a single loan with a single set of terms, but multiple lenders, each providing a portion of the funds. A *leveraged loan* is one extended to a speculative-grade borrower (i.e., a borrower rated below investment-grade, or below BBB–/Baa3). When market participants refer to "loans," they generally mean broadly syndicated (to 10 or more bank and nonbank investors) leveraged loans. They also typically mean senior secured loans, which sit at the topmost rank in the borrower's capital structure. And generally, they mean larger loans to larger companies.

Leveraged loans typically have maintenance and incurrence requirements and tests. Simply put, maintenance requirements are regular reviews of various operating performance measures, such as leverage, interest coverage, and so on. A certain corporate action is not required to "trigger" a review of these operating metrics. An incurrence requirement is a point in time review of specific operating metrics relative to pre-determined levels after an issuer has taken a specific action (i.e., triggers the review). Share-repurchases, divestitures, and special dividends are typical incurrence triggers.

Loans are a key part of financing packages by companies rated below investment-grade. A good estimate for the debt capitalization for a typical credit in the leveraged finance space is about 65% to 70% loans and 30% to 35% bonds, although variations can be significant.

Asset rich companies that have heavy capital expenditure (capex) requirements, such as cable companies that almost always have a new technology to invest in and develop, typically will have more than the average amount of bonds. Asset-rich names whose cash needs are driven by maintenance requirements, such as those in the chemical industry, typically rely more on the loan market as a source of funds. Asset-light sectors, such as restaurants, tend to have a heavier-than-average reliance on the bond market.

It is worth noting that the typical balance between bond and loan financing had evolved since 2001, with an increased proportion of bank loans and a lesser proportion of bonds (see Figure 3.1). This is due in part to the types of loans that were issued in the latter part of the period shown in the figure. Figure 3.2 shows that in 2007 more than $120 billion, or 20% of new loan issuance, were second lien or covenant-lite (cov-lite) loans, which many market participants have argued are really bonds disguised as loans. (Covenant-lite loans have incurrence tests but few, if any, maintenance requirements.) The market for second liens has since closed as of this writing, but previous issuance will probably have a downward influence on recoveries looking forward.

In terms of the issuers of loan securities, broadly speaking, corporate borrowers typically raise capital in the loan market for five reasons:

FIGURE 3.1   Issuance in the Leveraged Finance Market: Bond and Loan Supply as a Percentage of Total, 2001–2008

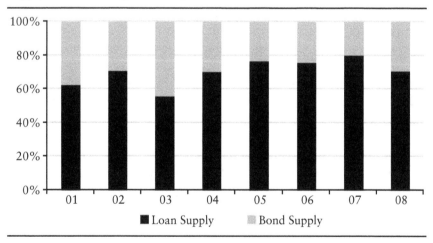

Data for this figure obtained from S&P LCD. Copyright © 2009 Standard & Poor's Financial Services LLC ("S&P"). Reproduction in any form is prohibited without S&P's prior written permission.

1. Refinance existing debt
2. Fund, at least partially, leveraged buyouts
3. Shareholder-friendly activities away from leveraged recapitalizations, such as special dividends
4. Corporate acquisitions
5. Corporate purposes and as a source of working capital

Table 3.3 shows the use of loan proceeds by reason from 1999 to 2008. On average, the two most common uses of loan proceeds over the period have been refinancing (31.9%) and acquisition financing (31.8%), but significant deviations from these averages are commonplace. For example, use of proceeds for leveraged buyouts (LBOs) has averaged 21.7% since 1999, but was the most common use of capital raised in the loan market in 2007 (37% of total). With regard to the concentration of loan issuers across industries, Figure 3.4 shows leveraged loans by the borrower's industry. There is clearly broad diversification across sectors, with healthcare having the largest percentage (about 10% of total). Most industries account for 3% to 7% of total loans.

FIGURE 3.2 Issuance of Second Lien and Cov-Lite Loans, in Absolute Dollar Terms and as a Percent of Total, 1997–2008

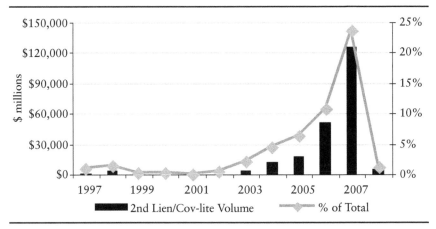

Note: As of October 8, 2008.
Data for this figure obtained from S&P LCD. Copyright © 2009 Standard & Poor's Financial Services LLC ("S&P"). Reproduction in any form is prohibited without S&P's prior written permission.

TABLE 3.3 Historical Use of Loan Proceeds, 1999–2008 ($ millions)

Year	Leveraged Buyout	Dividend/ Stock Repurchase	Refinance Existing Debt	Acquisition Financing	General Corporate Purposes/Working Capital	Total
1999	24,717	7,903	46,397	127,240	24,423	230,680
2000	21,094	4,082	58,807	70,582	25,225	179,790
2001	10,229	1,679	63,966	38,433	12,091	126,398
2002	11,128	3,345	81,257	36,688	7,777	140,195
2003	20,193	11,024	86,172	35,810	5,065	158,264
2004	47,564	28,922	114,691	67,404	9,403	267,984
2005	64,594	35,183	96,875	77,276	10,161	284,089
2006	122,046	48,809	104,893	165,471	39,574	480,793
2007	201,213	52,936	116,029	147,295	26,466	543,939
2008	69,107	3,174	30,621	85,309	10,666	198,877
Total	591,885	197,057	799,708	851,508	170,851	2,611,009

Data for this table obtained from S&P LCD. Copyright © 2009 Standard & Poor's Financial Services LLC ("S&P"). Reproduction in any form is prohibited without S&P's prior written permission.

FIGURE 3.4 Percentage of Syndicated Leveraged Loans by Industry

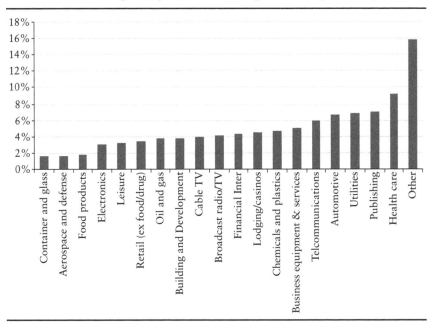

Note: As of October 3, 2008.
Data for this figure obtained from S&P LCD. Copyright © 2009 Standard & Poor's Financial Services LLC ("S&P"). Reproduction in any form is prohibited without S&P's prior written permission.

The Syndication Process

Syndication of loans first came to prominence in the 1970s, when governments of many developing countries, particularly from Latin America and Eastern Europe, took out large loans from Western banks, which were flush with petrodollar deposits. That period came to an end with a string of defaults in the 1980s. Companies and investors involved in M&A and LBO deals then became the most prominent borrowers, but that trend was dampened in the late 1980s by a number of events: the defaults of Federated and Ames, the collapse of the UAL loan syndicate, the stock market crash of 1987, and tighter Federal Reserve guidelines on banks holding highly leveraged transactions. But the syndication market rebounded strongly in the mid-1990s, led by general corporate borrowing and revived M&A activity.

Leveraged loans have been syndicated and sold to nonbank institutional investors since the late 1980s, but institutional investors only became a significant factor in the market beginning in 1995. Figure 3.5 shows the split of loans retained by banks (known as pro rata loans) versus those purchased by institutional investors since 1998.

Over time, the proportion of syndicated leveraged loans sold to institutional investors grew to the point where institutions purchased over 70% of loans in 2007. It fell to 50% in 2008 in the wake of the credit crunch, but the growing role of institutional investors in the loan market over time is the direct result of the high capital cost to banks of holding loans (banks often prefer to sell these loan assets in order to free up capital and clear their balance sheets). In addition, end investors are more efficient holders of loan assets, especially B-rated loans, and institutional purchases of loans are part of the general trend of commercial bank disintermediation.

Syndication allows a borrower to negotiate loan terms once, yet access multiple lenders. The process prevents conflicts in priority from arising, as would happen if a borrower serially negotiated loans. All lenders share equally in rights under the resulting credit agreement. The credit agreement is structured and the pricing process is managed by an arranger, typically a commercial or investment bank.

FIGURE 3.5   Syndicated Leveraged Loan Issuance, 1998–September 25, 2008

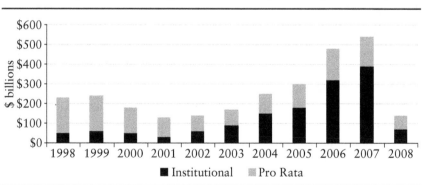

Data for this figure obtained from S&P LCD. Copyright © 2009 Standard & Poor's Financial Services LLC ("S&P"). Reproduction in any form is prohibited without S&P's prior written permission.

The loan market's ups and downs have fostered innovation in the design of syndicated loans. For example, loans may be *underwritten* or done on a *best-effort basis*. In the former, the arrangers guarantee that the entire loan will be placed, and must take onto their books (and thus fund) any portion that is not subscribed for by other banks or investors. In a best-effort deal, should the loan fail to be fully subscribed, the pricing or the size may be adjusted. In the wake of the 2008 market turbulence, most issues are likely to be done on a best-efforts basis until the market returns to a more operating structure.

A similar technique is the use of *market flex language*, which became more common after the turmoil of the Russian debt crisis of 1998. With market flex, borrowers typically give arrangers the flexibility to adjust loan terms and loan pricing to ensure that the loan would be fully subscribed, usually with an upper limit on what the borrower will accept. Typically, that means increasing the loan's spread above its reference benchmark. A *reverse market flex* tightens the spread in response to oversubscription or other market conditions.

Prospective borrowers interview potential arrangers as to their syndication strategy, loan terms, and their views on loan pricing. Once chosen, the arranger prepares an information memo or bank book containing information on the borrower, the borrower's industry, loan terms, and the borrower's financial projections. This document is confidential and made available to qualified banks and accredited investors only. It places readers of the document in the position of having private information about the company, bringing them "over the wall," the metaphorical dividing line between public and private information.

In fact, once a bank or institutional investor reads the bank book, it is forbidden from purchasing the borrower's public securities, such as common stock and bonds, until the information is stale or made public. Sometimes the bank book is stripped of financial projections and other private material for institutional investors that buy public securities and do not want to be restricted in their activities.

When a loan closes, its final terms are documented in a credit agreement and a security agreement. Afterward, liens that embody lender's rights to the borrower's collateral are perfected, with Uniform Commercial Code (UCC) registrations filed in relevant jurisdictions. However, credit agreements are often amended in ways ranging from the waiver of a specific covenant to complex changes in "RATS" (rate, amortization, term, and security). Minor changes require a simple majority vote to pass while RATS-level issues require 100% concurrence.

Loan Structure and Investors

We have spoken so far as if the borrower is taking out a single loan. Usually, the credit agreement includes a revolving line of credit (RC) and one or more term loans with increasing maturities: term loan A (TLA), term loan B (TLB), and so on. Sometimes the revolving line of credit can be drawn upon and converted into a term loan. Another classification of loans under the credit agreement is pro rata loans versus institutional loans. *Pro rata loans* are distributed to banks, and usually consist of the revolving line of credit and term loans maturing in three to five years. *Institutional loans* are distributed to nonbank institutional investors and usually include term loans maturing in five to seven years. Pro rata loans usually have significant amortization before maturity while institutional loans usually have a token 1% per year pay down before otherwise bullet maturities.

Major institutional investors include CLOs, hedge funds, and prime funds, although in the wake of volatility in 2008 the buyer base has evolved. Table 3.4 shows institutional loan purchases in 2007 and in the first three quarters of 2008. As can be seen in the table, in 2007 CLOs bought 57% of institutional loans, hedge funds, high-yield bond funds, and distressed debt funds accounted for 26% of institutional purchases, with prime funds, originally named when loans were commonly benchmarked to the prime rate rather than to the London Offered Bank Rate (LIBOR), buying 8% of the loans.[1] Finance companies and insurance companies accounted for 3% and 4% of total supply, respectively, with banks taking the remaining 2%. In the first three quarters of 2008, the percentage of purchases shifted, especially given the relative dormancy of CLOs, which accounted for only 38% of the purchases. The percentage of purchases made by prime rate funds and insurance funds also fell in the first three quarters of 2008 while hedge funds, high-yield bond funds, distressed debt funds, finance funds and banks all increased their percentage of purchases.

---

[1] LIBOR superseded the prime rate as the preferred reference rate in the 1990s as LIBOR was viewed as being more transparent and market-sensitive than prime.

TABLE 3.4 Institutional Loan Purchases in the Primary Market

Institution	Full Year 2007	First Quarter to Third Quarter 2008
CLOs	57%	38%
Hedge, distressed & HY funds	26%	29%
Prime rate funds	8%	5%
Insurance companies	4%	3%
Finance companies	3%	6%
Banks	2%	19%

Data for this table obtained from S&P LCD. Copyright © 2009 Standard & Poor's Financial Services LLC ("S&P"). Reproduction in any form is prohibited without S&P's prior written permission.

The Secondary Market

Banks, of course, have long sold portions of their loan portfolios, often in response to regulations regarding concentration of credit risk. But interest in the trading of syndicated loans has grown dramatically. Secondary trading volume grew from $50 billion in the first quarter of 2005 to $142 billion in second quarter 2008, as calculated by the Loan Syndications and Trading Association (LSTA).

One of the factors behind the rising interest in the secondary market for loans was the increasing amount of available information. Since loans are private contracts between lenders and borrowers, very little public information used to be available. That has changed since 1987. In that year, Loan Pricing Corporation (LPC) launched its flagship *Gold Sheets* weekly publication covering the loan market.[2]

In 1995, market participants, including banks, brokers, and investors, created the nonprofit LSTA. The LSTA has helped foster the development of a more liquid and transparent secondary market for bank loans by establishing market practices and settlement and operational procedures. The LSTA collects quotes on 2,500 U.S. loans on a daily basis. Table 3.5, taken from the LSTA website, shows the quotes for 25 syndicated bank loans that experienced the greatest price volatility for the week ending Friday, November 21, 2008.

---

[2] Available at the Loan Syndications and Trading Association web site, www.lsta.org.

TABLE 3.5 Biggest Movers during the Week Ending November 21, 2008

Name	Loan Rating Moody's/S&P	Coupon	Maturity	Average bid (pct. pts.)	Weekly change (pct. pts.)	Facility Size ($mm)
ADESA Inc.	Ba3/B+	L+225	21-Oct-13	61.33	-5.25	1490
Aleris International Inc.	Caa1/B	L+237.5	15-Dec-13	57.86	-5.81	1225
Avis Budget Car Rental LLC	Ba1/BB	L+125	1-Apr-12	38.71	-10.43	875
Burlington Coat Factory Warehouse Corp.	B2/CCC+	L+225	28-May-13	46.17	-6.67	900
Charter Communications	B1/B+	L+200	6-Mar-14	68.30	-5.40	6500
Community Health	Ba3/BB	+	1-May-14	75.56	-5.33	5700
Dex Media West	Ba2/BB	L+400	22-Oct-14	51.40	-6.40	950
Ford Motor	N.R./N.R.	L+300	15-Dec-13	34.40	-11.40	7000
General Motors Corp.	B1/B	L+275	27-Nov-13	35.33	-10.52	1500
Georgia Pacific Corp.	Ba2/BB+	L+175	22-Dec-12	78.39	-6.39	5250
HCA Inc.	Ba3/BB	L+225	6-Nov-13	74.82	-6.49	8800
Idearc	B2/B	L+200	17-Nov-14	34.64	-8.69	4750
Lear Corp.	N.R./N.R.	L+250	29-Mar-12	56.57	-7.54	1000
Masonite International	Caa3/CC	L+200	6-Apr-13	63.75	-6.57	1175
Michaels Stores Inc.	B2/B	L+225	31-Oct-13	53.90	-5.20	2344
Neiman Marcus Group Inc.	Ba3/BB+	L+175	6-Apr-13	65.14	-7.70	1900
OSI Restaurant Partners, Inc.	B3/B+	L+225	9-May-14	45.40	-6.85	1080
Swift Transportation Co Inc.	B1/B+	L+275	15-Mar-14	48.79	-6.50	1690

TABLE 3.5 (Continued)

Name	Loan Rating Moody's /S&P	Coupon	Maturity	Average bid (pct. pts.)	Weekly change (pct. pts.)	Facility Size ($mm)
Toys 'R' Us	B2/BB	L+425	19-Jul-12	64.69	–5.09	804
Travelport Inc	Ba2/BB	L+225	23-Aug-13	50.71	–7.50	1410
Tribune Co	Caa1/ CCC	L+300	17-May-14	28.90	–10.10	5515
Tropicana Opco	WR/N.R.	L+250	3-Jan-12	32.30	–7.70	1530
Venetian Macau US Finance Co LLC	B2/B	L+225	25-May-13	59.45	–5.85	100
Western Refining	B3/BB	L+175	31-May-14	67.67	–5.13	1125
Young Broadcasting	B2/B	L+225	3-Nov-12	55.30	–7.83	300
Total loans with at least one bid:	4913					
Average change in bids:	Change .01 percentage points					
Decliners	1248					
Advancers	111					
Unchanged	3554					

Note: These are the averages of indicative bid prices provided by bank loan traders and expressed as a percentage of the par, or face, value. Coupon, or interest rate, is in 1/100s of a percentage point over LIBOR, the benchmark London Interbank Offered Rate. All ratings are for specific loans and not for the company itself except as noted with an (a). These prices do not represent actual trades nor are they offers to trade; rather they are estimated values provided by dealers. Data for this table obtained from LSTA/Thomson Reuters Mark-to-Market Pricing.

LPC and LSTA also began gathering mark-to-market pricing data in the mid-1990s, and LSTA joined with S&P to create a secondary market index. S&P Leverage Commentary and Data (S&P LCD) was formed in 1996 and began publishing voluminous data on the market. LoanX (now part of Markit Partners) began offering loan pricing in 1999.

As in the primary market, institutions (including CLOs, insurers, and hedge funds) have come to play an increasingly important role. While many participants are simply adjusting their loan portfolios, others are clearly looking to take advantage of price movements and discrepancies, just as in other financial markets.

Historical secondary spreads, shown in Figure 3.7, put the 2008 downturn into perspective. Double- and single-B loan spreads have moved beyond their all-time wide levels set in March 2008 following the collapse of Bear Stearns. The average for all BB and B rated issuers stood at 761 basis points at of the end of September 2008, roughly 240 basis points wider than in the previous cyclical downturn (523 basis points).

Loans in the secondary market change hands either by assignment or by participation. With *assignment*, the buyer becomes the lender of record with all related rights and powers. However, the consent

FIGURE 3.7 Average Secondary Loan Spreads, January 1998–September 2008

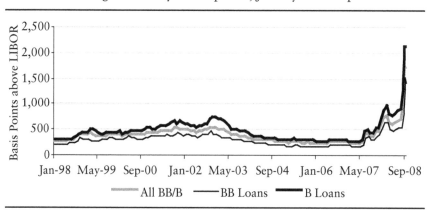

Data for this figure obtained from S&P LCD. Copyright © 2009 Standard & Poor's Financial Services LLC ("S&P"). Reproduction in any form is prohibited without S&P's prior written permission.

of the borrower is usually required. With *participation*, the buyer receives the right to repayment, but the original lender remains the lender of record and is responsible for collecting amounts from the borrower and forwarding them on to the participant. In this case, the borrower's consent is usually not required, but the buyer shoulders a greater credit risk because participation does not create a contractual link between the participant and the borrower. So the participant may be left with no recourse should the original lender become insolvent. As a consequence, CLOs buy loans via assignment.

To compare the balance of risk and reward relative to other asset classes, in Figure 3.8 we present the profiles of various asset classes. Note that the average loan market return is lower than alternative markets, but risk (as measured by standard deviation in "normal" market conditions) is also lower. As a result, with modest leverage, investors have achieved returns nearly equal to those available in other markets, but with less risk. It is important to note though, that leverage may be very difficult to come by in the wake of the 2008 credit crunch.

FIGURE 3.8 Risk-Reward Profiles of Various Asset Classes Relative to a Loan Portfolio, January 1997 to October 2008

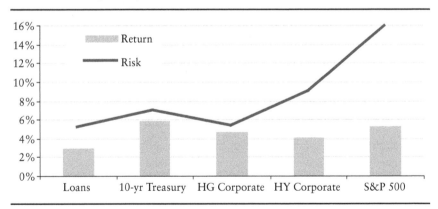

Note:
HG Corporate = High-grade corporate.
HY Corporate = High-yield corporate.
Data for this figure obtained from S&P LCD. Copyright © 2009 Standard & Poor's Financial Services LLC ("S&P"). Reproduction in any form is prohibited without S&P's prior written permission.

TABLE 3.6 Risk-Reward of Leveraged Loan Market Exposure Relative to Other Asset Classes

Asset Class	Leverage	Annual Return	Net Return[a]	Standard Deviation	Sharpe Ratio[b]
Loans	1×	5.11	5.11	1.99	0.83
	2×	10.21	6.25	3.97	1.70
	3×	15.32	7.39	5.96	1.99
10-yr Treasury		6.25		7.40	0.38
HG Corporate		6.84		4.74	0.71
HY Corporate		6.46		7.92	0.38
S&P 500		8.11		16.20	0.29

[a] Less cost of financing, assumed to be 10-year average annual return for three-month T-bill plus 50 bp.
[b] Based on net return and standard deviation (of net return).
Data for this table obtained from S&P LCD. Copyright © 2009 Standard & Poor's Financial Services LLC ("S&P"). Reproduction in any form is prohibited without S&P's prior written permission.

Table 3.6 contrasts the risk-reward profile of a loan portfolio with different levels of leverage compared to other assets (10-year Treasury, high-grade corporate bonds, high-yield corporate bonds, and the S&P 500). As the table shows, a loan portfolio leveraged 3× over this period returned about 7.4%, higher than most other risk assets. The Sharpe ratio was significantly higher as well.

AN OVERVIEW OF LOAN TERMS

Loan terms are embodied in loan credit agreements in three forms:[3]

---

[3] It is interesting to note that when Fitch compared loan agreements and bond indentures for speculative-grade credits, it counted 20 covenants for the former versus six for the latter. Fitch also found that debt limitations in bond indentures were usually subject to an incurrence test based on leverage or interest coverage tests. The loose definition of bond covenants made them ineffectual, in the rating agency's opinion. Restrictions on payments in bond indentures did not always include loans, advances, and investments. Bond debtors were also allowed to merge with few requirements or restrictions. Fitch's overall conclusion regarding bond indentures was that "the scope

- The borrower's representations and warranties
- Affirmative covenants
- Negative covenants

In this section, we ignore the specific form of loan terms and organize our discussion with respect to the underlying purpose of those terms. We divide loan terms into the following purposes, which we will discuss in detail:

- Preservation of collateral
- Appropriation of excess cash flow
- Control of business risk
- Performance requirements
- Reporting requirements

Moreover, in our discussion of loan terms, we continue to focus on loans to speculative-grade credits. For these loans, compliance with terms is typically tested on an ongoing basis. In contrast, for loans to investment-grade borrowers, compliance is often tested only upon the incurrence of some event, such as an acquisition or the issuance of additional debt. Furthermore, loans to speculative credits are almost always senior secured while loans to investment-grade credits are usually unsecured. Tight, perpetually tested loan terms and secured interest in collateral work to keep speculative-grade borrowers on a short leash.

Borrowers commonly breach loan terms, especially performance requirements such as interest coverage ratios. Borrowers also commonly ask permission to breach a loan term, such as for the sale of an asset. Both situations provide lenders with the opportunity to demand further concessions from the borrower.

In return for a waiver of a loan term and for not calling the loan immediately due and payable, lenders might, for example, discontinue advances under the revolving line of credit, curtail capital expenditures, increase mandatory amortization schedules, or increase the loan's spread. Banks usually renegotiate loan terms with borrowers

---

of the restrictions and the level of compliance required of the borrower are generally loose and add little value in protecting bondholders." See Mariarosa Verde, *Loan Preserver: The Value of Covenants*, Fitch, March 4, 1999.

long before bankruptcy or even severe impairment. This gives them the opportunity to speed up loan amortization or gain further control over the borrower's assets before bankruptcy occurs. Figure 3.9 shows concessions for the first three quarters of 2008. As can be seen, concessions were rising over this period.

Purposes of Typical Loan Terms

As noted above, there are five purposes for loan terms. We explain each in this section.

Preservation of Collateral

The borrower represents that lenders have a legal, valid, and enforceable security interest in the assets the borrower has pledged to secure the loan. Generally, this means all the assets of the firm, even assets acquired after the loan is closed, but sometimes a loan is only backed by specific assets. While investment-grade companies can get away with springing liens, which create security interests if the borrower is downgraded below investment-grade, speculative-grade borrowers typically pledge collateral as a precondition to receiving a loan.

Obviously, the value and liquidity of collateral are major factors in determining the credit quality of a loan. A large amount of liquid assets is better than a small amount of specialized assets that have little use to any party other than the borrower. Assets that fluctuate greatly in value are obviously less attractive. As a general rule, 50% of inventory and 80% of receivables can be readily financed while the loan value of plant, property, and equipment varies. Generally, senior secured loans make up half of a borrower's total liabilities and equity.

To maintain the lender's interest in the collateral, the borrower is forbidden from pledging collateral to other creditors. The borrower must also pay its taxes to prevent government authorities from gaining a superseding claim on pledged collateral. To protect the value of collateral, the borrower pledges to perform proper maintenance. And the borrower also pledges to insure collateral.

FIGURE 3.9 Average Covenant Relief: First Three Quarter of 2008

(A) Amendment fee

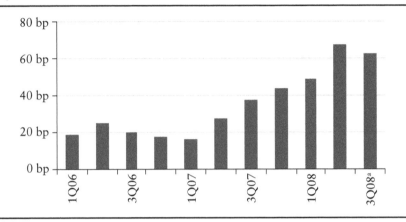

(B) Spread increase

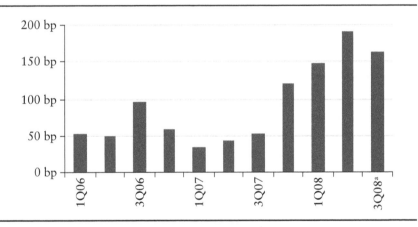

[a] As of September 25, 2008.
Data for these figures obtained from S&P LCD. Copyright © 2009 Standard & Poor's Financial Services LLC ("S&P"). Reproduction in any form is prohibited without S&P's prior written permission.

Appropriation of Excess Cash Flow

Unfettered, a borrower could take out a loan, sell its assets, dividend the proceeds of both the loan and the asset sale to equity holders, and leave lenders with an empty corporate shell. But borrowers are quite fettered. In fact, excess cash flow from the borrower's ordinary and extraordinary business activities must be used to prepay its loans.

"Excess cash flow" is typically defined as cash flow minus cash expenses, required dividends, debt repayments, capital expenditures, and changes in working capital. Typically, 50% to 75% of this must be used to prepay loans. Similarly, 50% to 100% of proceeds from new equity issuance, 100% of proceeds from new debt issuance, and 100% of asset sales (not already prohibited, as mentioned above) must be used to prepay loans. An acceptable level of annual capital expenditure is usually set out in the credit agreement.

In practice, troubled borrowers often approach lenders for permission to realize some proceeds from the sale of assets. Depending upon the borrower's circumstances, lenders generally agree, so long as the majority of proceeds from the asset sale are used to prepay loans.

Control of Business Risk

Lenders are obviously disadvantaged when a borrower's business becomes more risky. Less obvious, perhaps, is that the borrower's equity holders might gain an advantage if the borrower's business becomes more risky. An extreme example illustrates the differing incentives.

Suppose a company has declined in value to the point that its market value equals the par value of its bank loan. Lenders would like the borrower to offer itself up for sale and pay off the loan. In this case, the borrower's equity holders are assured of receiving zero residual value. Equity holders, on the other hand, would rather the firm sell its assets and buy lottery tickets. Most likely, this will be a losing proposition. But there is a chance that the winnings will be enough to not only pay off lenders, but also provide some residual value to equity holders.

From a lender's perspective, 100% assurance of payback is better than less-than-100% probability of payback. From a shareholder's perspective, a small positive probability of receiving residual value is better than zero probability of receiving any cash.

To control a borrower's business risk, loan documents place restrictions on the borrower's ability to take on more risk via investments, mergers, acquisitions, and the extension of guarantees. Borrowers are also prohibited from issuing more debt, even debt ranking below the loan in priority. Initially, this last requirement may seem unnecessary—how could debt subordinate to a loan negatively affect the loan lenders? The answer is that lenders do not want borrowers to increase their probability of default by becoming more levered, so they want to have control over any new borrower financing.

Performance Requirements

Violations of performance requirements, based on accounting measures, give lenders the right to accelerate a loan, making it become due and payable immediately. In practice, this threat gives lenders negotiating power over borrowers when these measures are violated. Banks would rather exercise control over a borrower early on and, by doing so, hopefully avoid more serious problems later. Accounting measures of performance usually address coverage, leverage, liquidity, tangible net worth, and capital expenditures.

The following are common variants:

- *Coverage.* Ratio of (1) cash flow or earnings to (2) debt service or fixed charges (debt service + amortization + capital expenditures + rent).
- *Leverage.* Ratio of (1) loan debt or total debt to (2) equity or cash flow.
- *Liquidity.* Current ratio of (1) cash + marketable securities + accounts receivable + inventory to (2) accounts payable + short term debt or the quick ratio, which is the current ratio without inventories in the numerator.
- *Tangible net worth.* Dollar amount of net worth – intangible assets.
- *Maximum capital expenditures.* Dollar amount of purchases of plant, property, and equipment.
- *Cash flow/net worth requirements.* Minimum dollar amounts of cash flow or net worth.

Many speculative-grade loans are made under the assumption that financial performance will improve. This is particularly the case in acquisition financing, where economies of scale or asset sales or other factors are expected to improve the financial performance of the combined entity going forward. In these cases, target financial ratios are tightened over time.

The calculation of these variables can vary from being generally accepted accounting principal (GAAP) based to being subject to harsher measures. For example, noncash revenue might be excluded from coverage calculations while noncash expenses are included.

Reporting Requirements

To facilitate the lender's monitoring of the borrower, the borrower is required to supply certain reports and documents, which may include:

- Quarterly and annual financial statements.
- Immediate notice of noncompliance with loan terms and periodic certification of compliance with loan terms.
- Budgets and financial projections, budget versus actual comparisons, and revised budgets.
- Accounts receivable analysis.
- Property, plant, and equipment appraisals.
- Financial statements, reports, and proxy statements sent to shareholders, the SEC, or other regulators.

Loan Interest Rates and Upfront Fees

Loan pricing, both interest rate and upfront fees, depends primarily on three factors:

1. Borrower's credit quality
2. New issue supply versus demand
3. Size of the loan

The effect of a loan's credit quality upon loan pricing is obvious. But, as we discussed earlier, the intrinsic credit risk of a borrower can at least be partially ameliorated by a loan's terms. New issue supply versus demand relates to the balance or imbalance between the amount of loans coming to market and the credit appetite of banks and institutional lenders. The driving technical in the loan market over the last few years had been the net cash inflow into single-purpose investment vehicles such as prime funds and CLOs.

As we learned earlier, in 2007, CLOs purchased 57% of all newly issued loans, but in the first three quarters of 2008, activity fell sharply as CLOs only accounted for 38% of loan purchases. Having been able to rely on CLOs to absorb more than half of the supply of institutional loans in the past, arrangers became dependent on this source of demand. When structured finance investors were faced with enormous losses on subprime mortgage exposures, their demand for CLO liabilities slowed to a crawl.

The effect of loan size is not completely obvious or consistent. Supply-demand factors work on an individual name basis just as they do for the market as a whole. In this respect, the larger the loan coming to market, the higher the spreads will have to be in order to clear the market. On the other hand, for purposes of liquidity with respect to future trading of a loan, investors prefer large loan sizes so that more investors and dealers will be familiar with the loan. In balancing these opposing factors, the wisdom in the market is that loans between $200 million and $2 billion price best.

Other factors affecting the attractiveness of a loan, if not actual loan pricing, include the borrower's equity investors, the relationship of the arranger to the borrower, and the expertise and reputation of the arranger. In addition, ownership by a leveraged buyout company with a reputation for quality transactions will help the borrower get better loan pricing. A loan arranger that is also an equity investor in the borrower is another positive factor. Finally, arrangers who have good records for either avoiding or working out problematic loans, and who provide good post-closing service to other lenders, can obtain better pricing for their borrowers.

Average upfront fees for pro rata loans averaged 54 basis points in 2007, jumping to 136 basis points by end of October 2008. These fees are deducted from the amount banks pay for the loan, so the loan is funded at par minus fees. Upfront fees for institutional loans were just about a thing of the past, but reached an average of 242 basis points in October 2008 (versus 73 basis points in 2007 and 3 basis points in 2006), due to the credit crunch.

Loan Credit Quality

In Figure 3.10 and Figure 3.11, we show two measures of loan credit quality for large (issuers with EBITDA greater than $50 million) syndicated corporate borrowers: leverage and interest coverage. Our leverage measure is total debt divided by EBITDA–earnings before deductions for interest, taxes, depreciation, and amortization.

As can be seen in the figure, this measure of leverage for large syndicated corporate borrowers returned to more normal levels in 2008, hovering near the 4× level, from the peak of almost 5× in 2007. However, the proportion of total debt made up of senior debt has remained elevated at 86%, versus 90% in 2007 and 69% in 2002 and 2003. While recovering from peak levels in 2007, these factors remain fundamental negatives: A higher leverage ratio represents a greater risk of bankruptcy for the corporation, and a higher proportion of senior debt represents less protection for the investors who are most concerned with protection of principal, which includes not only the other senior debt holders but also a debt holder below the senior debt in the capital structure.

Our interest coverage measure is EBITDA, with and without capital expenditure (capex), divided by total interest expense. As shown in Figure 3.11, this measure of borrower's interest coverage in the loan market also improved in 2008 over 2007 levels. Interest coverage peaked at 4.2× in 2004 but then declined to a six-year low of 2.8× in 2007 (both figures including capex). While improving, low interest coverage demonstrates another weakening fundamental characteristic of leveraged loans: interest coverage is simply a measure of a company's ability to service its debt on a year-to-year basis.

LOAN RECOVERY RATES

Studies of recovery rates confirm the advantage of a bank loan lenders' senior claim on the borrower's assets. A comprehensive study of ultimate recovery rates for roughly 3,500 defaulted loans and bonds issued since 1987 by over 720 nonfinancial U.S. corporations was published by Moody's.[4] Unlike prior recovery studies, which generally used a loan's or bond's postdefault trading level as a proxy for its

---

[4] Moody's, *Ultimate Recovery Database: Special Comment*, April 2007.

FIGURE 3.10 Average Leverage of Large Syndicated Corporate Borrowers

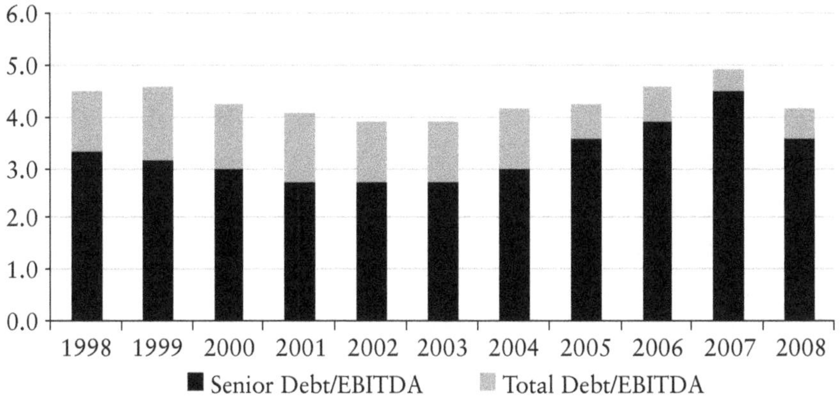

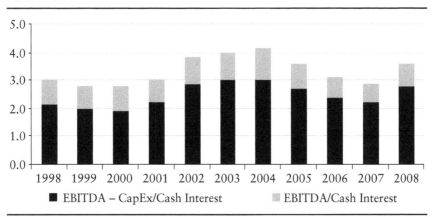

Note: As of October 31, 2008.
Data for this figure obtained from S&P LCD. Copyright © 2009 Standard & Poor's Financial Services LLC ("S&P"). Reproduction in any form is prohibited without S&P's prior written permission.

FIGURE 3.11 Average Interest Coverage of Large Syndicated Corporate Borrowers

Note: As of October 31, 2008.
Data for this figure obtained from S&P LCD. Copyright © 2009 Standard & Poor's Financial Services LLC ("S&P"). Reproduction in any form is prohibited without S&P's prior written permission.

TABLE 3.7 Average Recovery Rates by Assets, 1982–2007

Debt Type	Recovery Rates
Bank Loans	82%
Sr. Secured Bonds	65%
Sr. Unsecured Bonds	38%
Sr. Subordinated Bonds	29%
Subordinated Bonds	27%
Junior Subordinated Bonds	15%
All Bonds	37%

Data for this table obtained from Moody's.

recovery rate, Moody's discounted the actual amount received by the holder of a given piece of debt at the resolution of a credit event. The report by Moody's indicated high recoveries for loans in comparison to lower recoveries for bonds.

More specifically, Moody's found that defaulted loans recovered an average of 82% of par value, while defaulted bonds recovered an average of just 37%. This produces a loan-loss-to-bond-loss ratio of 29% [(1–82%)/(1–37%)]. Interestingly, Moody's found that loan recovery rates have a right-skewed distribution, while bond recovery rates have a left-skewed distribution. In fact, a majority of defaulted loans recovered 100% of their value. Defaulted bonds, in contrast, recovered less than 25% of their value more often than not.

Table 3.7 compares the average recovery rate of loans to those of various types of bonds. Notice how much the security and seniority matter: bank loans, being the most senior, recover 17% more value than senior secured bonds, which themselves recover 27% more value than their unsecured counterparts, on average. The recovery rate statistics noted above are based on the outstanding par of the loans and bonds at the time of default.

Keep in mind, however, that loan amounts decline because of:

1. Scheduled amortization.
2. Sweeps from excess cash flow and the sale of assets.
3. Forced amortization as a condition for waiving the right to call the loan due immediately upon a violation of a loan's covenants.

FIGURE 3.12 12-Month Trailing Loan and Bond Default Rates

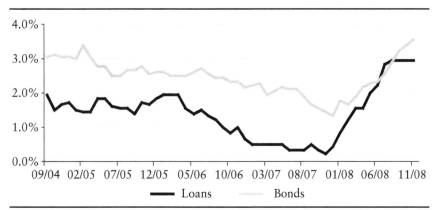

Note: As of October 7, 2008.
Data for this figure obtained from S&P LCD. Copyright © 2009 Standard & Poor's Financial Services LLC ("S&P"). Reproduction in any form is prohibited without S&P's prior written permission.

Structural features can make a significant difference in a loan's security, by providing lenders with tools to force amortization when things begin to go wrong. Given loan amortization, losses as a percent of the original loan amount are even smaller than would be indicated by these recovery rates.

Loan Recoveries in the Current Environment

In 2008 (through October 7, 2008), default rates in the leveraged finance markets continued to push higher off their lows at the end of 2007 as shown in Figure 3.12. The 12-month trailing default rate in the high-yield bond market as of early October 2008 was 3.3%, up from the prior low of 1.3% in December 2007. On the leveraged loan side, the rate of default as of early October 2008 was 2.9%, up from a low of 0.14% in November 2007.

In any period of rising defaults, the natural follow-up question is what are the prospects for recoveries? Will they be high or low? Let's take a look at some of the positive and negative factors that could impact recoveries.

FIGURE 3.13   Cov-Lite Loan Volume

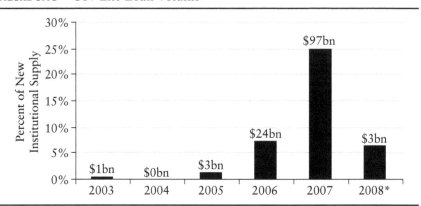

Note: New institutional money volume classified according to launch date. Data for this figure obtained from S&P LCD. Copyright © 2009 Standard & Poor's Financial Services LLC ("S&P"). Reproduction in any form is prohibited without S&P's prior written permission.

The Negative Factors

Key reasons why many expect recoveries to be relatively modest include:

- *Abundance of cov-lite loans.* One reason why many expect recoveries to be low (loss given default to be high) in the period during and following the credit crunch is because cov-lite loan issuance accounted for so much of total supply in 2006 and 2007 (see Figure 3.13). At the peak of the bull market, cov-lite loan supply totalled almost $100 billon, or about 20% of new money, institutional supply in 2007. In effect, issues with few, if any, maintenance requirements limit the ability of creditors to intervene early in a credit deterioration process. Instead, corporate managers retain flexibility to enhance the interest of some stakeholders (e.g., equity) at the expense of others.
- *Growth of second lien market.* What impact will the dramatic rise of second lien issuance (see Figure 13.14) in 2006 and 2007 have on recoveries? While this trend may have the biggest impact on the distribution of recoveries across capital structures, it likely will add an element of complexity and litigiousness to the bankruptcy

FIGURE 3.14 Second Lien Loan Volume

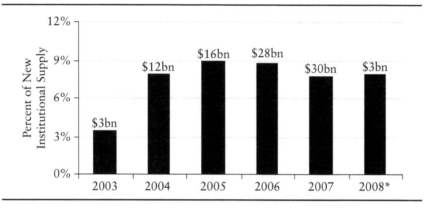

Note: New institutional money volume classified according to launch date. Data for this figure obtained from S&P LCD. Copyright © 2009 Standard & Poor's Financial Services LLC ("S&P"). Reproduction in any form is prohibited without S&P's prior written permission.

TABLE 3.8 Average Leverage of LBO Bond Deals in Select Sectors Since 2005

Industry	2005		2006		2007	
	Total Lev.	Sr. Lev.	Total Lev.	Sr. Lev.	Total Lev.	Sr. Lev.
Consumer	4.9	4.1	6.1	5.8	6.4	6.1
Health Care	5.8	3.6	6.8	4.5	7.2	6.2
Industrial	5.3	4.0	5.5	4.9	5.9	5.0
Media	—	—	7.2	6.9	9.1	7.7
Real Estate	—	—	—	—	7.0	6.0
Retail	—	—	—	—	7.2	6.2
Services	5.3	3.6	6.2	4.8	7.7	6.0
Technology	5.5	4.1	5.5	4.8	7.5	5.7
Telecom	5.4	4.3	6.0	6.0	7.9	7.9
Average	5.3×	4.0×	6.0×	5.1×	7.0×	6.1×

Note: As of April 29, 2008.
Data for this table obtained from UBS.

process, which could weigh on recoveries for the entire entity as well. Second-lien loan volumes fell dramatically in 2008 from 2007 levels, primarily due to the tightness in the capital market.

■ *Aggressively structured LBO deals.* Capital structures have become increasingly leveraged since 2005, in part due to "aggressively" structured LBO deals. In Table 3.8, we highlight how leverage for the average LBO bond deal has climbed—total leverage from 5.3× in 2005 to 7.0× in 2007, and senior leverage up 2.1× from 2005 to 2007. Moreover, many of the deals were done at the peak of the bull market—a time when companies were generating record earnings and receiving premium valuations. One or both of these factors may not be sustainable in a more normal (or weaker) economic or market environment. Also noteworthy is that a number of aggressively leveraged deals were done in cyclical sectors, such as industrials and the technology space. This could have an upward influence on the pace of defaults and a downward influence on recovery potential.

The key point here is that relative to historic norms, there can be a number of factors that can exert an upward influence on loss given defaults (LGD).

FIGURE 3.15   Historical Prices and Default Rates for High-Yield Bonds

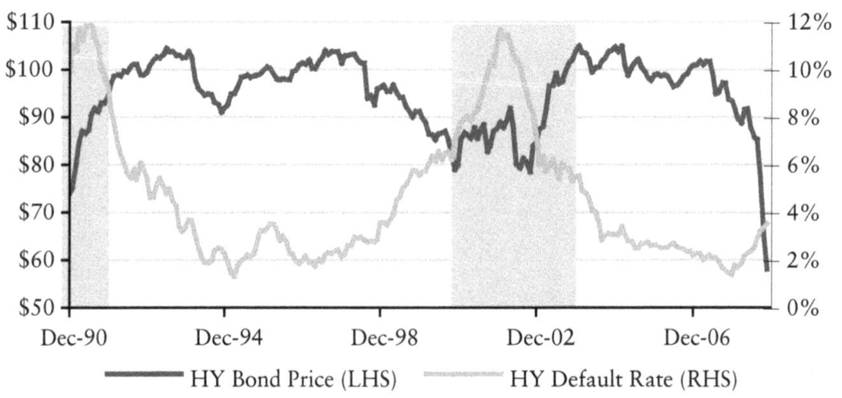

Note: As of October 31, 2008. Default rate for HY Bonds beginning from 2001; default rate prior to 2001 is for the overall high-yield market. Data for this figure obtained from Moody's and *Yield Book*.

FIGURE 3.16   Historical Prices and Default Rates for Leveraged Loans

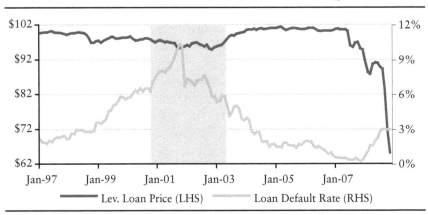

Note: As of October 24, 2008. Default rate for Lev. Loans beginning from 2001; default rate prior to 2001 is for the overall high-yield market.

Data for this figure obtained from Moody's and S&P LCD. Copyright © 2009 Standard & Poor's Financial Services LLC ("S&P"). Reproduction in any form is prohibited without S&P's prior written permission.

The Positive Factors

Although the factors noted above will certainly have a negative influence on recovery prospects, it does not mean that losses will be higher than normal per se. There are also several factors at work that can exert a downward influence on LGDs as well. The key factors likely to limit LGD include:

- *Dollars at risk are typically not par value.* Recovery may be less important than LGD for someone thinking about adding exposure to the loan market if dollar prices are already low. In Figures 3.15 and 3.16, we present the average price for a broad portfolio of bonds and loans, respectively. We juxtapose these prices against the default rate in each market, and find that typically when the default rate is low, prices are close to par even if the default rate is expected to rise in the future. While most consider LGD to be the difference between par and expected recovery, for someone looking to add new exposure to the market, a more realistic approach might be the difference between market price and expected recovery. For example, given a standard LGD (about 30 points in the loan market, 60 points in the bond market), based on the bond and loan prices in Figures 3.15 and 3.16, prices are already consistent with a low recovery. A recovery of 70% was needed to generate a LGD of 30 points for a typical loan in 2007 (prices at par), but as of October 2008, recoveries of less than 50% would result in the same LGD given dollar prices at the time.

■ *Asset-light credits.* A number of filings in the past were by asset-lite credits. For example, names such as Global Crossing (15.4% family recovery) and Iridium (4.1%) were arguably "business plans" that were able to take advantage of a frothy market and raise debt financing instead of venture capital or private equity at the time. More recently, companies may be heavily levered, but by-and-large they are beyond the "business plan" stage. Table 3.9 highlights a number of issuers that had relatively low recoveries following a default.

■ *Distressed money waiting on the sideline.* While recoveries ultimately depend on negotiation, litigation, and so on, many holders prefer not to take part in that process. After all, the average loan portfolio manager—someone responsible for deciding if overweighting double-B energy names or single-B gaming credits makes more sense in the current environment—does not have the time to participate in bankruptcy proceedings. As such, post-

TABLE 3.9 Select Issuers that had Low Postdefault Recovery Rates in the Previous Cycle

Issuer	Industry	Date of Default	Total Recovery
Adelphia	Media	3/27/02	27.8%
Enron	Energy	12/1/01	21.1%
Global Crossing	Telecom	1/28/02	15.4%
Hayes Lemmerz	Automotive	12/5/01	37.6%
Iridium	Telecom	8/13/99	4.1%
Owens Corning	Manufacturing	10/5/00	33.4%
WorldCom	Telecom	7/21/02	28.0%

Note: Total recovery across all assets.
Data for this table obtained from UBS.

FIGURE 3.17 Amount Raised by Private Equity Funds for Distressed Debt Investing

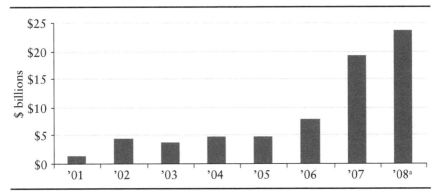

Note: As of May 1, 2008.
[a] Annualized figure.
Data for this figure obtained from Thomson Financial.

TABLE 3.10 Average Ultimate and Postdefault Trading Recovery Rates

Debt Type	Ultimate Recovery	Trading Recovery	Diff
Bank Loans	82%	70%	12%
Sr. Sec. Bonds	66%	52%	14%
Sr. Unsec. Bonds	39%	37%	2%

Note: Ultimate recovery data from 1987–2007; Trading recovery data from 1982–2007. Both issuer-weighted.
Data for this table obtained from Moody's.

bankruptcy prices in the secondary market may be an appropriate recovery metric for many. And given how sharply distressed funds have grown in recent years (see Figure 3.17), that bid may be stronger than it has been in the past. Historically, the difference between ultimate recovery and 30-day post bankruptcy prices has been 12% for loans and 14% for senior secured bonds (see Table 3.10), so there may be room for compression. And, away from the secondary market, additional distressed capital on the sideline may result in an increased willingness and ability of junior claimholders to preserve recovery prospects through capital injections (i.e., essentially take out senior portions of the capital structure at par to control the bankruptcy process).

To summarize, what is worse for recovery prospects, corporate business plans that (somehow) received debt financing or asset-heavy companies with cov-lite loans? Low-dollar prices or over-levered capital structures? There are many factors that are likely to weigh on recovery prospects, but some factors that negatively impacted recoveries in the past may not exert much influence in the future. In addition, there are other factors that should have a positive influence.

LOAN DEFAULT RATES

More surprising than differences in loan-bond recoveries are differences in loan-bond default rates.

The Pace of Defaults

Table 3.11 shows defaults according to year of issuance by broadly syndicated institutional loan borrowers that make public filings to the Security and Exchange Commission. Each row of the table shows how many borrowers took out loans in a particular year, and how many of those borrowers subsequently defaulted on those loans. For example, 137 borrowers took out loans in 2000, and of those, 11 defaulted in 2001, 15 in 2002, 2 in 2003, and 1 in 2004. Note that a data point in the analysis incorporates all of a borrower's institutional loans, so multiple institutional loans by the same borrower are treated as a single data point in the statistics.

Total defaults in any particular year are shown in the bottom row of Table 3.11. Note that the staggering 61 defaults over 2001 and 2002 almost match the 65 defaults over the other eight years combined. The number of borrowers increased significantly in the years following that high-default period, while defaults trended lower until 2008. For year end 2008, there were 86 U.S. corporate defaults, surpassing the previous peak year, 2001.

Figure 3.18 shows the changes in of loan defaults another way, by the 12-month rolling average of loan defaults. The rate is calculated two ways: the number of defaulting loans in the past 12 months divided by the total number of loans outstanding, and the par value of defaulting loans divided by the total par value of loans outstanding.

TABLE 3.11 Number of Public Filers and Subsequent Defaulters

Year of Origination	Public Filers	1998	1999	2000	2001	2002	2003	2004	2005	2006	2007	2008[a]
1998	189	1	7	11	7	6	4	—	—	—	—	—
1999	166		—	7	13	3	2	2	—	—	—	—
2000	137			—	11	15	2	1	—	—	—	—
2001	115				2	3	—	1	—	—	—	—
2002	165					1	3	2	—	—	—	3
2003	288						—	3	2	2	—	3
2004	451							—	8	1	—	6
2005	496								1	1	—	11
2006	564									1	1	12
2007	529										2	4
Totals	3100	1	7	18	33	28	11	9	11	5	3	36

[a] As of October 14, 2008.

Data for this table obtained from S&P LCD. Copyright © 2009 Standard & Poor's Financial Services LLC ("S&P"). Reproduction in any form is prohibited without S&P's prior written permission.

FIGURE 3.18   12-Month Rolling Default Average

Data for this figure obtained from S&P LCD. Copyright © 2009 Standard & Poor's Financial Services LLC ("S&P"). Reproduction in any form is prohibited without S&P's prior written permission.

By either measure, loan defaults are picking up, but remain below the 2000–2003 levels.

A Look at the Effect of Seasoning

With regard to default risk after a period of "seasoning," Table 3.12 shows cumulative default rates, as well as the variability in default rates among borrowers from different issuance years (also referred to as *issuance cohorts* or *vintages*).

For example, the default history of the 2003 issuance cohort shows that 10 issuers defaulted over the six year period leading to a cumulative default rate of 3.5%. The cumulative default rate is calculated as the number of defaulting borrowers (3 + 2 + 2 + 3 = 10) divided by the total number of borrowers (288), generating a 3.5% default rate. These defaults occurred over approximately 5.5 years, as 2003 issuance cohort loans were made, on average, on July 1, 2003, and the loans are tracked through 2008.

We cut the timeline short at six years of seasoning since the vast majority of defaults occur within that length of time.

TABLE 3.12 Cumulative Default Rates of 10 Issuance Cohorts

Year of Origination	Public Filers	Year 1	Year 2	Year 3	Year 4	Year 5	Year 6	Cumulative Default Rate
1998	189	1	7	11	7	6	4	19.0%
1999	166	0	7	13	3	2	2	16.3%
2000	137	0	11	15	2	1	0	21.2%
2001	115	2	3	0	1	0	0	5.2%
2002	165	1	3	2	0	0	0	3.6%
2003	288	0	3	2	2	0	3	3.5%
2004	451	0	8	1	0	6		3.3%
2005	496	1	1	0	11			2.6%
2006	564	1	1	12				2.5%
2007	529	2	4					1.1%
Totals	3100	8	48	56	26	15	9	

Data for this table obtained from S&P LCD. Copyright © 2009 Standard & Poor's Financial Services LLC ("S&P"). Reproduction in any form is prohibited without S&P's prior written permission.

After six years of seasoning, loans issued in 1998 and 2000 exhibited the highest cumulative default rates (19.0% and 21.2%, respectively) on account of a relative high number of defaults in their second and third years outstanding, respectively. Loans issued in 2001 exhibited the lowest cumulative default rate (5.2%) with only six defaults in the first six years of seasoning. The 1999, 2000, 2003, and 2004 cohorts had their first defaults after a year of seasoning. The important things to note here is that lifetime default curves vary widely by vintage, and that it is difficult to tell whether a vintage is likely to be "money-good" until it has seasoned for a couple of years.

Defaults Across the Bond and Loan Markets

In Table 3.13, we weight cumulative default rates by number of issuers for the 10 loans mentioned previously and compare the results to those of BBB, BB, and B senior unsecured bond issuers. For the bond data, we rely on another arm of Standard & Poor's, namely Ratings Direct, to provide issuer-weighted default rates. The period covered

TABLE 3.13 Average Cumulative Default Rates, Loans versus Bonds

Seasoning	Year 1	Year 2	Year 3	Year 4	Year 5	Year 6
Loans	1.1%	3.3%	5.2%	6.3%	7.3%	7.8%
BBB Sr. Unsecured	0.3%	0.7%	1.2%	1.8%	2.5%	3.2%
BB Sr. Unsecured	1.1%	3.1%	5.6%	8.0%	10.1%	12.1%
B Sr. Unsecured	5.0%	10.9%	15.9%	19.8%	22.6%	24.7%

Data for this table obtained from S&P LCD. Copyright © 2009 Standard & Poor's Financial Services LLC ("S&P"). Reproduction in any form is prohibited without S&P's prior written permission.

is considerably longer (1981–2006) than the previous period, but both datasets are underpinned by weak macroeconomic conditions for roughly 20% of the period covered. Defaults spiked in each recession, thus this parity makes comparison reasonable. The key takeaway here is a basic one: leveraged loans default less frequently than bonds rated BB and lower (i.e., high-yield bonds).

One explanation for what is going on here is that loan ratings are generally more up-to-date than bond ratings. Rating agencies tend to have a bias against making rating changes. Thus, if a company's fortunes have changed, positively or negatively, its ratings do not necessarily fully reflect that current credit condition. Many companies taking out loans, however, do not have existing ratings, so there is no ratings history to restrain a rating analyst's judgment. Also, many loan packages are accomplished in the context of a complete top-to-bottom restructuring of all the issuer's debt. Thus, a new loan has the effect of starting the ratings process over with a clean slate.

Lender Liability

Bank loan participants have a special relationship with borrowers, as indicated by their receipt of private information in the bank book and as discussed earlier when we covered loan terms. The downside of a lender's relationship with a borrower is the risk of "lender liability," a set of legal theories and claims under which a borrower may sue a lender.

In its most basic form, lender liability arises if a lender violates an implied or contractual duty of good faith and fair dealing towards the borrower. But a higher standard of conduct is demanded of the lender if, through its influence over the borrower, the lender has assumed fiduciary responsibilities. This fiduciary responsibility might even extend to the borrower's other creditors and subject the lender to claims from them, too.

In asserting its contractual rights, a lender must be careful to maintain an arm's length relationship with the borrower and avoid becoming the borrower's *de facto* consultant, advisor, officer, or board of directors. Finally, a lender subjects itself to liability if it fails to sell seized collateral in a commercially reasonable manner.

One punishment open to courts against lenders who have misbehaved is to subordinate their claim against the borrower to that of other creditors of the borrower. CLOs mitigate this risk by limiting their investment in revolving loans so that failure to fund a loan cannot be the basis of a lender liability assertion.

SUMMARY

The leveraged loan market will likely continue to be a dynamic space in the years ahead. This is primarily due to the volatility of the broader credit markets and the inflow of new investors, such as equity hedge funds and private equity funds, seeking opportunities outside of their traditional asset classes. As such, understanding the basics (such as who uses leveraged loans, loan structures and terms, the size and growth of the market, and the syndication process) and the risks (such as defaults and recoveries) are crucial for keeping up with the market. Similar to the high-yield bond market, investing in the leveraged loan market has always been credit-intensive, requiring a solid understanding of a company's business fundamentals, corporate management, stability of financing, and so on. That said, successful participation in the leveraged loan market is not just about a deep understanding of credit fundamentals. The structure of a loan and trading/hedging strategies now play a critical role in determining the ultimate profitability of exposure to a particular credit.

Structured Market

4

Collateralized Loan Obligations

Collateralized loan obligations (CLOs) have been around for more than 20 years and until September 2007 purchased two-thirds of all U.S. leveraged loans. A CLO issues debt and equity and uses the funds it raises to invest in a portfolio of leveraged loans. It distributes the cash flows from its asset portfolio to the holders of its various liabilities in prescribed ways that take into account the relative seniority of those liabilities. We will fill in this definition over the next few pages, and rest assured, we do not take anything for granted.

To properly explain CLOs, we break them down into their four moving parts: assets, liabilities, purposes, and credit structures. We explain each building block in detail and create a framework for understanding CLOs that puts old and new CLO variants in context. Next, we define the roles of the different parties to a CLO. This will conclude our initial pass at CLOs. We then circle back, emphasizing particular topics of importance to CLO investors: the cash flow credit structure, the advantages of CLO equity, and how CLO equity fits into an existing portfolio.

UNDERSTANDING CLOs

A CLO can be well described by focusing on its four important attributes: *assets*, *liabilities*, *purposes*, and *credit structures*. Like any company, a CLO has assets. With a CLO, these are corporate loans, most always leveraged loans rated speculative grade. And like any company, a CLO has liabilities. With a CLO, these run the gamut of preferred shares to AAA rated senior debt. Beyond the seniority and subordination of CLO liabilities, CLOs have additional structural credit protections, which fall into the category of either *cash flow* or *market value* protections. Finally, every CLO has a purpose that it was created to fulfill, and these fall into the categories of *arbitrage* or *balance sheet*. In this section, we are going to look at the different types of loans CLOs hold, the different liabilities they issue, the two different credit structures they employ, and, finally, the two purposes for which CLOs are created.

Assets

CLO assets are usually performing leveraged loans. But some CLOs have been comprised of defaulted and distressed loans and some have been comprised of investment-grade loans. Instead of buying loans, some CLOs have gained exposure to loans by selling credit protection on loans or loan obligors via credit default swaps. As will be explained in Chapter 7, in these transactions, the CLO obligates itself to pay what is essentially the credit loss associated with a default.

Liabilities

Any company that has assets also has liabilities. In the case of a CLO, these liabilities have a detailed and strict ranking of seniority, going up the CLO's capital structure as equity or preferred shares, subordinated debt, mezzanine debt, and senior debt. These *tranches* of notes and equity are commonly labeled Class A, Class B, Class C, and so forth going from top to bottom of the capital structure. They run the gamut from the most secured AAA rated tranche with the greatest amount of subordination beneath it, to the most levered, unrated equity tranche. Table 4.1 shows a simplified tranche structure for a CLO owning leveraged loans.

TABLE 4.1   Simple, Typical CLO Tranche Structure

Tranche	Percent of Capital Structure	Rating	Coupon
Class A	77.5%	AAA	LIBOR + 26
Class B	9%	A	LIBOR + 75
Class C	2.75%	BBB	LIBOR + 180
Class D	2.75%	BB	LIBOR + 475
Preferred Shares	8%	NR	Residual Cash Flow

Special purposes entities like CLOs are said to be "bankrupt remote." One aspect of the term is that they are new entities without previous business activities. They therefore cannot have any legal liability for sins of the past. Another aspect of their "remoteness from bankruptcy" is that the CLO will not be caught up in the bankruptcy of any other entity, such as the manager of the CLO's assets, or a party that sold assets to the CLO, or the banker that structured the CLO.

But another, very important aspect of a CLO's bankruptcy remoteness, is the absolute seniority and subordination of the CLO's debt tranches to one another. Even if it is a certainty that some holders of the CLO's debt will not receive their full principal and interest, cash flows from the CLO's assets are still distributed according to the original game plan dictated by seniority. The CLO cannot go into bankruptcy, either voluntarily or through the action of an aggrieved creditor. In fact, the need for bankruptcy is obviated because the distribution of the CLO's cash flows, even if the CLO is insolvent, has already been determined in detail at the origination of the CLO.

But within the stipulation of strict seniority, there is great variety in the features of CLO debt tranches. The driving force for CLO structurers is to raise funds at the lowest possible cost. This is done so that the CLO's equity holder, who is at the bottom of the chain of seniority, can get the most residual cash flow.

Most CLO debt is floating rate off LIBOR, but sometimes a fixed rate tranche is structured. Sometimes a CLO employs short-term debt in its capital structure. When such debt is employed, the CLO must have a stand-by liquidity provider, ready to purchase the CLO's short-term debt should it fail to be resold or roll in the market. A CLO will only issue short-term debt if its cost, plus that of the liquidity provider's fee, is less than the cost of long-term debt.

Sometimes a financial guaranty insurer will wrap a CLO tranche. Usually this involves a AAA rated insurer and the most senior CLO tranche. Again, a CLO would employ insurance if the cost of the tranche's insured coupon plus the cost of the insurance premium is less than the coupon the tranche would have to pay in the absence of insurance. To meet the needs of particular investors, sometimes the AAA tranche is divided into *senior* AAA and *junior* AAA tranches.

Some CLOs do not have all their assets in place when their liabilities are sold. Rather than receive cash that the CLO is not ready to invest, tranches might have a delay draw feature, where the CLO can call for funding within some specified time period. This eliminates the negative carry the CLO would bear if it had to hold uninvested debt proceeds in cash. An extreme form of funding flexibility is a revolving tranche, where the CLO can call for funds and return funds as its needs dictate.

Purposes

CLOs are created for one of two purposes: balance sheet or arbitrage. These purposes also dictate how a CLO acquires its assets.

Balance Sheet

A bank holding loans desires to (1) shrink its balance sheet, (2) reduce required regulatory capital, (3) reduce required economic capital, or (4) achieve cheaper funding costs. The bank sells loans to the CLO. Unless the bank is very poorly rated, CLO debt would not be cheaper than the bank's own source of funds. But selling the loans to a CLO removes them from the bank's balance sheet and therefore lowers the bank's regulatory capital requirements. This is true even if market practice requires the bank to buy some of the equity of the newly created CLO.

Arbitrage

An asset manager specializing in loans wishes to gain assets under management and management fees. Investors wish to have the expertise of an asset manager. Assets are purchased in the market place from many different sellers and put into the CLO. CLOs are another means, along with mutual funds and hedge funds, for a money manager to provide a service to investors. The difference is that instead of all the investors sharing the fund's return in proportion to their investment, investor returns are also determined by the seniority of the CLO tranches they purchase.

These two purposes differentiate CLOs on the basis of how they acquire their assets and focus on the motivations of assets sellers, asset managers, and capital note issuers. But from the point of view of CLO investors, all CLOs have a number of common purposes, which explain why many investors find CLO debt and equity attractive.

One purpose is the division and distribution of the risk of the CLO's assets to parties that have different risk appetites. Thus, both a AAA investor and a BB investor can invest in leveraged loans. Often CLO debt provides a higher spread than comparable investments.

For CLO equity investors, the CLO structure provides a leveraged return without some of the nasty consequences of borrowing via repurchase agreement (repo) from a bank. CLO equity holders own stock in a company and are not liable for the losses of that company. Equity's exposure to the CLO asset portfolio is therefore capped at the cost of equity minus previous equity distributions. Instead of short-term bank financing, financing via the CLO is locked in for the long term at fixed spreads to LIBOR. The CLO structure allows investors to purchase an interest in a diversified portfolio of loans, which they otherwise would not be able to purchase. Table 4.2 summarizes the CLO purposes we have discussed.

TABLE 4.2 CLO Purposes

	Balance Sheet	Arbitrage
Provide bank sellers with cheap funding or regulatory capital relief or economic capital relief.	X	
Provide asset managers with assets under management and CLO investors with asset management services.		X
Divide and distribute the risk of the loans to parties with differing appetites for risk.	X	X
Provide equity investors with leveraged exposure to loans with nonrecourse term financing.	X	X
Provide debt investors with high ratings-adjusted yields.	X	X
Provide investors with a diversified investment portfolio, perhaps of hard-to-access assets.	X	X

Credit Structures

Beyond the seniority and subordination of CLO liabilities, CLOs have additional structural credit protections, which fall into the category of either *cash flow* or *market value* protections.

The *market value credit structure* is less often used, maybe 5% of the time, but easier to explain, since it is analogous to an individual's margin account at a brokerage. Every asset in the CLO's portfolio has an *advance rate* limiting the amount that can be borrowed against that asset. Advance rates are necessarily less than 100% and vary according to the market value volatility of the asset. For example, the advance rate on a B rated loan would be less than the advance rate on a Baa rated loan. The rating of the Baa loan indicates that its market value will fluctuate less that the B rated loan. Therefore, the CLO can borrow more against it. The sum of advance rates times the market values of the associated assets is the total amount the CLO can borrow.

The credit quality of a market value CLO derives from the ability of the CLO to liquidate its assets and repay debt tranches. Thus, the market value of the CLO's assets are generally measured every day, advance rates are then applied, and the permissible amount of debt calculated. If this comes out, for example, to $100 million, but the CLO has $110 million of debt, the CLO must do one of two things. It can sell a portion of its assets and repay a portion of its debt until the actual amount of debt is less than the permissible amount of debt. Or the CLO's equity holders can contribute more cash to the CLO. If no effective action is taken, the entire CLO portfolio is liquidated, all debt is repaid, and residual cash given to equity holders. The market value credit structure is analogous to an individual being faced with a collateral call at his brokerage account. If he does not post additional collateral, his portfolio is at least partially liquidated.

The *cash flow credit structure* does not have market value tests. Instead, subordination is sized so that the *postdefault cash flow* of assets is expected to cover debt tranche principal and interest with some degree of certainty. Obviously, the certainty that a Aaa CLO tranche, with 23% subordination beneath it, will receive all its principal and interest is greater than the certainty a BB CLO tranche, with only 8% subordination beneath it, will receive all its principal and interest.

All cash flow CLOs have a feature that improves the credit quality of their senior tranches. In the normal course of events, if defaults are not "too high" (a phrase we will shortly explain in detail), cash coupons come in from the CLO's asset portfolio. These moneys are first applied to the CLO's administrative costs, such as those for its trustee and its manager, if it has one. Next, these moneys are applied to interest expense of the CLO's seniormost tranche. Next, moneys are applied to interest expense on the CLO's second most senior tranche and successively moving down the capital structure until all interest on all debt tranches is paid. If the CLO has a manager, an additional fee to that manager might be paid next. Finally, left over, or residual, cash flow is given to the CLO's equity holders.

But what if defaults are "too high" as we promised earlier to explain? Also, how do we know whether defaults are too high? There are two series of tests, the most important of which is shown next. The key to these tests is that defaulted assets are excluded or severely haircut (counted at a fraction of their par amount) in the definition of *asset par*:

Class A par coverage test = Asset par/Class A par

Class B par coverage test = Asset par/(Class A par + Class B par)

Class C par coverage test
= Asset par/(Class A par + Class B par + Class C par)

... and so on, for all the debt tranches.

To pass these tests, par coverage must be greater than some number, perhaps 120% for the class A par coverage test, perhaps only 105% for the class C par coverage test. The more defaulted assets a CLO has, the more likely it will be to fail one or more of these tests. Failure of a par coverage test requires that cash be withheld from paying interest on lower-ranking debt tranches. Instead, cash must be used to pay down principal on the CLO's senior-most debt tranche. If enough cash is available to pay down the senior-most tranche so that the par coverage test is in compliance, remaining cash can be used to make interest payments to lower-ranking tranches and on down the line to the CLO's equity holders. We discuss the cash flow credit structure in much more depth later in this chapter.

TABLE 4.3   CLO Structural Matrix

Assets	Liabilities	Purpose	Credit Structure
Leveraged loans	Fixed/Floating rate	Arbitrage	Cash flow
Investment-grade loans	PIK/Non-PIK	Balance sheet	Market value
Defaulted and distressed loans	Guaranteed/ Unenhanced		
	Short term/Long term		
	Delayed draw/ Revolving		

A CLO Structural Matrix

Table 4.3 shows the four CLO building blocks and a variety of options beneath each one. This way of looking at CLOs encompasses all the different kinds of CLOs that have existed in the past and all the kinds of CLOs that are currently being produced. Any CLO can be well described by asking and answering the four questions implied by Table 4.3:

- What are its assets?
- What are the attributes of its liabilities?
- What is its purpose?
- What is its credit structure?

Parties to a CLO

A number of parties and institutions contribute to the creation of a CLO. This section discusses the most important roles.

A CLO is a distinct legal entity, usually incorporated in the Cayman Islands, and is the *issuer*. Its liabilities are called CLOs, so one might hear the seemingly circular phrase "the CLO issues CLOs." Offshore incorporation enables the CLO to more easily sell its obligations to U.S. and international investors and escape taxation at the corporate entity level. When a CLO is located outside the United

States, it will typically also have a Delaware *coissuer*. This entity has a passive role, but its existence in the structure allows CLO obligations to be more easily sold to U.S. insurance companies.

Asset managers select the initial portfolio of an arbitrage CLO and manage it according to prescribed guidelines contained in the CLO's *indenture*. Sometimes an asset manager is used in a balance sheet CLO of distressed assets to handle their work-out or sale. A variety of firms offer CLO asset management services including hedge fund managers, mutual fund managers, and firms that specialize exclusively in CLO management.

Asset sellers supply the portfolio for a balance sheet CLO and typically retain its equity. In cash CLOs, the assets involved are usually smaller-sized loans extended to smaller-sized borrowers. In the United States, these are called "middle market" loans and in Europe these are called "small and medium enterprise (SME)" loans.

Investment bankers and structurers work with the asset manager or asset seller to bring the CLO to fruition. They set up corporate entities, shepherd the CLO through the debt-rating process, place the CLO's debt and equity with investors, and handle other organizational details. A big part of this job involves structuring the CLO's liabilities: their size and ratings, the cash diversion features of the structure, and, of course, debt tranche coupons. To obtain the cheapest funding cost for the CLO, the structurer must know when to use short-term debt or insured debt or senior/junior AAA notes, to name just a few structural options. Another part of the structurer's job is to negotiate an acceptable set of eligible assets for the CLO. These tasks obviously involve working with and balancing the desires of the asset manager or seller, different debt and equity investors, and rating agencies.

Monoline bond insurers or financial guarantors typically only guarantee the seniormost tranche in a CLO. Often, insurance is used when a CLO invests in newer asset types or is managed by a new CLO manager.

Rating agencies approve the legal and credit structure of the CLO, perform due diligence on the asset manager and the trustee, and rate the various seniorities of debt issued by the CLO. Usually two or three of the major rating agencies (Moody's, Standard & Poor's, and Fitch) rate the CLO's debt. Dominion Bond Rating Service (DBRS) is a recent entrant in CLO ratings.

Trustees hold the CLO's assets for the benefit of debt and equity holders, enforce the terms of the CLO indenture, monitor and report upon collateral performance, and disburse cash to debt and equity investors according to set rules. As such, their role also encompasses that of collateral custodian and CLO paying agent.

ELABORATIONS AND DETAILS

Having laid down a general framework for understanding CLOs and discussing the two most popular kinds of CLOs and the roles of various parties to a CLO, we turn to three specific CLO topics in greater detail: (1) the cash flow credit structure, (2) purchasing CLO equity, and (3) how CLO equity fits into an existing portfolio.

The Cash Flow Credit Structure

The cash flow credit structure is the dominant credit enhancement mechanism in CLOs, being roughly 95% of all CLOs. The specifics of a CLO's cash flow structure determine the risks taken on by various classes of CLO debt and equity and therefore the return profiles of those classes.

To understand the cash flow credit structure, one must understand *cash flow waterfalls*. There are two waterfalls in a cash flow CLO: one for collateral interest and another for collateral principal. The cash flow waterfalls decide the order in which CLO creditors get paid and thus enforce the seniority of one creditor over another. Embedded in the waterfalls are *coverage tests*, which can divert cash from subordinated creditors and redirect it to senior CLO creditors. The most important of these are the par *coverage tests*:

Class A par coverage test = Asset par/Class A par

Class B par coverage test = Asset par/(Class A par + Class B par)

... and so on, for all the debt tranches.

The par of defaulted loans is reduced or excluded from asset par in the numerator of par coverage tests.

Here is a simple, typical interest waterfall in which collateral interest is applied to CLO creditors in the following order:

1. To the trustee for base fees and expenses.
2. To the asset manager for base fees.
3. To Class A for interest expense.
4. If Class A coverage tests are failed, to Class A for principal repayment until Class A coverage tests are met.
5. To Class B for interest expense.
6. If Class B coverage tests are failed, to the seniormost outstanding tranche (which could be Class A or, if Class A has been paid in full, Class B) for principal repayment until Class B coverage tests are met.
7. To Class C for interest expense.
8. If Class C coverage tests are failed, to the seniormost outstanding tranche for principal repayment until Class C coverage tests are met. (Steps 7 and 8 are repeated for remaining debt tranches.)
9. An additional coverage test that determines whether an amount of collateral interest must be reinvested in additional collateral.
10. Additional fees to the trustee.
11. Additional fees to the asset manager.
12. To the equity tranche, in accordance with any profit sharing agreement with the asset manager.

Note that coverage tests force a decision to be made about whether to pay interest to a class or pay down principal on the seniormost outstanding tranche.

Here is a simple, typical principal waterfall in which collateral principal is applied to CLO creditors in the following order:

1. Amounts due in steps 1 through 8 of the interest waterfall that were not met with collateral interest.
2. During the CLO's reinvestment period, to purchase new collateral assets.
3. After the reinvestment period, for principal repayment of tranches in order of their priority.
4. Amounts due in 9 through 12 of the interest waterfall.

Diversion of collateral interest can greatly increase protection to senior CLO tranches. Debt tranches can receive all their principal and interest even if collateral losses surpass the amount of subordination below them in the capital structure. The benefit of coverage tests to senior tranches depends on how soon the tests are breeched. The earlier diversion begins, the more collateral interest that can be diverted over the remaining life of the collateral. The amount of cash that can be diverted is smaller if tests fail late in the life of the CLO.

But it is possible for a CLO manager to circumvent the protection of cash flow diversion. *Par building* trades artificially shore up par coverage tests by replacing relatively high price collateral with relatively low price collateral. For example, if a CLO manager sells $2 million of bonds at par he can buy $3 million par of bonds selling at 67%. This would inflate Asset Par by $1 million in the numerator of the par coverage test. Done in enough size, it could prevent a CLO from violating par coverage tests and keep cash flowing down the CLO's waterfall to the manager and equity holders.

Rating agencies and CLO debt investors pushed through a number of structural enhancements to the cash flow credit structure. Beginning in 2002, the calculation of asset par in the numerator of the par coverage tests in some CLOs was haircut if collateral assets were downgraded or purchased too cheaply. Par credit given to defaulted assets was also reduced. Reinvestment coverage tests (such as the one shown as step 9 in the previous interest waterfall) came into use. Delays in sending cash to equity holders and faster amortizations of debt tranches were also put into place. While no CLO has all these structural enhancements, they all have some of these enhancements and together they are an important part of a CLO's cash flow credit structure.

Why Buy CLO Equity?

There are four reasons that investors purchase CLO equity:

1. The nonrecourse term financing that CLOs provide to CLO equity is a very good thing.
2. The cash flow CLO structure is very forgiving to CLO equity holders; providing significant return even when CLO debt holders are destined to receive less than their due.

3. CLO equity holders receive two valuable options that further increase the value of their investment, the rights to "sell out early" or "wait and see."
4. CLO equity can be used as a *defensive investment strategy.*

We explain on each of these reasons next.

Nonrecourse Term Financing

CLOs don't just provide financing to CLO equity holders. They deliver *nonrecourse term financing* because CLO equity holders own stock in a company and are not liable for the losses of that company. With term financing, because the financing rate does not change, the financing cannot be withdrawn, and a cash flow CLO cannot be forced to liquidate its assets.

CLO equity is a leveraged position in the assets of a CLO, with the CLO's debt tranches providing the financing for equity holders. CLO equity receives whatever cash flow remains after satisfaction of debt claims. Equity sustains the risk of collateral asset payment delays and credit losses, but also receives the upside if CLO assets generate cash flow in excess of debt tranche requirements. Meanwhile, debt tranche holders only have recourse to the CLO's assets, and cannot make any additional claims against equity holders. CLO equity holders are not at risk for anything beyond their initial investment.

CLO equity holders receive financing that is in place for up to 12, or even 15, years. Moreover, the financing rate is locked in, usually at a spread above LIBOR. CLO debt is subject to early amortization only if asset quality deteriorates according to objective measures (primarily par coverage tests). In such cases, principal repayment is due only to the extent the asset portfolio provides cash flow, and asset sales are never required.

These features are in stark contrast to the terms available in the repo market or in other short-term secured financing arrangements. In those, financing rates can fluctuate and higher levels of security (larger collateral haircuts) can be demanded at the pleasure of the creditor. In fact, financing can be completely withdrawn with little warning. Collateral assets are subject to sale by the creditor to meet what are essentially margin calls, and creditors have recourse to the borrower if the collateral is insufficient to extinguish the debt. CLO equity holders avoid all these risks.

The Forgiving Nature of CLO Financing

CLO equity will receive payments in any realistic collateral default scenario, even in scenarios where debt holders receive less than their full principal and interest. Unless collateral losses are large and immediate, CLO equity will initially receive cash flow. Later, coverage tests may become binding and redirect collateral cash flows to pay down debt holders or purchase new assets. So some cash flow will leak out of the CLO structure to equity holders in scenarios where CLO debt holders are not repaid in full. How much flows through depends on the timing of collateral losses and the strictness of the CLO structure in cutting off cash flow to equity holders.

To demonstrate the leakage of cash flow to equity holders, we selected a recently issued and typical CLO. We compared cash flows of the equity tranche to those of the CLO's lowest debt tranche, a floating rate BB debt under a scenario of delayed defaults. Table 4.4 shows a default scenario based on increasing defaults.

This will be our base case default scenario, which we will adjust by multiplying it by 0, 1, 2, 3, and so on to create more stressful scenarios. But note that no matter how high a factor we multiply the scenario by, there are never any defaults in the CLO's first year. This allows equity to receive the maximum cash flow possible in its first year.

TABLE 4.4 CDR Scenario

Year	Defaults
1	0.0%
2	0.5%
3	1.0%
4	1.0%
Thereafter	1.0%

FIGURE 4.1   Equity and BB Debt Under CDR Scenarios

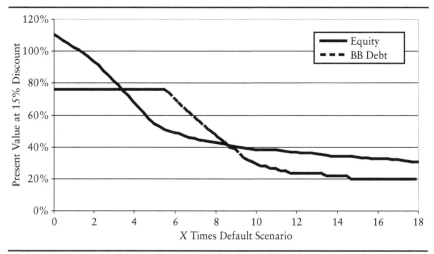

Data for this figure obtained from Intex Solutions.

Figure 4.1 shows the results of multiplications of this default scenario. We discount cash flows by 15% to achieve a present value (PV).
The PV of equity immediately deteriorates with greater defaults. But
at 5.0 times the default scenario, the PV of equity flattens out significantly. This is because most of equity's value comes from cash flows
in the early years of the CLO. Meanwhile, BB debt maintains its PV
until 5.75 times the default scenario, after which it rapidly loses PV.
At 8.75 times the default scenario, the PV of the BB tranche actually
crosses below the PV of equity. So with this particular CLO in this
particular default pattern, we have the case where one is better off
owning equity in both low and high default scenarios.

CLO Options

The value of equity is also enhanced by two different call options that
equity holders have on the CLO's assets. The simplest to understand
option is in the market value of the CLO's assets. After a noncall
period, CLO assets can be liquidated. To the extent proceeds from
the liquidation exceed the cost of repaying debt and other expenses,
equity holders benefit dollar-for-dollar. Certainly, if the market value
of the CLO assets is less than the par value of the CLO's debt, equity

holders would not want to liquidate assets. And a cash flow CLO is never forced to sell collateral before that collateral's maturity. Nor does the market value of CLO collateral affect CLO equity distributions. Equity holders in a market value-challenged CLO will keep receiving cash flow, so long as coverage tests are not violated.

CLO equity holders also have a call option on the postdefault cash flows of a CLO's asset portfolio. If CLO asset cash flow exceeds debt tranche requirements, the equity tranche also gains dollar-for-dollar. And if postdefault cash flow is insufficient to satisfy debt tranches, CLO equity "loses" the same amount of return whether the CLO debt service shortfall is $1 million or whether it is only $1. Whereas the strike price of CLO equity's market value option is the amount necessary to retire the CLO's debt and repay the CLO's other senior expenses, the strike price of CLO equity's postdefault cash flow option is the cash flow necessary in each payment period to service CLO debt.

So CLO equity holders have two similar options:

1. An option on the market value of assets in the CLO portfolio, which is exercised by liquidating and unwinding the CLO
2. An option on the postdefault cash flow of the CLO asset portfolio, which is reaped by simply waiting to see how actual defaults and coverage tests interact to produce equity cash flow

Like all option holders, CLO equity tranche holders are long volatility. They benefit if the underlying has greater market risk and if the underlying has greater postdefault cash flow risk. This is because all underlying collateral asset outcomes below the strike price have the same result for the option holder, i.e., the option is worthless. But volatility on the upside creates greater and greater returns for the option holder.

Market value and postdefault cash flow optionalities increase the value of CLO equity. A CLO manager would never liquidate a CLO unless there was considerable upside for CLO equity holders. A CLO manager might refrain from selling a credit-deteriorated asset in order to avoid crystallizing a loss and retain a potential upside benefit for equity holders. And, in fact, some CLO managers have intentionally purchased riskier assets to take advantage of CLO equity's cash flow optionality.

CLO Equity as a Defensive Strategy

Obviously, investors do not know what the future may bring. Furthermore, it seems to us that prognostications based on the most careful analysis of past economic experience may prove incorrect. Those few who share such uncertainty may consider CLO equity as a defensive investment.

Here's what we mean. Rather than invest $100 in high-yield loans or investment-grade structured finance assets on an un-levered basis, the concerned investor should consider purchasing CLO equity that controls $100 of those assets. The remainder can be stored in whatever safe harbor asset one prefers: Treasury bills, inflation-indexed Treasuries, or AAA LIBOR floaters.

The resulting risk profile will not have all the upside potential as if one had dedicated the portfolio completely to the CLO's underlying assets. But the downside risk will be significantly mitigated.

CLO Equity in a Portfolio

CLO equity investors want to understand how their investment will behave relative to other assets in their portfolio. Consequently, there has been a good deal of research published on historic CLO equity returns, particularly with regard to the monthly volatility of equity returns, their Sharpe ratios (i.e., the average monthly return on CLO equity minus the risk-free return divided by the standard deviation of monthly CLO equity returns), and the correlation of CLO equity returns to the returns of other assets. Unfortunately, the calculation of these variables is so fundamentally flawed that the results that have been reported to investors are useless. The reason is quite simple: the secondary market for CLO equity is undeveloped. As a result, there are no monthly prices for CLO equity. It follows that one cannot calculate monthly CLO equity returns, the monthly volatility of CLO equity returns, or a CLO equity Sharpe ratio. Nor can one correlate monthly CLO equity returns with those of other assets.

But what if CLO equity was traded on the New York Stock Exchange, and the bid-ask spread was 0.125%, and we had daily traded prices for every single CLO equity ever issued? What then? Well, in that world, we could certainly compute monthly and even daily price volatility as well as Sharpe ratios and return correlations with other assets. But if these computations were available, how much weight should we give them in terms of predicting future CLO equity performance, especially the performance of new and recently created CLO equity? The important question here is, "What can history teach us about future CLO equity returns?"

To answer this question, one first has to think about determinates of CLO equity returns. These factors are:

1. The collateral's promised yield
2. The CLO's funding cost
3. The amount of leverage in the CLO structure
4. The cash flow structure of the CLO
5. The influence of the CLO manager
6. The collateral's default and recovery performance

Given that these factors are determinates of CLO equity returns, which ones are subject to historical analysis? Or to put it another way, of these six factors, for which do we care about past values and for which do we care only about current values? We look into each of the six inputs to CLO equity returns below:

1. *The collateral's promised yield or the cash flow from the CLO's portfolio in the absence of collateral defaults.* If the CLO has purchased its initial portfolio, the CLO equity investor need only look at the portfolio's weighted average coupon or weighted average spread. If the CLO is in the process of buying its collateral portfolio, the CLO equity investor would best look at current spreads in the respective collateral markets. The long-term history of collateral spreads does not offer much insight to the CLO equity investor, with the exception of being perhaps an indicator of collateral reinvestment risk.
2. CLO *funding cost or the cost of the CLO's own debt.* Historic CLO spreads do not matter at all to the returns of new CLO equity. We only care about the levels at which CLO debt can be placed today. Old CLO liability spreads do not help us predict returns on new CLO equity.
3. *The amount of leverage in the CLO structure.* Past CLO leverage ratios do not change the fact of current rating agency and debt

investor requirements. Past leverage ratios do not matter to the future performance of today's CLO equity.

4. *The cash flow structure of the CLO, including coverage tests and equity caps that determine cash distributions to CLO equity holders.* CLO structures today are dramatically different from ones executed two years ago and they even differ from CLO structures executed one year ago. How structures used to be has no effect on how today's structures are going to affect CLO equity returns.

5. *CLO manager influence.* A manager's historic total return performance or default-avoidance performance may help predict future CLO equity returns. But perhaps a stronger factor influencing CLO equity performance is any bias shown to equity or debt investors by the manager in previous CLOs. While managers' historical behavior may be important in predicting CLO equity returns, we view it as a nonquantifiable and nonmodelable factor.

6. *Collateral defaults and recoveries.* Of all the factors influencing CLO equity returns, the one most open to an appeal to history is collateral defaults and recoveries. In analyzing potential CLO equity returns, we should be very interested in the historic average and the historic volatility of default rates and recovery rates. This does not mean that we do not consider today's economic conditions or underwriting standards in estimating future default and recoveries. But past experience, in good times, bad times, and average times is a good place to start when thinking about future collateral defaults and recoveries.

Thus, history makes little difference with respect to most of the factors affecting CLO equity returns. Only current levels matter. Given this, how applicable would historic CLO equity price volatility, Sharpe ratios, and return correlation with other assets be to *new* CLO equity offerings, even if these measures could be reasonably calculated? It seems to us that the measures would be of little guidance to an investor considering a CLO equity purchase today.

The answer to predicting the performance of a new CLO is to model the CLO's collateral spread, funding cost, leverage and structure, and then to test it under different default and recovery assumptions. This is nothing more than what bankers already present in every

CLO pitch book. We simply recommend looking at the default and recovery scenarios provided mindful of the historic default experience of the CLO's assets and current underwriting standards. This, we hope, sounds like a very ordinary, even mundane, suggestion. We now turn to predicting how CLO equity will complement an existing portfolio.

An Equity Correlation Short Cut

Figure 4.2 shows the graph of CLO underlying returns and CLO equity returns under the simplifying assumptions that (1) CLO equity does not receive any cash flow until the claims of CLO debt holder are completely satisfied; and (2) CLO equity holders do not take advantage of certain optionalities inherent in their position. (We explained the benefit of these factors to CLO equity earlier in this chapter.)

The figure's horizontal axis depicts returns on the CLO's underlying assets. In our example, the best case is that the CLO portfolio suffers no defaults and returns its promised yield of 10%. In the worst case, all the assets in the CLO's portfolio default without any recovery and the portfolio's return is –100%. The thin line going up at a 30-degree angle represents the tautology that the return of the underlying CLO assets depends on the return of the underlying CLO assets. Therefore, it also goes from –100% to +10%.

FIGURE 4.2   Underlying Asset and CLO Equity Return

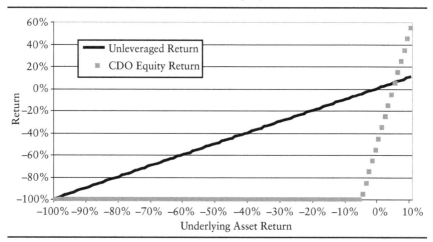

In graphing CLO equity return, we assume that equity contributes 10% of the funding for the CLO's asset portfolio and that 90% of the CLO portfolio is funded with CLO debt costing an average of 5%. The thick line in Figure 4.2, which moves horizontally along the bottom of the graph and becomes a rising dotted line at the right of the exhibit, represents CLO equity returns.

There are two distinct regions in Figure 4.2 with respect to the return correlation of CLO equity and the CLO's underlying assets. On the right side of the figure, when CLO equity return varies between –100% and +55%, there is a strict mathematical relationship based on the excess cash flow from the underlying CLO collateral over that which is necessary to service the CLO's debt. All of this excess goes to CLO equity and every extra dollar of excess cash flow is an extra dollar of return to CLO equity. In this region, at the right of the figure, the return correlation between CLO assets and CLO equity is a perfect 1.0.

Between CLO underlying returns of –100% and –5%, CLO equity's return is flat-lined at a –100% loss in our example. This is due to, as we have said, the nonrecourse nature of CLO equity. As equity holders in a corporate entity, CLO equity holders are not responsible for the debts of the CLO and can only lose the purchase price of their equity investment. In this region, the return correlation between CLO assets and CLO equity is zero.

The simple, and pretty good, answer to the correlation of CLO equity returns and the CLO asset portfolio is thus: when CLO equity is not completely wiped out, the return correlation is 1.0; and when CLO equity is wiped out, the return correlation is zero. These correlations are based on the cash flows of the CLO equity and CLO assets over their lives, as opposed to monthly price movements. We've argued why this is the only reasonable way to look at CLO equity returns.

Having correlated CLO equity returns to the returns of the underlying CLO assets, it is simple to compare the return correlation of the underlying CLO assets to what might be in an investor's existing portfolio through the traditional practice of using monthly returns, as we show in Table 4.4. So, if CLO equity is firmly in-the-money, its return correlation with the loans in its portfolio is 1.0. The table shows the monthly return correlation of high-yield loans

TABLE 4.4   Monthly Asset Return Correlations

	HY Loans	HY Bonds	IG Bonds	S&P 500	U.S. Treasuries
High-yield loans	1.00				
High-yield bonds	0.48	1.00			
Investment-grade bonds	–0.06	0.23	1.00		
S&P 500	0.14	0.51	0.02	1.00	
U.S. Treasuries	–0.11	0.04	0.91	–0.09	1.00

Data for this table obtained from UBS Fixed Income Research.

to other assets, which is our proxy for the return correlation of CLO equity with those same assets. Note that historically, the correlation of high-yield loans (and therefore in-the-money CLO equity) to the S&P 500 has been very low, while the correlation of high-yield loans (and therefore in-the-money CLO equity) to investment-grade bonds and U.S. Treasuries has been negative.

Recall the simplifying assumptions we made in order to create Figure 4.2: CLO equity receives no cash unless CLO debt is repaid in full and CLO equity does not make use of the options it holds. These assumptions lower CLO equity return. Thus, if one uses the return and correlation assumptions of Table 4.4 to size the optimum amount of CLO equity in a portfolio, one will underallocate to CLO equity because these benefits are not factored in. This process therefore determines the *minimum amount* of CLO equity that is optimal in a portfolio.

SUMMARY

In this chapter on cash CLOs, we used a building block approach to explain and define CLOs. The four parts of a CLO are its assets, liabilities, purpose, and credit structure. Many different combinations of these four elements have been put together to create CLOs, but as of this writing the most common types of CLOs are arbitrage-purpose cash flow-credit structure CLOs backed by leveraged loans. So we went into detail on these CLOs and the cash flow credit structure. Finally, we made a four-part case for buying CLO equity and discussed its contribution to an existing portfolio.

5

CLO Returns

In the previous chapter, we described the fundamental of collater- alized loan obligations (CLOs). In this chapter, we look at CLO returns. We begin by investigating the resiliency of CLO returns to defaults and recoveries. More specifically, we analyze 1,575 tranches from 340 CLOs issued from 2003 to 2007 that are covered by Moody's Wall Street Analytics (MWSA) modeling service. Although when modeling CLO returns, the focus is primarily on defaults and recoveries, when there is dislocation in the credit markets, two other factors demand attention: (1) the size of the CLO's triple-C asset bucket and (2) the price at which the CLO reinvests in new collateral loans. We investigate those factors in the second part of the chapter.

DEFAULT AND RECOVERY SCENARIOS

Table 5.1 shows the 26 default and recovery scenarios we made in modeling the CLOs using MWSA. In modeling CLOs, defaults can be quantified in a number of ways. The *conditional default rate* (CDR) is the annualized value of the unpaid principal balance of newly defaulted loans over the course of a month as a percentage of the total unpaid balance of the pool at the beginning of the month. Note in Table 5.1 that when we test CLOs with higher CDRs, we also stress them with lower loan recoveries in the event of default. We also specify bond recoveries for those CLOs that are allowed to invest a portion of their portfolios in those assets.

In creating our scenarios, we attempted to correlate default and recovery rates. In the very mild default scenario of 0.5% CDR, we use the highest average recoveries of recent years. For loans, this was

TABLE 5.1   Default and Recovery Scenarios (percent)

Conditional Default Rate	Loan Recovery	Bond Recovery
0	na	na
0.5	90	60
1	87	57
1.5	84	54
2	82	52
2.5	79	49
3	76	46
3.5	73	43
4	71	41
4.5	68	38
5	65	35
5.5	64	34
6	63	33
6.5	62	32
7	61	31
7.5	60	30
8	59	29
9	58	28
10	57	27
12	56	26
14	55	25
16	54	24
18	53	23
20	52	22
22	51	21
25	50	20

Data for this table obtained from MWSA.

around 90% in 1996 and for bonds this was around 60% in 1985, 1987, and 1996.[1]

To give context to the CDRs in Table 5.1, 5% CDR approximates the highest cumulative default rate of U.S. institutional loans since that market developed in 1995. Loans originated in 2000 had a cumulative default rate over 4.5 years of 21.0%.[2] Loan underwriting had significantly deteriorated and 2000-vintage loans were exposed to the U.S. recession of 2000–2001. The 21.0% cumulative default rate of 2000-vintage loans compares to an average of 7.7% across all other vintages 1995–2003. In our cash flow modeling, a 5% CDR over 4.5 years produces a cumulative default rate of 20.6%. The 65% loan recovery rate we associate with 5% CDR is the average recovery rate of loans defaulting from 2001 to 2003.

Another default "landmark" in Table 5.1 is 10% CDR. Over four years, this CDR produces a 34.4% cumulative default rate, which is a little higher than the 33.9% high-yield bond default rate that prevailed in the depths of the Great Depression 1932–1935.[3] Over five years, this same 10% CDR produces 41% cumulative defaults, equal to the worst five-year single B rated high-yield bond default rate since 1970.[4] Higher default rates, further down the rows in the table, have no basis in historical experience for either leveraged loans or high-yield bonds.

Other modeling assumptions that we made in using MWSA were:

---

[1] Moody's annual default studies publish recovery details for the previous two years. We use Moody's series of average trading prices after default as our measure of recovery.

[2] Steve Miller, Robert Polenberg, Aditi Mahendroo, *1Q08 Institutional Loan Default Review*, S&P LCD, April 2008.

[3] Lea V. Carty and Dana Lieberman, *Historical Default Rates of Corporate Bond Issuers, 1920–1996*, Moody's Investors Service, January 1997. Page 9 discusses the worst four-year period 1932–1935. W. Braddock Hickman, the grandfather of default study research, found a rate of 48.9% over the same period in *Corporate Bond Quality and Investor Experience*, NBER, 1958. The considerable difference could be because Moody's focused on Moody's-rated bonds.

[4] Kenneth Emery, Sharon Ou, Jennifer Tennant, Frank Kim, and Richard Cantor, *Corporate Default and Recovery Rates, 1920–2007*, Moody's, February 2008.

- Default reinvestment.
- Prepay loans at 15% per annum, bonds at 5%.
- Reinvest principal proceeds in accordance with the CLO's current portfolio attributes with respect to the percentage of bonds versus loans, weighted average spreads, weighted average coupon, price, etc.

Defaulting reinvestment is, of course, unambiguously conservative in comparison to not defaulting reinvestment. A low prepayment rate is conservative as prepaid assets are not unavailable to default. Our choice of 15% loan prepayments reflects what some in the industry think is a low lifetime prepayment rate. Assuming that reinvestment mirrors the current portfolio's parameters captures the manager's investment style, although it may not reflect current market conditions.

Example Results

The results of default and recovery scenarios in terms of the present value of future CLO tranche cash flows were generated by MWSA. Internal rates of returns (IRRs) were not computed because at the stresses we put the CLOs through, we knew the negative IRR results that would be generated would be hard to interpret.[5] Instead, we show CLO tranche present values as a percent of current outstanding par, thereby creating a present value price. Because we are assuming the certainty of particular stress scenarios, we used MWSA to discount cash flows for all tranches at LIBOR. This allows comparison of results across tranches of different ratings. In the results that we report in this chapter, a "PV @ LIBOR" of 100 means that the CLO's future cash flows, when discounted at LIBOR, are equal to the CLO's outstanding par balance. If so, the tranche's IRR is LIBOR if purchased at par. A present value greater than or smaller than 100 indicates the price necessary to produce a LIBOR return. Figure 5.1 shows results for one CLO from 2005.

---

[5] Which is worse, a –10% IRR over one year or a –5% IRR over two years? We're not sure, either.

FIGURE 5.1   Present Value Results for a 2005 CLO

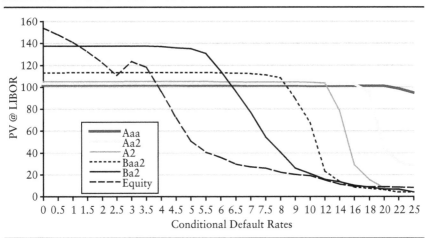

Data for this figure obtained from Moody's Wall Street Analytics.

Looking at the figure, it's easy to identify the CLO's tranches. The line with the highest present value in the 0% CDR case is, of course, the equity tranche. The next two highest present values are the Ba2 and Baa2 tranches. Neither tranche suffers a loss at 0% CDR; the difference in their present values is the result of the higher coupon of the Ba2 tranche relative to the Baa2 tranche. Aaa, Aa, and A tranche present values are very close to each other at 0% CDR because the difference in their coupons is not enough to cause their present values to be very different. Looking to the right of Figure 5.1, one sees where each tranche eventually "breaks" or returns less than full principal and interest, causing their present values to decline. For the Ba tranche, this is at 4.5% CDR and 68% recovery on loans. For the two Aaa tranches of this CLO, loss of some interest occurs at 22% CDR, and 51% loan recovery.

Figure 5.2 shows results for 61 Baa2 CLOs issued in 2005. Coupon spreads above LIBOR for these CLOs range from 170 to 285 basis points, thus creating differences in present values in the 0% CDR case. The first CLO to default on a portion of its coupon does so at 4% CDR. That same CLO's present value falls to 100 at 5% CDR. The two strongest Baa2 CLOs begin defaulting on a portion of their coupons at 12 to 14% CDR.

FIGURE 5.2 Present Value of 62 Baa2 CLOs from 2005

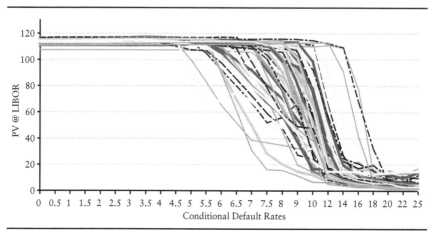

Data for this figure obtained from Moody's Wall Street Analytics.

Some of the difference in the relative strength of these Baa2 tranches is explained by the CLO's *weighted average rating factor* (WARF) triggers. WARF is a rough guide to the asset quality of the CLO portfolio and is meant to incorporate the probability of default for each of the assets backing a CLO. CLOs with higher WARF triggers (and, therefore, lower collateral ratings) must be structured to withstand the higher collateral losses those lower ratings imply. Another factor is the maximum limit for high-yield bonds in these CLOs. CLOs with larger "bond buckets" must also be able to withstand higher collateral losses. Still another factor is the pattern and extent of collateral losses to date, which affects the current strength of tranches.

Present Value Results for 340 CLOs

Table 5.2 shows the distribution of the CLO debt tranches we studied by vintage and original ratings. In all, we looked at 1,575 tranches from 340 CLOs issued in the years 2003 to 2007.

In Tables 5.3 and 5.4, we show average present value results for each vintage and rating of debt tranches shown in Table 5.2. Rather than show every one of the 26 scenarios run using MWSA, we focus on scenarios where the average present value for CLOs of a particu-

TABLE 5.2 Number of CLO Tranches in Study

CDO Tranche	2003	2004	2005	2006	2007	Total
Aaa	38	61	109	193	110	511
Aa2	18	20	58	106	69	271
A2	21	29	65	113	68	296
Baa2	24	31	62	102	64	283
Ba2	12	17	42	82	61	214
Total	113	158	336	596	372	1575

Data for this table calculated using Moody's Wall Street Analytics.

lar rating and vintage first falls below 100. This implies an IRR of less than LIBOR if the CLO was purchased at par today.

In Table 5.3, we show present values under a 0% CDR scenario. As we only look at floating rate debt tranches, differences in average present values reflect coupon spreads above LIBOR. Therefore, in the 0% CDR scenario, the present values of lower-rated, higher-coupon tranches are always greater than the present values of higher-rated, lower-coupon tranches.

Moving down the panels of Tables 5.3 and 5.4, we see that the average present values sometimes rise for particular combinations of vintages and ratings. This happens if enough tranches represented in a cell of the panel extend their maturities, but still pay all principal and interest. The above-LIBOR coupon received over a longer time period present values to a greater amount. Eventually, as one goes down the panels to higher CDRs, present values decline.

Recall that our 5% CDR scenario replicates the worse loan performance since the U.S. institutional loan market developed in 1995. This was the 2000 loan vintage which had a cumulative default rate of 21.0% over 4.5 years. Our 5% CDR scenario produces a similar cumulative default rate of 20.6% over 4.5 years. In that scenario, we use a 65% recovery rate, the loan recovery rate of 2001–2003.

Results for the 5% CDR scenario are shown in the third panel of Table 5.3. Note that all average debt tranche present values are above 100, implying an IRR greater than LIBOR if the CLO was purchased today at par. Ba2 tranches are down significantly from the present values in the 0% CDR case, indicating that they are not

TABLE 5.3   Average Present Value for 340 CLOs, by Vintage and Original Rating

(A) 0% CDR

CDO Tranche	2003	2004	2005	2006	2007	Average
Aaa	102	102	101	102	102	102
Aa2	105	104	103	103	104	104
A2	109	107	106	106	108	107
Baa2	117	115	113	113	118	115
Ba2	148	136	136	134	138	136

(B) 2.5% CDR, 79% Loan Recovery, 49% Bond Recovery

CDO Tranche	2003	2004	2005	2006	2007	Average
Aaa	102	102	101	102	102	102
Aa2	105	104	103	103	104	104
A2	109	108	106	106	108	107
Baa2	117	115	114	114	118	115
Ba2	149	137	137	135	138	137

(C) 5% CDR, 65% Loan Recovery, 35% Bond Recovery

CDO Tranche	2003	2004	2005	2006	2007	Average
Aaa	102	102	101	101	102	101
Aa2	105	104	103	103	104	104
A2	109	108	106	106	108	107
Baa2	118	112	113	112	118	114
Ba2	141	129	124	123	120	124

returning all promised coupon. But Ba2 present values are still well above higher-rated tranches, which might indicate that if one expects a repeat of 2000 default and recovery conditions, Ba CLO tranches offer the best return, even if they do not return all their promised coupon.

However, let's take a step back and poke at the Ba results a little. MWSA's cash flow model, just like any other we know about, is driven by defaults and recoveries. It does not take into account

TABLE 5.3 (continued)

(D) 6% CDR, 63% Loan Recovery, 33% Bond Recovery

CDO Tranche	2003	2004	2005	2006	2007	Average
Aaa	102	102	101	101	101	101
Aa2	105	104	103	103	103	103
A2	109	108	106	105	107	106
Baa2	118	110	109	111	115	112
Ba2	121	117	105	102	95	103

(E) 7.5% CDR, 60% Loan Recovery, 30% Bond Recovery

CDO Tranche	2003	2004	2005	2006	2007	Average
Aaa	102	102	101	101	101	101
Aa2	105	104	103	103	103	103
A2	109	108	105	103	105	105
Baa2	112	96	96	100	104	101
Ba2	66	64	56	51	48	53

(F) 10% CDR, 57% Loan Recovery, 27% Bond Recovery

CDO Tranche	2003	2004	2005	2006	2007	Average
Aaa	102	101	101	101	101	101
Aa2	105	104	102	102	102	102
A2	109	103	96	96	101	99
Baa2	59	45	54	52	49	52
Ba2	24	20	24	20	18	21

Data for this table calculated using Moody's Wall Street Analytics.

collateral downgrades. But in a 5% CDR environment, we would expect a lot of leverage loan downgrades. Downgrades affect CLO cash flows because after a certain point, CCC assets are not given credit in overcollateralization tests. Thus, collateral downgrades added to collateral defaults would cause CLO overcollateralization triggers to trip sooner, cutting off cash flow to lower debt tranches sooner. How much sooner? It depends on leverage loan downgrades. So, the bottom line is that investors looking for a pickup in spread to

TABLE 5.4 Average Present Value for 340 CLOs, By Vintage and Original Rating

(A) 16% CDR, 54% Loan Recovery, 24% Bond Recovery

CDO Tranche	2003	2004	2005	2006	2007	Average
Aaa	102	101	100	100	100	100
Aa2	93	96	85	87	90	89
A2	32	29	31	25	26	28
Baa2	11	8	12	10	7	10
Ba2	10	8	10	8	10	9

(B) 20% CDR, 52% Loan Recovery, 22% Bond Recovery

CDO Tranche	2003	2004	2005	2006	2007	Average
Aaa	101	99	98	98	99	98
Aa2	43	47	44	47	47	46
A2	9	10	12	10	9	10
Baa2	7	5	6	7	5	6
Ba2	7	6	7	8	7	7

(C) 25% CDR, 50% Loan Recovery, 20% Bond Recovery

CDO Tranche	2003	2004	2005	2006	2007	Average
Aaa	95	91	93	92	94	93
Aa2	29	30	31	33	32	32
A2	5	7	6	6	6	6
Baa2	5	4	4	5	3	4
Ba2	4	4	4	5	5	5

Data for this table calculated using Moody's Wall Street Analytics.

Aaa CLOs in a 5% CDR environment would be safer moving up the capital structure from Ba2 to Baa2 or A2 CLOs.

The other default "landmark" we mentioned was 10% CDR, which replicates Great Depression speculative-grade bond defaults. This is shown in the last panel of Table 5.3. What is interesting is in that extreme default scenario, an investor is better off with Aa2 CLOs than Aaa CLOs. Not all the Aa2 CLOs pay full interest and principal, which we can tell because their average present values decrease from the 0% CDR case. But higher coupons on the Aa2 CLOs that do pay make up for this and Aa2 CLO present values are greater than Aaa CLOs present values. As most Aa2 CLO tranches are nonpay-in-kind (nonPIK), they would not be negatively affected by our concern about leverage loan downgrades causing overcollateralization triggers to trip.

Present Value Standard Deviation

As we explained, Tables 5.3 and 5.4 show average present values for all the CLOs from a particular vintage and original rating. Table 5.5 delves deeper and shows the standard deviation among CLO present values in the 5% CDR scenario, which replicates the worse default and recovery environment for leverage loans since the inception of that market in 1995. Ba2 CLOs have the highest present value standard deviation. Present value standard deviation is significantly reduced in the Baa2 tranches and further reduced as one continues up in rating. Present value standard deviations for 2007 Aa2 and A2 CLOs are high because of the broad range of coupon spreads for those CLOs.

It's interesting to consider the risk of buying a bad Baa2 CLO versus a bad Aaa CLO. Suppose "bad" is defined as a CLO that returns one standard deviation below average present value in the 5% CDR scenario. Such a bad Baa2 CLO would return 114 (the average Baa2 PV across all vintages in the third panel of Table 5.3) minus 7.7 (the average Baa2 standard deviation across all vintages in Table 5.5), or

TABLE 5.5 Present Value Standard Deviations for 5% CDR, 65% Loan Recovery, 35% Bond Recovery

CDO Tranche	2003	2004	2005	2006	2007	Average
Aaa	1.0	0.6	0.4	0.6	0.7	0.6
Aa2	0.9	0.5	0.5	0.5	2.1	1.3
A2	0.9	0.9	1.2	1.9	3.9	2.6
Baa2	1.2	15.1	5.2	6.1	6.6	7.7
Ba2	7.6	15.7	16.1	13.2	15.0	15.0

Data for this table calculated using Moody's Wall Street Analytics.

TABLE 5.6   Present Value Standard Deviations for 10% CDR, 57% Loan Recovery, 27% Bond Recovery

CDO Tranche	2003	2004	2005	2006	2007	Average
Aaa	0.9	0.7	0.3	0.4	0.5	0.5
Aa2	0.9	0.6	6.1	2.5	5.8	4.4
A2	3.2	10.1	18.6	20.2	16.6	17.8
Baa2	21.4	27.4	29.2	26.0	29.3	27.3
Ba2	8.1	8.3	25.0	22.7	15.4	19.9

Data for this table calculated using Moody's Wall Street Analytics.

106.3. An average Aaa CLO would return 101. One is better off with a bad Baa2 CLO than an average Aaa CLO! However, if one defines a "bad" CLO as one which performs two standard deviations below average, the result changes. The bad Baa2 CLO would return 114 − 2 × 7.7 or 98.6. A bad Aaa CLO would return 101 − 2 × 0.6, or 99.8. In that case, one is better off with a bad Aaa CLO than a bad Baa2 CLO.

Table 5.6 provides standard deviations in the 10% CDR scenario, which replicates Great Depression high-yield bond defaults. Except for Aaa CLOs, present value standard deviations have significantly increased, showing an increasing divergence of performance among CLOs of the same vintage and original rating. For an investor expecting Great Depression defaults and unsure of his or her ability to pick out an average CLO or one that will perform one to two standard deviations below average, Aaa tranches are the ones to buy.

CLO Debt Tranche "Breakpoints"

It's handy to define the strength of CLOs by their ability to withstand defaults and default losses. We'll first look at CLOs in terms of their "coupon break points" or the combination of CDR and recovery which cause a CLO tranche to fail to return promised coupon. We continue to test CLOs using the combinations of CDRs and recoveries in Table 5.1. In determining coupon break points, we accept the small tolerance of losing one point of present value. In other words, the present value must decline 1 from the 0% CDR present values shown in the first panel of Table 5.3 before we declare a "coupon break point." This is basically a 10 basis point loss in yield on a security with a 10-year weighted average life (WAL).

Table 5.7 shows the CDR at which CLOs of a particular vintage and original rating lose one point of present value. There are big differences in the CDR coupon breakpoints across vintages. For example, 2007 Aaa CLOs have coupon break points at 12 CDR while 2003 Aaa CLOs have coupon break points at 22 CDR. There is even a discontinuity in the 2004 vintage where Baa2 CLOs have a lower average coupon breakpoint than Ba2 CLOs. This is caused by the mix of CLOs having Baa2 tranches, but not Ba2 tranches.

Table 5.7 is a very different way to look at CLO performance than we have shown so far, and we would argue that it is a wrong way to look at CLO performance. It focuses on what was lost rather than what was received. We would argue that it is better to receive 10% IRR, even if one was promised an IRR of 12%, rather than receive a promised 5% IRR.

We would argue that the information provided in Table 5.8 is more relevant to an investor. It shows the combination of CDR and recovery which cause a CLO tranche's present value to fall below 100. Since we discount CLO cash flows by LIBOR, this shows when the average IRR in each combination of vintage and rating falls below LIBOR for CLOs purchased at par. An investor can find the lowest rating that satisfies their worst case CDR scenario and obtain their highest return. Of course, these are averages, and a bad CLO in a particular vintage and rating combination would perform worse. We also repeat our warning that rating downgrades may speed up the point at which cash flow is cut off to lower-rated tranches.

TABLE 5.7 CDR Where Average Present Value Declines One Point

CDO Tranche	2003	2004	2005	2006	2007	Average
Aaa	22	18	16	16	12	16
Aa2	14	16	10	10	7.5	10
A2	12	10	8	6.5	6.5	7
Baa2	7	4	5.5	5.5	5.5	5.5
Ba2	5	4.5	4	4	3.5	4

Data for this table calculated using Moody's Wall Street Analytics.

TABLE 5.8   CDR Where Average Present Value Declines Below 100

CDO Tranche	2003	2004	2005	2006	2007	Average
Aaa	22	20	16	18	18	18
Aa2	16	16	14	12	14	14
A2	12	12	10	10	12	10
Baa2	9	7.5	7.5	8	8	8
Ba2	7	7	6.5	6.5	6	6.5

Data for this table calculated using Moody's Wall Street Analytics.

TABLE 5.9   Weighted Average Life at 0% CDR

CDO Tranche	2003	2004	2005	2006	2007	Average
Aaa	3.4	4.5	5.3	6.4	7.5	6.0
Aa2	5.9	6.4	7.7	9.0	10.4	8.7
A2	6.2	6.9	8.2	9.6	11.0	9.1
Baa2	6.5	7.3	8.7	10.0	11.4	9.4
Ba2	6.7	6.7	9.0	10.5	11.8	10.1

Data for this table calculated using Moody's Wall Street Analytics.

Buying CLOs at a Discount: Optimum CDR and Weighted Average Life

We have shown CLO present values as a percent of outstanding principal balance, implicitly assuming CLOs are purchased at par. Since we discount at LIBOR, a present value of 100 means the CLO returns LIBOR. But CLO have traded at substantial discounts to par. An important question is how fast the discount will be earned, i.e., what is the WAL of the CLO? Table 5.9 shows average WALs for CLOs in the 0% CDR case.

However, Aaa CLOs, and 2005–2007 Aa2 and A2 CLOs sold at a discount have higher average returns in CDRs greater than 0%. A positive CDR is optimal if it shortens the WAL of a discount CLO without causing the tranche to fail to pay full principal and coupon. In Table 5.10 we show optimum CDRs for particular CLO tranches. These CDRs produce the shortest average WALs for CLOs of particular combinations of vintage and rating without causing loss of principal or coupon. We also show the resulting WAL at these CDRs, which can be compared to the CDRs in Table 5.9 to see how much WAL is shortened.

Discount Aaa tranches are better off in Great Depression type CDRs of 10% or more. Looking from Table 5.9 to Table 5.10, average WAL across all Aaa vintages shrinks from 6.0 to 3.2 years. A price discount is earned over about half the amount of time. If a Aaa CLO was purchased at a price of 94, the discount would be earned over six years in a 0% CDR scenario and return 100 basis points a year. In higher CDR scenarios, the discount would be earned over 3.2 years and return 188 basis points a year.

Aa2 and A2 CLOs issued in 2005 through 2007 behave the same as Aaa CLOs in that higher CDRs cause their WALs to shorten, thereby reducing the time over which a price discount is earned and increasing return. Baa2 and Ba2 CLOs and Aa2 and A2 CLOs issued in 2003 and 2004 all lengthen in higher CDRs.

DISTRESSED LOAN PRICES, OVERFLOWING TRIPLE-C BUCKETS, AND CLO RETURNS

When market participants model CLO returns, they focus primarily on defaults and recoveries. But since the dislocation in the credit markets, two other factors demand attention: the size of the CLO's triple-C asset bucket and the price at which the CLO reinvests in new collateral loans.

At depressed loan prices, a dollar can buy $1.05, $1.10, even $1.15 or more of loan par. The increased par amount also provides more dollars of interest income every coupon period. But overflowing triple-C buckets can cut off cash flow to lower CLO tranches and redirect it to senior tranches. In this section we look at the separate and joint effects of reinvestment prices and triple-C buckets on different CLO tranches.

Low reinvestment prices help CLO tranches withstand higher defaults and lower recoveries, but the benefit is muted for senior tranches. Equity benefits the most. High triple-C buckets obviously help senior tranches by diverting cash flow their way. But a high triple-C bucket also helps lower debt tranches in CDR modeling by cutting off reinvestment and potential losses on reinvested principal.

TABLE 5.10 Optimal CDRs and the Weighted Average Life They Produce CDR%/(WAL)

CDO Tranche	2003	2004	2005	2006	2007	Average
Aaa	16–20 (2.8)	16 (3.1)	14 (3.2)	14 (3.3)	10 (3.8)	14 (3.2)
Aa2	0–3.5 (5.9)	0–1.5 (6.4)	9 (6.8)	9 (6.9)	7 (7.3)	9 (6.7)
A2	0–2.5 (6.2)	0–1 (6.9)	7–7.5 (7.7)	6 (8.8)	6 (9.3)	6.5 (8.1)
Baa2	0 (6.5)	0–1 (7.3)	0–1 (8.7)	0–0.5 (10.0)	0–0.5 (11.4)	0–0.5 (9.4)
Ba2	0–1.5 (6.7)	0–1 (6.7)	0 (9.0)	0–0.5 (10.5)	0–1.0 (11.8)	0–1.0 (10.1)

Data for this table calculated using Moody's Wall Street Analytics.

For equity, low reinvestment prices help more than high triple-C buckets hurt.

We first show the effect of reinvestment price and triple-C buckets separately. Then, we go through each CLO tranche and look at joint effects.

Reinvestment Scenarios

"Cheap" loans allow CLO managers to build collateral par and earn more dollars of interest coupon. We studied a few CLOs issued in 2007, and present the results of one representative CLO.[6] The 26 default and recovery scenarios we analyzed using MWSA are the same as used earlier in this chapter and shown in Table 5.1. Note that, once again, as CDR increases, our assumed recovery rates decrease, reflecting what we think the reality would be. In our modeling, we default reinvestments, prepay loans and bonds at 15% and 5%, respectively, and assume that collateral assets mature at the CLO's maturity.

Figure 5.3 shows the present value of Baa2 tranche cash flows discounted at LIBOR plus whatever that tranche's coupon spread (vertical axis) at different CDRs (horizontal axis). The four curves represent different reinvestment cases and all scenarios assume a 0% triple-C bucket. The figure shows how different reinvestment scenarios affect the returns of the Baa2 tranche of the CLO. For CDRs below 8.0%, the CLO has a present value of 100 in all four reinvestment assumptions. The interpretation is that since we are discounting at LIBOR plus the coupon spread of the CLO, the CLO is paying all required principal and interest. At 8.0% CDR, a coupon break occurs in the 100% price reinvestment case. This is shown by its present value being less than 100 on the vertical axis. But in the 85% price reinvestment case, the tranche does not break coupon until 10% CDR. Hence, lower reinvestment prices allow the Baa2 tranche to withstand greater defaults and still pay required principal and interest.

Triple-C Bucket Scenario

Most CLO structures react to the presence of triple-C-rated loans in their asset portfolio via overcollateralization tests. Generally, any

---

[6] The analysis was performed using the MSWA.

FIGURE 5.3   Baa2 Cash Flows Discounted at LIBOR + Coupon Spread under Different Reinvestment Prices

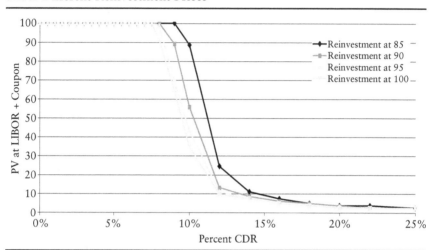

Data for this table calculated using Moody's Wall Street Analytics.

amount of triple-C assets above a specified percentage of total collateral assets (5–7.5%, typically) is treated as "triple-C excess" and counted at market value in the tests. This increases the chances of overcollateralization tests being tripped and redirecting cash flow away from subordinate tranches to more senior tranches. We looked at the effect of different sized triple-C buckets upon CLO returns assuming that the CLO's triple-C bucket tolerance was 7.5% of total assets and that the market value of excess triple-C assets was 65%. We also assumed, for now, that reinvestment was made at par.

Figure 5.4 shows the present value of Baa2 tranche cash flows discounted at LIBOR plus the tranche's coupon spread at different CDRs and different triple-C bucket levels. Again, we see that the curves have different coupon break points. The 0% triple-C bucket scenario breaks coupon at 8% CDR, while the 25% triple-C bucket scenario breaks at 11% CDR. Hence, a higher triple-C bucket allows this tranche to withstand greater defaults and still pay required principal and interest. One may be surprised to find this effect so far down the CLO's capital structure, and be even more surprised to learn that we find the same effect in the CLO's Ba2 tranche. We'll explore this phenomenon in detail later.

FIGURE 5.4 Baa2 Cash Flows Discounted at LIBOR + Coupon Spread under Different Triple-C Buckets

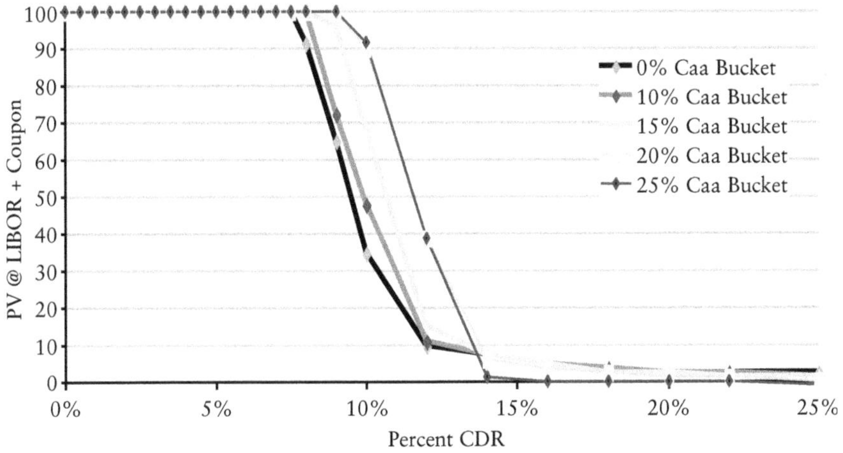

Data for this table calculated using Moody's Wall Street Analytics.

Combined Effect

We now show the combined effect of reinvestment prices and triple-C buckets on all the tranches of a CLO. For each CLO tranche, we find the highest CDR the tranche can withstand and still pay all required principal and interest.

The super senior Aaa tranche of the CLO we examined never breaks coupon under any CDR/reinvestment/triple-C bucket scenario we studied. Even in the highly stressed 25% CDR and 50% loan recovery scenario, the senior most tranche was still able to repay all its principal and coupon in any reinvestment and triple-C bucket scenario.

Table 5.11 shows that higher triple-C buckets help the Aa1 tranche withstand higher CDR stress. (Note that this is a junior AAA tranche as per S&P.) At 100 reinvestment/0 triple-C bucket, the tranche breaks coupon at 18% CDR, but when the triple-C bucket rises to 25%, the tranche can withstand 20% CDR before breaking coupon. This can be attributed to the fact that a higher triple-C bucket creates a lower overcollateralization ratio, which in turn may trigger cash diversion and pay down the principal of senior CLO tranches. Due to early principal repayment, senior tranches have lower WALs and can withstand higher CDRs. A similar trend can be seen for Aa2 and A2 tranches as well. Note that reinvestment prices have no effect on the Aa1 tranche. This is because at CDRs of 18 to 20%, reinvestment is cut off, making reinvestment price moot. Reinvestment prices make a little difference for Aa2 and A2 tranches when CDR is 10 to 14%.

TABLE 5.11 Coupon Break CDRs for Aa1, Aa2, and A2 Tranches

Aa1	Reinvestment Price (%)			
Caa Bucket Size (%)	100	95	90	85
0	18	18	18	18
10	20	20	20	20
15	20	20	20	20
20	20	20	20	20
25	20	20	20	20

Aa2	Reinvestment Price %			
Caa Bucket Size (%)	100	95	90	85
0	14	16	16	16
10	16	16	16	16
15	16	16	16	16
20	16	16	16	16
25	18	18	18	18

A2	Reinvestment Price %			
Caa Bucket Size (%)	100	95	90	85
0	10	10	10	12
10	10	10	10	12
15	12	12	12	12
20	12	12	12	12
25	12	12	12	12

Data for this table calculated using Moody's Wall Street Analytics.

We tested all combinations of reinvestment prices and triple-C buckets. However, it makes sense to consider the probable correlation of reinvestment prices and triple-C buckets. It is likely that when reinvestment prices are low, triple-C buckets will be swollen. The economic conditions that cause a lot of loan downgrades are the very ones that will depress loan prices, and vice versa. If loan prices are high, we expect CLO triple-C buckets to be modest. The most likely combinations of triple-C buckets and loan reinvestment prices in our exhibits are those lying along the diagonal from upper left to lower right. As we go down the CLO capital structure, a high triple-C bucket helps tranches less. After all, these are the tranches from which cash flow is being diverted. This can be seen in Table 5.12 when we look at coupon break CDRs for the Baa2 CLO tranche. Although the triple-C bucket assists the Baa2 CLOs to withstand higher CDRs, the range of CDRs, 7.5 to 9.0%, is tight across the scenarios.

One might assume that increasing the triple-C bucket would harm the Ba2 tranche, causing it to break at a lower CDR because of cash flow being diverted away from it. But Table 5.13 shows coupon break CDRs staying the same or increasing as triple-C buckets increase. In the most surprising case, at a 90% reinvestment price, the Ba2 tranche breaks at 5.5% CDR when the triple-C bucket is 0%, but at 7.5% CDR when the triple-C bucket is 25%.

What is going on? The answer lies in the fact that as triple-C bucket rises, the dollar amount of collateral loan loss decreases because reinvestment is cut off. Table 5.14 shows the dollar amount of collateral losses at different triple-C bucket levels and different

TABLE 5.12 Coupon Break CDRs for Baa2 Tranche

Baa2	Reinvestment Price (%)			
Caa Bucket Size (%)	100	95	90	85
0	7.5	7.5	8	9
10	8	8	8	9
15	8	8	8	9
20	9	9	9	9
25	9	9	9	9

Data for this table calculated using Moody's Wall Street Analytics.

TABLE 5.13   Coupon Break CDRs for Ba2 Tranche

Baa2		Reinvestment Price (%)		
		100	95	90	85
Caa Bucket Size (%)	0	na	na	na	na
	10	na	na	na	na
	15	na	na	na	na
	20	na	na	na	na
	25	22	22	22	22

Data for this table calculated using Moody's Wall Street Analytics.

CDR scenarios, assuming loan reinvestment is at 90%. We can see that across all CDR scenarios, as we increase the triple-C bucket to 20% or higher, the actual loss amount of collateral decreases. In the 8% CDR scenario, as the triple-C bucket is increased from 0 to 25%, collateral dollar loss goes down from $149.15 million to $58.82 million (i.e., it decreases by 61%). The reason is that the higher triple-C bucket trips overcollateralization tests, which results in cash flow being diverted to pay down the principal of higher tranches instead of being invested in new collateral assets. Thus, the collateral amount to which the CDR is applied keeps getting smaller. Actual collateral dollar loss is reduced, which helps all tranches.

Now let's look at the equity tranche. Increasing the triple-C bucket affects the cash flows of the equity tranche in different ways, such that it:

- Diverts cash flow away from equity tranche as the OC trigger is tripped, hurting equity.
- Lowers reinvestment by diverting cash flow to pay down debt tranche principal, again hurting equity.
- Reduces actual collateral dollar losses by limiting reinvestment, which helps equity.

We assume that the price paid for the CLO's equity tranche is the undiscounted amount of its next two years' cash flow, assuming 2% CDR, 82% recovery, 0% triple-C bucket, and reinvestment at a loan price of 100%. This sum is used to compare the present values

TABLE 5.14 Dollar Amount of Collateral Loss for Reinvestment at 90% Price Scenario

CDR (%)	Caa Bucket Size ($)				
	0	10	15	20	25
0.0	—	—	—	—	—
0.5	14,191,381	14,191,381	14,191,381	14,020,574	13,096,899
1.0	7,751,778	7,751,778	7,751,778	7,645,915	7,064,532
1.5	13,382,341	13,382,341	13,382,341	13,189,237	12,136,873
2.0	20,149,479	20,149,479	20,150,347	19,846,712	18,202,065
2.5	28,178,982	28,178,982	28,184,474	27,741,419	25,386,833
3.0	37,344,058	37,344,058	37,358,088	36,747,807	33,550,313
3.5	47,583,840	47,583,840	47,611,697	46,857,599	40,917,695
4.0	58,656,005	58,656,005	58,704,139	57,744,540	50,280,580
4.5	70,817,706	70,817,706	70,894,777	69,647,835	58,115,675
5.0	83,832,223	83,832,223	83,948,376	82,465,184	65,911,787
5.5	93,648,512	93,648,512	93,800,097	92,177,530	67,965,345
6.0	103,665,612	103,665,612	103,858,802	99,226,308	67,094,778
6.5	113,984,724	114,131,225	114,671,131	101,361,850	60,832,172
7.0	125,391,577	125,573,847	126,172,106	61,978,065	55,439,570
7.5	137,262,953	137,515,063	138,169,977	54,513,458	54,513,458
8.0	149,148,982	149,600,663	150,630,975	58,821,285	58,821,285
9.0	105,631,795	104,345,199	168,577,678	66,178,831	66,178,831
10.0	104,453,850	102,531,998	98,108,998	73,553,449	73,553,449
12.0	111,124,629	105,819,705	96,574,877	86,477,880	86,477,880
14.0	121,719,378	115,439,288	106,117,931	98,955,409	98,955,409
16.0	129,817,297	122,579,830	114,521,308	111,003,280	111,003,280
18.0	135,819,260	135,755,441	126,641,089	122,639,416	122,639,416
20.0	148,675,473	139,285,667	138,344,572	133,882,237	133,882,237
22.0	160,894,827	149,299,255	149,572,533	144,750,489	144,750,489
25.0	164,094,476	164,094,476	164,180,416	158,877,588	158,877,588

Data for this table calculated using Moody's Wall Street Analytics.

TABLE 5.15   LIBOR Break CDRs for Equity

Ba2	Reinvestment Price (%)			
	100	95	90	85
Caa Bucket Size (%) 0	4.5	5.5	5.5	7.5
10	5	5.5	5.5	7.5
15	5	5.5	5.5	7.5
20	5	5.5	6	7.5
25	5	7.5	7.5	7.5

Data for this table obtained from Moody's Wall Street Analytics and UBS.

of future cash flows in all triple-C/reinvestment scenarios. Looking at the LIBOR-break CDRs in Table 5.15, we see that increasing the triple-C bucket in lower loan price scenarios hurts the equity tranche. For example, keeping loan price constant at 85 cents to a dollar, we see that with 0% triple-C bucket, the equity can take 10% CDR stress before breaking either LIBOR or principal, but as we increase the triple-C bucket to 20%, equity breaks LIBOR and principal at 6.5% CDR. But overall, the negative effect of the diverted cash flow and low reinvestment exceeds the positive effect of lower dollar collateral loss, resulting in a higher triple-C bucket hurting the equity tranche.

Shortening WAL with Higher Triple-C Buckets

Earlier in this chapter we showed how higher CDRs can increase the total return of CLO tranches. Collateral defaults trip overcollateralization triggers, causing cash flow to be redirected to pay down senior tranche principal and shorten those tranches' weighted average lives. Tranches purchased at a discount earn that discount over a shorter period, increasing their total return. Large triple-C buckets have the same effect.

Table 5.16 shows the shortening of average life in years when the triple-C bucket increases from 0 to 25%. We show results in the 10% CDR case, where all tranches receive their full principal and coupon. The average lives of the tranches shown decrease 0.6 to 5.6 years when the triple-C bucket increases from 0 to 25%.

TABLE 5.16 Decline in WAL as the Caa bucket increases from 0 to 25%, 10% CDR

Tranche	Reinvestment Price (%)			
	100	95	90	85
Aaa	1	1.2	1.8	5.6
Aa1	0.7	0.8	1.1	4.9
Aa2	0.6	0.7	1.1	5.2
A2	0.8	1	1.4	5.6

Data for this table calculated using Moody's Wall Street Analytics.

The shortening of WAL is greatest in the 85% reinvestment case. This is because in the 0% triple-C case, the low cost of loans allows CLO tranches to pass their overcollateralization tests more easily, avoid principal pay down, and remain outstanding longer. But when the triple-C bucket is 25%, the tranches fail their OC tests more easily, are prohibited from reinvestment, and the benefit from a low reinvestment cost is negated.

SUMMARY

In this chapter, we looked at two issues regarding CLO returns: (1) the resiliency of CLO returns to defaults and recoveries and (2) the impact of CLO's triple-C asset bucket size and price at which the CLO reinvests in new collateral loans.

With respect to return resiliency, we looked at 1,575 tranches from 340 CLOs rated Aaa to Ba2 issued in the years 2003 to 2007. We tested Aaa to Ba2 CLOs in a 5% CDR scenario, which replicates the worst U.S. leverage loan performance since the market began in 1995. On average, every vintage and rating combination has a greater-than-LIBOR return. In a 10% CDR scenario, which replicates the defaults of high-yield bonds in the Great Depression, Aaa, Aa2, and most A2 vintages return more than LIBOR.

We discussed the variability of individual CLO results among these vintage and rating averages. In the 5% CDR scenario, one can be a little unlucky in the selection of a particular Baa2 CLO and still do better than buying Aaa CLOs. In the 10% CDR scenario, individual CLO performance varies drastically, and Aaa CLOs provide the only consistent performance.

We showed the CDRs at which CLO vintage and rating combinations begin to lose their coupon. But we argued that the coupon received is more important than the coupon foregone. It can be better to receive a partial coupon from a Ba2 CLO than a full coupon from a Aaa CLO. To put all CLOs to the same test, we showed the CDRs at which various combinations of CLO vintages and ratings fail to return LIBOR.

Acknowledging that all our present value calculations assume CLOs are purchased at par, we discussed the relationship between CDR and weighted average life. Higher CDRs first shorten the average life of higher-rated CLOs; still higher CDRs reduce realized coupon and principal. Until CDR becomes so high that coupon and principal are impacted, higher CDR can raise the realized yield of a higher-rated CLO purchased at a discount. We showed optimal CDR across CLO vintage and rating.

With respect to the impact of CLO's triple-C asset bucket size and price at which the CLO reinvests in new collateral loans, we found that rising triple-C bucket levels affect CLO tranche cash flows. This is due to the fact that in most CLOs, the haircut associated with the triple-C bucket triggers overcollateralization tests and affects cash flows to the tranches.

We found that increasing the triple-C bucket size affects different debt tranches differently. For the CLO we studied, the seniormost tranche never had a coupon break across any of the different stress scenarios. For the Aa1, Aa2 and A2 tranches, increasing triple-C bucket helped these tranches withstand higher stress. The trend was similar, albeit less pronounced in the Baa2 tranche, as the positive effect of diverted cash flow decreases as we come down the capital structure.

Surprisingly, for the Ba2 tranche also, a rising triple-C bucket helped the tranche withstand higher CDRs. This can be attributed to the fact that as the triple-C bucket grows, the dollar amount of loss in collateral decreases due to low the level of reinvestment of amortizing collateral. The CDR is applied to a smaller amount of remaining collateral assets.

Finally, for the equity tranche, an increasing triple-C bucket has multiple effects, but overall the negative effect of the diverted cash flow and low reinvestment exceeds the positive effect of lower collateral dollar loss. Higher triple-C buckets hurt the equity tranche, although perhaps not as much as some would assume.

6

CLO Portfolio Overlap

CLO portfolios, even from CLOs issued in different years, tend to have a lot of underlying loan borrowers in common. This is the result of loan repayments causing CLO managers to continually be in the market buying loans for their CLOs. Thus, portfolio differences due to CLO vintage are muted. CLO managers' practice of allocating loan purchases across all their CLOs causes additional borrower overlap among CLOs managed by the same manager.

The average "name" or "credit" overlap among the 32 CLOs we study in this chapter is 45% of par. The average overlap among CLOs from the same vintage is 44%, and the average collateral overlap among CLOs managed by the same manager is 81%. We also look at CLO and collateral vintage. We find that different vintage CLOs have similar collateral vintage distribution. For the 2003 to 2007 CLOs that we study, 2007 collateral was within a tight range of 55% to 58%, and 2006 collateral ranged from 24% to 29%. At the same time, small loan allocations, and the necessity of filling several CLOs with collateral, keep single-name concentrations within individual CLO portfolios small. The average number of separate credits in the CLOs that we study is 250.

We first present several measurements related to collateral overlap and single-name concentration. We look at collateral overlap in CLOs between individual CLOs, between CLO managers, and between CLO vintages. We also look at collateral vintage across CLO vintage. Next, we look at the most common credits across CLOs and across CLO managers. Finally, we look at the relative risks of collateral overlap and single-name concentration.

COLLATERAL OVERLAP IN U.S. CLOs

To study collateral overlap among managers and vintages, we selected 32 CLOs from seven different managers, spanning vintages from 2003 to 2007, as shown in Table 6.1. The collateral portfolios of these CLOs range from $290 million to $1.1 billion.

TABLE 6.1 CLOs in Study by Vintage

Vintage	Manager	CLO
2003	Deerfield Capital Management	Forest Creek CLO
2003	Invesco	Sagamore CLO
2003	Octagon Investment Partners	Octagon Investment Partners V
2003	Octagon Investment Partners	Octagon Investment Partners VI
2003	Prudential Investment Management	Dryden V
2003	Sankaty Advisors	Avery Point CLO
2003	Sankaty Advisors	Castle Hill III CLO
2003	Sankaty Advisors	Race Point II CLO
2004	American Express Asset Management	Centurion VII 2004
2004	David L Babson & Company	Babson CLO 2004-I
2004	Deerfield Capital Management	Long Grove CLO
2004	Invesco	Champlain CLO
2004	Octagon Investment Partners	Octagon Investment Partners VII
2004	Prudential Investment Management	Dryden VII
2005	American Express Asset Management	Centurion IX
2005	American Express Asset Management	Centurion VIII 2005
2005	David L Babson & Company	Babson CLO 2005-I
2005	David L Babson & Company	Babson CLO 2005-II
2005	Octagon Investment Partners	Octagon Investment Partners VIII
2005	Prudential Investment Management	Dryden VIII

TABLE 6.1   (continued)

Vintage	Manager	CLO
2006	David L Babson & Company	Babson CLO 2006-I
2006	David L Babson & Company	Babson CLO 2006-II
2006	Deerfield Capital Management	Bridgeport CLO
2006	Invesco	Saratoga CLO I
2006	Octagon Investment Partners	Octagon Investment Partners IX
2006	Prudential Investment Management	Dryden XI
2007	American Express Asset Management	Centurion XV
2007	David L Babson & Company	Babson CLO 2007-I
2007	Deerfield Capital Management	Bridgeport CLO II
2007	Octagon Investment Partners	Octagon Investment Partners XI
2007	Prudential Investment Management	Dryden XVIII
2007	Sankaty Advisors	Race Point IV CLO

Data obtained from Intex Solutions.

To determine whether two CLOs contain the same credit, we first looked at the "Issuer" data field in Intex Solutions' asset detail. Intex Solution provides up-to-date asset detail, current as of the CLO's last trustee report. Unfortunately, as Intex Solution relies on trustee-reported data, it does not have one unique issuer identifier across all CLOs. Nor does it group affiliated legal entities, such as holding companies and their subsidiaries. Hence, we mapped various Intex Solution issuer names to common issuer names.

To quantify single-name risk, we look at the percent of a CLO's collateral par that is made up of obligations of the same credit. For a particular credit, collateral overlap between two CLOs is defined as the *average* percentage of that single name in the two portfolios. Because Calpine Corp. makes up 1.2% of Centurion IX's portfolio and 0.4% of Babson 2005-II's portfolio, the collateral overlap of Calpine between the two CLOs is calculated as 0.8%. The total collateral overlap between Centurion IX and Babson 2005-II is the sum of these single-name collateral overlaps, or 52%, as shown in Table 6.2.[1]

Table 6.2 shows the collateral overlaps among 32 CLOs. In the table, CLOs are grouped by manager. The average overlap between any two CLOs in our pool is 45% and the range is 26% to 95%. The rightmost column in the table shows the average collateral overlap between a particular CLO and the other 31 CLOs.

Table 6.3 summarizes the findings of Table 6.2 by manager, averaging the collateral overlap of CLOs from different managers. For example, the average collateral overlap between CLOs managed by American Express and CLOs managed by Babson is 44%. The diagonal of the table shows the collateral overlap among CLOs managed by the same manager. For example, American Express-managed CLOs have an average 81% collateral overlap with one another. The "average" column at the far right of the table measures each manager's overlap against all the other managers.

Table 6.3 shows that, by far, the greatest collateral overlap occurs among the CLOs managed by the same manager. CLOs managed by Invesco have the highest average overlap at 91%, while the average overlap between CLOs managed by the same manager is 81%. The average overlap between CLOs managed by different managers is 41%. These data suggest that owning two CLOs managed by the same manager do not provide the same collateral diversification as owning CLOs from different managers. Interestingly, Prudential has only a 68% collateral overlap across five of its Dryden CLOs,

---

[1] There are two ways to do the overlap calculation: The methodology used in this study averages the two CLOs' exposures to a credit. Other researchers take a different approach. In those studies, the minimum of the two CLO's exposure to the credit is calculated. A simple example shows the correctness of our approach. Suppose CLO A and CLO B own the same 50 credits, but not in the same amounts. For 25 credits, CLO A has 3% exposure, while CLO B has 1% exposure. For the other 25 credits, CLO A has 1% exposure while CLO B has 3% exposure. Our esteemed competitors measure each collateral overlap as 1% and sum all 50 to get 50% collateral overlap. We measure each collateral overlap at 2% and sum all 50 credits to get a 100% collateral overlap. Which methodology is right? Well, if all the credits in CLO A default, 100% of the credits in CLO B would default, and vice versa. On CLOs in this study, the other methodology would underestimate collateral overlap by 13%.

TABLE 6.2 Percent of Collateral Overlap: Borrowers Common to any Two CLOs Grouped by Manager

	Amex				Babson						Deerfield				Invesco			Octagon						Prudential					Sankaty				Average
	Centurion CDO VII	Centurion CDO VIII	Centurion CDO IX	Centurion CDO XV	Babson CLO 2004-I	Babson CLO 2005-I	Babson CLO 2005-II	Babson CLO 2006-I	Babson CLO 2006-II	Babson CLO 2007-I	Forest Creek CLO	Long Grove CLO	Bridgeport CLO	Bridgeport CLO II	Sagamore CLO	Champlain CLO	Saratoga CLO I	Octagon Investment Partners V	Octagon Investment Partners VI	Octagon Investment Partners VII	Octagon Investment Partners VIII	Octagon Investment Partners IX	Octagon Investment Partners XI	Dryden V	Dryden VII	Dryden VIII	Dryden XI	Dryden XVIII	Avery Point CLO	Castle Hill III	Race Point II CLO	Race Point IV	Average
Amex Centurion CDO VII		87	88	74	44	49	51	42	44	45	45	44	45	43	46	48	51	42	44	43	45	41	42	37	41	44	41	38	48	45	50	48	48
Centurion CDO VIII			91	71	43	49	51	43	44	45	43	42	43	41	47	49	51	42	44	43	44	41	42	37	41	44	43	41	50	45	52	49	48
Centurion CDO IX				73	44	51	52	44	45	46	44	43	43	41	49	50	53	42	43	43	44	42	42	37	41	44	42	41	50	46	52	49	49
Centurion CDO XV					36	41	42	35	36	38	35	35	37	35	40	42	44	33	33	34	36	32	34	26	31	37	34	34	43	36	45	46	40
Babson Babson CLO 2004-I						74	76	71	78	79	37	40	39	40	44	47	47	33	35	34	35	36	35	35	40	42	39	36	42	38	43	42	45
Babson CLO 2005-I							89	74	74	74	44	45	46	44	51	53	51	38	41	41	41	41	42	40	45	45	41	41	45	41	46	45	50
Babson CLO 2005-II								74	73	76	45	45	45	44	54	55	53	38	40	39	40	41	40	39	44	45	45	43	47	42	49	45	50
Babson CLO 2006-I									75	78	38	39	39	38	47	48	46	34	37	35	36	35	36	31	36	38	38	37	44	37	44	43	45
Babson CLO 2006-II										88	39	40	37	37	47	47	48	35	36	37	37	36	38	34	38	39	41	37	43	38	42	41	46
Babson CLO 2007-I											39	40	38	38	48	48	49	35	37	37	37	36	37	34	39	41	41	38	43	37	42	42	47
Deerfield Forest Creek CLO												91	86	82	44	45	45	34	38	37	37	34	33	37	41	40	36	39	41	39	42	42	44
Long Grove CLO													89	86	44	44	45	34	36	36	35	33	32	38	43	42	38	41	44	39	44	40	45
Bridgeport CLO														87	44	44	44	33	36	35	35	34	33	35	38	40	36	38	43	39	43	41	44
Bridgeport CLO II															42	43	43	33	36	34	34	33	32	33	38	40	34	38	43	40	43	41	43

137

TABLE 6.2 (continued)

		Amex				Babson						Deerfield				Invesco			Octagon						Prudential					Sankaty				Average
		Centurion CDO VII	Centurion CDO VIII	Centurion CDO IX	Centurion CDO XV	Babson CLO 2004-I	Babson CLO 2005-I	Babson CLO 2005-II	Babson CLO 2006-I	Babson CLO 2006-II	Babson CLO 2007-I	Forest Creek CLO	Long Grove CLO	Bridgeport CLO	Bridgeport CLO II	Sagamore CLO	Champlain CLO	Saratoga CLO I	Octagon Investment Partners V	Octagon Investment Partners VI	Octagon Investment Partners VII	Octagon Investment Partners VIII	Octagon Investment Partners IX	Octagon Investment Partners XI	Dryden V	Dryden VII	Dryden VIII	Dryden XI	Dryden XVIII	Avery Point CLO	Castle Hill III	Race Point II CLO	Race Point IV	Average
Invesco	Sagamore CLO																90	90	38	39	39	40	38	38	38	43	45	43	44	46	41	47	45	47
	Champlain CLO															90		93	40	41	41	42	38	40	38	43	46	44	44	48	43	50	49	48
	Saratoga CLO I															90	93		41	41	42	42	40	41	38	43	47	45	45	50	44	51	52	49
Octagon	Octagon Investment Partners V																			90	85	88	85	79	28	35	36	34	31	38	37	39	36	44
	Octagon Investment Partners VI																				87	86	84	78	30	36	39	35	32	39	38	40	37	45
	Octagon Investment Partners VII																					88	83	80	29	37	38	36	35	39	38	40	38	45
	Octagon Investment Partners VIII																						86	83	29	37	38	36	34	38	40	39	38	46
	Octagon Investment Partners IX																							81	29	37	39	37	33	39	38	39	37	45
	Octagon Investment Partners XI																								27	34	38	34	34	39	38	39	39	44

138

TABLE 6.2 (continued)

	Amex				Babson						Deerfield				Invesco			Octagon						Prudential					Sankaty				Average
	Centurion CDO VII	Centurion CDO VIII	Centurion CDO IX	Centurion CDO XV	Babson CLO 2004-I	Babson CLO 2005-I	Babson CLO 2005-II	Babson CLO 2006-I	Babson CLO 2006-II	Babson CLO 2007-I	Forest Creek CLO	Long Grove CLO	Bridgeport CLO	Bridgeport CLO II	Sagamore CLO	Champlain CLO	Saratoga CLO I	Octagon Investment Partners V	Octagon Investment Partners VI	Octagon Investment Partners VII	Octagon Investment Partners VIII	Octagon Investment Partners IX	Octagon Investment Partners XI	Dryden V	Dryden VII	Dryden VIII	Dryden XI	Dryden XVIII	Avery Point CLO	Castle Hill III	Race Point II CLO	Race Point IV	Average
Prudential Dryden V																									73	66	58	56	40	32	41	39	38
Dryden VII																										78	71	69	42	34	43	40	44
Dryden VIII																											73	71	46	36	47	44	45
Dryden XI																												69	42	35	44	42	43
Dryden XVIII																													43	32	44	43	42
Sankaty Avery Point CLO																														73	95	84	47
Castle Hill III																															76	64	42
Race Point II CLO																																85	48
Race Point IV																																	46

Data for this table obtained from Intex Solutions. Calculations by UBS CDO Research.

TABLE 6.3 Collateral Overlap Among Managers

Manager	Amex	Babson	Deerfield	Invesco	Octagon	Prudential	Sankaty	Average
Amex	81%	44%	41%	47%	40%	39%	47%	49%
Babson		77%	41%	49%	37%	39%	42%	47%
Deerfield			87%	44%	34%	38%	41%	47%
Invesco				91%	40%	43%	47%	52%
Octagon					84%	34%	39%	44%
Prudential						68%	41%	43%
Sankaty							80%	48%

Data for this table obtained from Intex Solutions. Calculations by UBS CDO Research.

which is the lowest among the managers. We understand that it is Prudential's policy to limit collateral overlap across their CLOs. At 39%, Prudential also has the second lowest average overlap with other CLO managers, with Octagon having the lowest at 38%.

Obviously, if two manager's CLOs are 68% overlapped with another, it means that the CLOs are 32% not overlapped with each other. That provides a lot of opportunity for managers to distinguish themselves from one another. Equity, of course, is very exposed to a manager's unique asset selection. But even AAA tranches do not have enough subordination beneath them to be unconcerned about the unique credits that a CLO manager purchases.

Table 6.4 also summarizes the findings from Table 6.2, but this time by vintage. In this table, we average collateral overlap of CLOs across different vintages. For example, the average collateral overlap between 2003 vintage CLOs and 2004 vintage CLOs is 45%. The diagonal of the table shows the collateral overlap of CLOs within the same vintage. For instance, 2005 vintage CLOs have an average of 51% collateral overlap with one another. The "average" column at the far right of Table 6.4 measures each vintage's overlap against all the other vintages.

The average collateral overlap of CLOs from the same vintage is 44%, with all results in a tight range of 38% to 51%. The average collateral overlap of CLOs from different vintages is 46%. Therefore, CLOs from different vintages have nearly the same collateral overlap as CLOs from the same vintage. Furthermore, it appears that having the same manager produces higher collateral overlap between CLOs than does being in the same vintage year.

TABLE 6.4 Collateral Overlap Among Vintages

Vintage	2003	2004	2005	2006	2007	Average
2003	45%	45%	45%	44%	43%	43%
2004		42%	50%	47%	45%	44%
2005			51%	48%	47%	47%
2006				42%	44%	44%
2007					38%	42%

Data for this table obtained from Intex Solutions. Calculations by UBS CDO Research.

COLLATERAL VINTAGE VS. DEAL VINTAGE

What is the relationship between CLO vintage and collateral vintage? Is a 2007 CLO likely to have a very different distribution of collateral vintage than a 2005 CLO? To answer this question, we looked at 26 CLOs[2] from 2003 to 2007 and the collateral vintages within those CLOs. Table 6.5 lists the various CLOs we looked at and shows the distribution of collateral vintages for each CLO. Table 6.6 summarizes our results by looking at the average collateral vintage distribution for different CLO vintages.

We found that irrespective of vintage, each CLO had a similar vintage collateral distribution. On an average, across all CLOs, 59% collateral is made up of 2007 loans and around 25% of 2006 loans. Looking across different CLO vintages, the average percentage of 2007 collateral in 2003–2006 CLOs ranged from 55 to 58%. For 2007 CLOs, the average was 70%. This can be explained by the fact that there were large numbers of loan prepayments prior to mid-2007. In fact, the repayment rate, including scheduled amortization and prepayments, for four years prior to the second quarter of 2007 was nearly 50%. This meant CLO managers continually bought current vintage loans for their CLOs.

FAVORITE CLO CREDITS

There are 1,113 unique borrowers represented in the 32 CLO portfolios we examined, so that across all CLOs, the average par exposure to any particular credit is 0.09%. But Table 6.7 shows the 10 highest single-name exposures across the 32 CLOs. The biggest common holding across all of our sampled CLOs is Univision Communications Inc. On average, it comprises 1.2% of each CLO's portfolio and is present in 31 CLOs. The top 10 credits average between 0.8 and 1.2% of each CLO portfolio.

Table 6.8 shows the highest single-name exposures across CLOs from the seven managers. The most popular names for any given manager are generally in the top 10 or 15 across all managers, with

---

[2] We could identify vintage for 75% or more of the collateral in 26 CLOs. We assume that this vintage mapping is also representative of the remaining unmapped collateral.

EXHIBIT 6.5 Percentage of Vintage Collateral in CLOs grouped by Deal Vintages

Deal Vintage	Deal Name	Collateral Vintage					
		2003	2004	2005	2006	2007	2008
2003	Race Point II CLO	0.00%	4.45%	10.90%	27.28%	56.41%	0.96%
	Octagon Investment Partners VI	0.00%	8.44%	11.70%	26.14%	50.90%	2.82%
	Octagon Investment Partners V	0.00%	6.82%	10.86%	24.58%	54.83%	2.91%
	Castle Hill III	0.00%	4.31%	15.63%	29.25%	50.01%	0.79%
	Sagamore CLO	2.16%	1.26%	11.21%	25.72%	58.14%	1.51%
	Forest Creek CLO	0.12%	4.71%	13.92%	28.82%	51.97%	0.47%
	Dryden V	0.00%	4.01%	6.20%	26.90%	60.66%	2.23%
2004	Babson CLO 2004-I	0.00%	5.56%	7.80%	24.77%	57.77%	4.09%
	Dryden VII	0.00%	2.34%	7.44%	19.79%	69.02%	1.40%
	Long Grove CLO	0.27%	5.32%	14.32%	24.62%	55.21%	0.26%
	Centurion CDO VII	0.00%	4.23%	14.21%	25.70%	54.81%	1.05%
	CHAMPLAIN CLO	1.01%	1.75%	8.60%	24.72%	62.45%	1.46%
	Octagon Investment Partners VII	0.16%	8.70%	8.89%	29.23%	50.13%	2.89%

143

EXHIBIT 6.5 (continued)

Deal Name		Collateral Vintage					
		2003	2004	2005	2006	2007	2008
2005	Dryden VIII	0.00%	1.53%	8.43%	16.80%	72.22%	1.02%
	Centurion CDO VIII	0.00%	5.26%	17.75%	24.33%	51.56%	1.10%
	Centurion CDO IX	0.00%	5.49%	16.13%	25.72%	51.57%	1.09%
	Octagon Investment Partners VII	0.15%	5.15%	9.66%	27.34%	54.26%	3.44%
	Babson CLO 2005-I	0.00%	5.13%	12.73%	26.74%	54.51%	0.88%
	Babson CLO 2005-II	0.00%	3.69%	14.15%	23.20%	58.39%	0.58%
2006	Bridgeport CLO	0.00%	3.46%	8.75%	34.61%	52.90%	0.28%
	Octagon Invest Partners IX	0.00%	3.53%	9.72%	28.88%	54.52%	3.35%
	Saratoga CLO I	0.00%	1.55%	8.70%	23.56%	64.86%	1.33%
2007	Bridgeport CLO II	0.00%	2.54%	8.90%	24.06%	64.21%	0.29%
	Octagon Investment Partners XI	0.00%	2.33%	7.16%	27.01%	60.47%	3.04%
	Cent CDO XV	0.00%	2.04%	8.86%	15.44%	71.62%	2.04%
	Dryden XVIII	0.00%	0.00%	3.44%	13.14%	81.94%	1.48%

Data for this table obtained from Intex Solutions. Calculations by UBS CDO Research.

TABLE 6.6 Percentage of Vintage Collateral Among Vintages

		Collateral Vintage					
		2003	2004	2005	2006	2007	2008
Deal Vintage	2003	0.33%	4.86%	11.49%	26.96%	54.70%	1.67%
	2004	0.24%	4.65%	10.21%	24.80%	58.23%	1.86%
	2005	0.02%	4.38%	13.14%	24.02%	57.08%	1.35%
	2006	0.00%	2.85%	9.06%	29.02%	57.43%	1.65%
	2007	0.00%	1.73%	7.09%	19.91%	69.56%	1.71%

Data for this table obtained from Intex Solutions. Calculations by UBS CDO Research.

TABLE 6.7 Most Common Borrowers in Sampled CLOs

Rank	Borrower	Average (%)	Number of CLOs with Exposure	Number of Managers with Exposure
1	Univision Communications Inc.	1.2%	31	7
2	Georgia-Pacific Corp.	1.1%	31	7
3	HCA Inc.	1.1%	31	7
4	Idearc Media	1.0%	31	7
5	Community Health Systems Inc.	0.9%	29	7
6	TXU Corp.	1.0%	26	6
7	Royalty Pharma	0.8%	31	7
8	Calpine Corp.	0.8%	31	7
9	SunGard Data Systems Inc.	0.8%	30	7
10	Metro-Goldwyn-Mayer Inc.	0.8%	27	6

Data for this table obtained from Intex Solutions. Calculations by UBS CDO Research.

a few exceptions. For example, First Data Corp makes up 1.5% of Babson's CLO assets. While First Data Corp is present in 11 non-Babson CLOs, it has a significant presence ($53 million in total) across all six Babson-managed CLOs.

The bottom three rows of Table 6.8 show the total number of borrowers across all the CLOs managed by a single manager, the average number of borrowers per CLO, and the manager's average CLO size. The table shows that Octagon has the lowest number of total borrowers than any other manager. Recall that Octagon CLOs also have the lowest collateral overlap with other CLOs. Octagon's CLOs are apparently comprised of a smaller number of more unique names than other CLOs.

SINGLE-NAME RISK AND TRANCHE PROTECTIONS

Now that we have quantified collateral overlap across CLOs and collateral diversification within CLOs, what do we make of it? How do we combine these factors and measure single-name risk? And how can we measure and compare single-name risk for CLO tranches at different points in the CLO capital structure? For example, an investor's CLOs might own $15 million of Georgia-Pacific and $30 million of Univision Communications. Does the CLO investor bear twice the risk to Univision as to Georgia-Pacific? Not necessarily. Suppose the investor owns senior tranches of CLOs that hold Univision, but subordinate tranches of CLOs that hold Georgia-Pacific. A Univision default might have less of an impact on senior CLO tranches than the default of Georgia-Pacific would have on subordinate tranches.

This discrepancy in the dollar amount and significance of exposure might arise even if an investor consistently purchased CLO tranches of the same seniority. This would be the case if Georgia-Pacific-owning CLOs happen to suffer more collateral losses than CLOs owning Univision, thus making the former more sensitive to future collateral losses. The collateral overlap problem can be summarized as follows: How does a CLO investor weigh the amount of exposure a CLO has to a single name against the credit protection a tranche has against that single name? And, even more difficult, how does a CLO investor aggregate the balance of exposure and protection to a single name across a portfolio of CLOs? Our suggestion is to look at the CLO's excess overcollateralization.

TABLE 6.8 Most Common Borrowers by Manager

Rank	Amex	Percent	Babson	Percent
1	Univision Communications Inc.	1.3%	First Data Corp.	1.5%
2	Calpine Corp.	1.2%	Univision Communications Inc.	1.3%
3	Charter Communications Holding Co. LLC	1.0%	Metro-Goldwyn-Mayer Inc.	1.2%
4	Michaels Stores Inc.	0.9%	Las Vegas Sands Corp.	1.1%
5	Metro-Goldwyn-Mayer Inc.	0.9%	Cengage Learning	1.0%
6	Community Health Systems Inc.	0.8%	Realogy Corp.	0.9%
7	Delphi Corporation	0.8%	SunGard Data Systems Inc.	0.9%
8	Nielsen Company	0.8%	Freescale Semiconductor Inc.	0.8%
9	Graphic Packaging Corp.	0.8%	HCA Inc.	0.8%
10	Cablevision Systems Corp.	0.7%	Georgia-Pacific Corp.	0.8%
	Total number of borrowers	413	Total number of borrowers	476
	Avg. number of borrowers per CLO	316	Avg number of borrowers per CLO	309
	Avg. CLO size ($ million)	$758	Avg CLO size ($ million)	$614

TABLE 6.8 (continued)

Rank	Deerfield	Percent	Invesco	Percent
1	TXU Corp.	1.3%	TXU Corp.	2.1%
2	Capital Automotive LP	1.3%	Idearc	1.9%
3	Royalty Pharma Finance Trust	1.2%	Univision Communications Inc.	1.9%
4	HCA Inc.	1.2%	Georgia-Pacific Corp.	1.7%
5	Las Vegas Sands Corp.	1.2%	Royalty Pharma Finance Trust	1.6%
6	Georgia-Pacific Corp.	1.1%	Cequel Communications Inc.	1.5%
7	Univision Communications Inc.	1.0%	Biomet Inc.	1.5%
8	UPC Financing Partnership	1.0%	Freescale Semiconductor Inc.	1.4%
9	Sabre Holdings Corp.	0.9%	DJO Finance LLC	1.3%
10	Community Health Systems Inc.	0.9%	Lyondell Chemical Company	1.3%
	Total number of borrowers	344	Total number of borrowers	298
	Avg. number of borrowers per CLO	280	Avg. number of borrowers per CLO	269
	Avg. CLO size ($ million)	$433	Avg. CLO size ($ million)	$327

TABLE 6.8 (continued)

Rank	Octagon	%	Prudential	%
1	Capital Automotive LP	1.4%	HCA Inc.	1.9%
2	Georgia-Pacific Corp.	1.3%	Georgia-Pacific Corp.	1.6%
3	Ford Motor Co.	1.3%	Community Health Systems Inc.	1.6%
4	Community Health Systems Inc.	1.2%	TXU Corp.	1.5%
5	HCA Inc.	1.2%	Idearc	1.4%
6	Discovery Communications Inc.	1.1%	Las Vegas Sands Corp.	1.3%
7	Seminole Tribe of Florida	1.1%	Univision Communications Inc.	1.3%
8	Idearc	1.1%	Reynolds & Reynolds Co.	1.3%
9	Tribune Co.	1.1%	Mylan Laboratories Inc.	1.1%
10	Calpine Corp.	1.1%	Freescale Semiconductor Inc.	1.1%
	Total number of borrowers	275	Total number of borrowers	298
	Avg. number of borrowers per CLO	200	Avg. number of borrowers per CLO	159
	Avg. CLO size ($ million)	$390	Avg. CLO size ($ million)	$475

TABLE 6.8 (continued)

Rank	Sankaty	Percent
1	Georgia-Pacific Corp.	1.4%
2	Las Vegas Sands Corp.	1.2%
3	Ford Motor Co.	1.2%
4	Warner Music Group	1.2%
5	Idearc	1.1%
6	Graham Packaging Co.	1.1%
7	HCA Inc.	1.1%
8	Oshkosh Truck Corp.	1.0%
9	Enterprise GP Holdings LP	1.0%
10	Freescale Semiconductor Inc.	1.0%
	Total number of borrowers	321
	Avg. number of borrowers per CLO	242
	Avg. CLO size ($ million)	$479

Data for this table obtained from Intex Solutions. Calculations by UBS CDO Research.

EXCESS OVERCOLLATERALIZATION AND EXCESS OVERCOLLATERALIZATION DELTA

A tranche's *excess* overcollateralization (excess OC) is the excess of collateral par over the outstanding par amount of that tranche plus all the tranches above it in seniority. For a CLO with $100 of collateral, $70 of Tranche A, $10 of Tranche B, and $10 of Tranche C, excess OC for Tranches A and C are:

$$\text{Tranche A excess OC} = \text{Collateral} - \text{Tranche A} = \$100 - \$70 = \$30$$

$$\text{Tranche C excess OC} = \text{Collateral} - \text{Tranches A, B, and C}$$
$$= \$100 - \$90 = \$10$$

An intuitive interpretation of excess OC is that it is the amount of par the CLO could lose before the tranche is collateralized exactly 100%. Note that excess OC increases with the par amount of collateral and decreases with the outstanding par amount of the tranche and more senior tranches.

Now suppose that this CLO has a $2 investment in Univision Communications. Each tranche's excess OC delta with respect to Univision is the amount its excess OC would decrease if Univision suddenly defaulted without any recovery. To calculate each tranche's excess OC *delta* with respect to Univision, we compare the par amount of Univision to that tranche's excess OC as shown below:

Tranche A excess OC Univision Delta = $2/$30 = 6.7%
Tranche C excess OC Univision *Delta* = $2/$10 = 20.0%

The excess OC deltas show that Tranche A would lose 6.7% of its excess OC if Univision defaulted without recovery, while Tranche C would lose 20% of its excess OC. In other words, because of the difference in tranche subordination, Tranche C is three times as exposed to Univision as Tranche A (20.0% vs. 6.7%). Note that excess OC delta increases with the dollar amount of the single-name risk and decreases with the amount of the tranche's excess OC. In this manner, excess OC delta takes into account both single-name concentration and the amount of OC protection the tranche has.

Senior tranche and subordinate tranche excess OC deltas are comparable. Thus, if an investor holds tranches of different seniorities, excess OC delta allows summarizing exposure to a particular name across different CLO tranches. The concentration of a particular credit across different CLO tranches can be gauged by averaging the credit's excess OC deltas or by looking at the range of the credit's excess OC deltas.

SENIOR AND SUBORDINATE EXCESS OC DELTAS

Table 6.9 shows senior tranche excess OC deltas for each of the most common names in the CLOs we examined, excluding Champlain CLO.[3] The first row of the table, for Univision Communications, shows how much senior tranche excess OC would decline if Univi-

---

[3] We exclude Champlain CLO in our senior and subordinate excess OC deltas study because this CLO has revolving senior tranches in its capital structure, which makes it hard to calculate its excess OC.

sion defaulted without any recovery. The decline in excess OC varies from 3.3 to 16.2% and averages 5.9%. The bottom row of the table shows the decline in excess OC if all 10 credits defaulted without any recovery. The amounts for the different CLOs range from 28.4 to 137.5% and averages 48.1%.

Table 6.9 combines the effects of collateral overlap across CLO portfolios with the effect of single-name concentration within a particular CLO. Collateral overlap is addressed because we are looking at the 10 most common credits across all CLOs. Single-name concentration is addressed because we are looking at the concentrations of those names within each individual CLO portfolio.

It is obviously a remote possibility that all 10 credits in Table 6.9 would default and almost an impossibility that all 10 credits would default with zero recovery. Yet, in even this latter scenario, apart from Dryden XVIII, senior tranche excess OC would not be completely eaten through for any of the CLOs. Except for Dryden XVIII, each senior tranche would still have greater than 100% OC coverage. The table also does not capture protection from the diversion of excess spread to protect the senior tranche. We therefore find it very difficult to get excited about single-name risk at the senior tranche level for healthy CLOs.

Table 6.10, on the other hand, shows much more severe excess OC deltas for the subordinate tranches of these same CLOs. The excess OCs for Univision across all the CLOs varies from 9.1 to 31.1%, and averages 18.0%. Subordinate tranche excess OC would be significantly reduced by the default of Univision Communications.

The loss of all 10 credits at 100% severity would cause most of the subordinate tranches in the 30 CLOs to lose all their excess OC. Overcollateralization of each subordinate tranche would therefore fall below 100%. Again, it is obviously a remote possibility that all 10 credits would default, and almost an impossibility that all 10 credits would default with zero recovery. The subordinated notes of Dryden XVIII, the CLO with the highest subordinated tranche excess OC, would still be covered, even if all 10 credits defaulted, as long as they had a 46% recovery.

In our study, the 10 most common names produce an average excess OC delta of 139%.

TABLE 6.9 Percentage of Senior Tranche Excess Overcollateralization Deltas

	Avery Point CLO	Babson CLO 2004-I	Babson CLO 2005-I	Babson CLO 2005-II	Babson CLO 2006-I	Babson CLO 2006-II	Babson CLO 2007-I	Bridgeport CLO	Bridgeport CLO II	Castle Hill III	Centurion CDO 8	Centurion CDO 9	Centurion CDO VII	Centurion CDO XV	Dryden V	Dryden VII
Univision Communications Inc.	3.3	7.5	4.3	5.7	5.9	6.7	7.8	5.4	5.4	0.0	5.5	6.6	5.4	7.6	4.0	7.0
Georgia-Pacific Corp.	5.8	4.2	3.2	2.8	3.8	4.7	4.6	4.8	5.4	10.2	0.7	2.8	1.0	0.0	2.8	12.2
HCA Inc.	4.5	6.1	1.5	1.8	3.3	5.0	6.1	7.5	6.4	4.1	3.0	3.6	3.0	0.0	8.4	13.0
Idearc Media	3.9	3.1	5.0	5.9	2.6	3.6	3.4	4.3	4.3	7.4	3.0	3.6	2.8	0.0	5.7	8.4
Community Health Systems Inc.	2.8	1.9	1.8	1.1	2.6	4.1	2.7	3.6	5.2	0.0	3.6	4.3	3.6	3.9	2.2	8.2
TXU Corp.	3.2	2.3	2.5	2.1	4.5	4.4	4.2	7.6	7.6	3.8	1.9	2.6	1.9	2.3	7.3	13.2
Royalty Pharma	2.4	0.0	4.6	5.5	2.7	0.8	2.1	6.1	5.2	4.5	2.1	2.5	2.5	2.8	2.3	6.2
Calpine Corp.	2.9	1.4	1.9	2.2	2.5	2.1	1.4	3.1	3.1	2.5	4.8	6.8	5.3	5.7	0.0	7.0
SunGard Data Systems Inc.	3.1	3.9	2.4	5.7	4.0	2.5	7.8	5.3	0.0	0.0	2.6	3.1	2.7	2.6	5.6	7.6
Metro-Goldwyn-Mayer Inc.	2.2	5.4	7.8	6.3	3.5	4.2	6.3	3.2	2.7	4.1	3.0	3.1	5.4	3.5	2.2	3.8
Total	34.0	35.8	35.0	39.1	35.5	38.1	46.5	50.8	45.1	36.6	30.2	39.0	33.6	28.4	40.5	86.6

TABLE 6.9 (continued)

	Dryden VIII	Dryden XI	Dryden XVIII	Forest Creek CLO	Long Grove CLO	Octagon Invest Partners IX	Octagon Investment Partners V	Octagon Investment Partners VI	Octagon Investment Partners VII	Octagon Investment Partners VIII	Octagon Investment Partners XI	Race Point II CLO	Race Point IV	Sagamore CLO	Saratoga CLO I	Average
Univision Communications Inc.	5.0	6.6	16.2	6.8	5.5	4.1	4.8	6.5	4.5	3.3	4.9	3.7	4.0	8.7	10.3	5.9
Georgia-Pacific Corp.	6.7	9.0	15.4	10.7	6.2	6.6	4.7	8.1	8.5	6.2	6.1	3.8	4.1	6.7	8.6	5.8
HCA Inc.	6.2	11.4	13.9	6.7	6.1	6.7	6.3	9.1	6.7	4.4	5.1	4.5	3.8	2.8	1.6	5.6
Idearc Media	5.4	6.5	15.3	7.9	4.2	4.7	6.3	6.4	6.7	4.1	5.1	3.9	4.0	9.6	7.9	5.3
Community Health Systems Inc.	7.4	7.8	23.4	6.5	5.3	6.5	5.3	8.3	7.9	4.9	5.9	2.8	4.8	0.0	0.3	4.8
TXU Corp.	1.8	7.5	16.2	9.0	5.5	0.0	0.0	0.0	0.0	0.0	0.0	3.3	3.5	9.8	10.1	4.4
Royalty Pharma	3.4	3.3	10.2	13.6	5.8	5.4	4.7	6.4	5.2	3.7	4.6	3.5	4.0	6.9	8.7	4.6
Calpine Corp.	3.6	4.2	14.1	2.2	2.3	4.3	5.0	4.7	6.6	5.8	4.9	2.9	4.2	5.0	4.2	4.1
SunGard Data Systems Inc.	3.6	3.5	12.8	4.9	4.8	4.6	2.3	5.2	4.4	4.1	3.1	4.3	4.0	0.7	2.2	4.0
Metro-Goldwyn-Mayer Inc.	0.9	0.0	0.0	8.9	4.2	5.3	4.7	7.4	4.8	3.0	4.6	0.5	1.1	0.0	0.0	3.6
Total	43.8	59.8	137.5	77.2	49.9	48.1	44.1	62.2	55.4	39.4	44.4	33.4	37.5	50.1	54.0	48.1

Data for this table obtained from Intex Solutions. Calculations by UBS CDO Research.

TABLE 6.10 Percentage of Subordinate Tranche Excess Overcollateralization Deltas

	Avery Point CLO	Babson CLO 2004-1	Babson CLO 2005-I	Babson CLO 2005-II	Babson CLO 2006-I	Babson CLO 2006-II	Babson CLO 2007-I	Bridgeport CLO	Bridgeport CLO II	Castle Hill III	Centurion CDO 8	Centurion CDO 9	Centurion CDO VII	Centurion CDO XV	Dryden V	Dryden VII
Univision Communications Inc.	9.3	24.6	12.0	22.5	23.4	21.3	22.4	18.0	20.0	—	18.8	29.4	18.0	22.1	18.7	13.0
Georgia-Pacific Corp.	16.3	13.8	8.9	11.2	14.8	14.9	13.4	15.9	19.7	—	2.3	12.4	3.3	0.0	13.0	22.6
HCA Inc.	12.7	19.9	4.2	7.2	12.8	15.9	17.8	24.9	23.6	—	10.5	16.2	10.1	0.0	39.0	24.1
Idearc Media	10.9	10.4	14.0	23.4	10.2	11.4	9.9	14.2	15.8	—	10.3	16.2	9.3	0.0	26.3	15.6
Community Health Systems Inc.	8.0	6.3	5.1	4.5	10.4	12.8	7.8	12.0	19.1	—	12.5	19.3	11.9	11.3	10.2	15.2
TXU Corp.	9.1	7.5	6.9	8.5	17.9	13.8	12.2	25.1	27.8	—	6.5	11.8	6.3	6.8	33.7	24.4
Royalty Pharma	6.8	0.0	12.9	21.7	10.7	2.7	6.1	20.1	18.9	—	7.1	11.0	8.3	8.2	10.6	11.4
Calpine Corp.	8.2	4.6	5.3	8.6	10.0	6.5	4.1	10.3	11.4	—	16.5	30.2	17.7	16.6	0.0	12.9
SunGard Data Systems Inc.	8.6	12.9	6.7	22.4	15.9	7.9	22.7	17.6	0.0	—	8.8	13.8	9.0	7.5	25.9	14.0
Metro-Goldwyn-Mayer Inc.	6.3	17.7	21.8	24.7	13.8	13.3	18.1	10.6	9.9	—	10.3	13.9	18.1	10.2	10.4	7.0
Total	96.2	117.7	97.8	154.7	139.9	120.5	134.4	168.9	166.1	—	103.5	174.3	112.0	82.7	188.0	160.2

TABLE 6.10 (continued)

	Dryden VIII	Dryden XI	Dryden XVIII	Forest Creek CLO	Long Grove CLO	Octagon Invest Partners IX	Octagon Investment Partners V	Octagon Investment Partners VI	Octagon Investment Partners VII	Octagon Investment Partners VIII	Octagon Investment Partners XI	Race Point II CLO	Race Point IV	Sagamore CLO	Saratoga CLO I	Average
Univision Communications Inc.	10.6	22.9	25.4	16.2	18.9	9.2	13.4	13.5	9.1	12.7	15.6	8.7	13.3	24.5	31.1	18.0
Georgia-Pacific Corp.	14.2	31.4	24.1	25.5	21.3	15.0	13.1	16.9	17.2	23.9	19.4	9.0	13.8	18.8	26.0	15.7
HCA Inc.	13.3	39.5	21.7	16.0	20.8	15.1	17.7	18.9	13.5	16.9	16.1	10.6	12.6	7.8	5.0	16.2
Idearc Media	11.4	22.6	24.0	18.7	14.5	10.6	17.8	13.3	13.6	16.0	16.1	9.1	13.5	27.0	24.0	15.0
Community Health Systems Inc.	15.7	27.2	36.7	15.5	18.0	14.6	15.0	17.3	16.0	19.1	18.7	6.6	16.1	0.0	1.0	13.5
TXU Corp.	3.8	26.2	25.4	21.5	18.8	0.0	0.0	0.0	0.0	0.0	0.0	7.9	11.6	27.4	30.4	13.0
Royalty Pharma	7.2	11.3	16.1	32.4	20.0	12.1	13.3	13.3	10.5	14.3	14.6	8.3	13.3	19.3	26.4	13.0
Calpine Corp.	7.6	14.7	22.0	5.1	8.0	9.7	14.2	9.8	13.3	22.5	15.5	6.9	14.0	13.9	12.6	11.8
SunGard Data Systems Inc.	7.6	12.2	20.0	11.7	16.4	10.4	6.5	10.9	8.9	15.7	9.7	10.1	13.4	2.0	6.6	11.9
Metro-Goldwyn-Mayer Inc.	1.9	0.0	0.0	21.2	14.4	12.0	13.1	15.4	9.7	11.5	14.5	1.1	3.5	0.0	0.0	10.8
Total	93.4	207.9	215.5	183.8	171.1	108.7	124.3	129.3	111.9	152.5	140.1	78.3	125.2	140.7	163.1	138.8

Data obtained from Intex Solutions. Calculations by UBS CDO Research.

EQUITY TRANCHES AND DISTRESSED TRANCHES

The same logic applies to the equity tranches as well. Excess OC for the subordinate tranche becomes the residual amount of par for the equity piece of the CLO.

Table 6.10 also has applicability to the equity tranches of these CLOs. Excess OC for the subordinate debt tranche is also the residual amount of par available for the equity tranche after all the debt tranches are satisfied. Thus, each excess OC delta in Table 6.10 shows the reduction in residual par available to the equity tranche if the credit defaults without any recovery. For example, for Babson 2004-1, the default of all 10 names without recovery would reduce the subordinate tranche's excess OC by 100% and it would eliminate the payment of collateral principal to the equity tranche.

Whereas excess OC delta for the subordinate debt tranche quantifies the potential deterioration of coverage above 100%, for the equity tranche, the same statistic quantifies the potential deterioration of par otherwise applicable to equity. This same analysis is valid for any distressed CLO tranche that does not have 100% par coverage and therefore no excess par coverage.

SUMMARY

CLOs have many of the same underlying credits in common. The greatest collateral overlap is among CLOs having the same manager, because most managers distribute loan purchases across all their CLOs. High loan repayment rates cause CLOs to have recent vintage collateral regardless of the CLO's vintage. Across different managers, the typical CLO owns between 159 and 316 individual credits. Excess overcollateralization delta is a measure to take into account single-name risk in the context of the CLO tranche's collateral protection. The combined excess OC delta to the 10 most common names shows that single-name risk is minor for senior tranches, but of greater concern for subordinated debt tranches and, of course, equity.

Three

Synthetic Markets

7

Credit Default Swaps and the Indexes

The synthetic markets have grown rapidly in both size and popularity, and now dominate the volume of trading activity in the corporate credit markets. In this chapter, we provide an overview of single-name credit default swaps (CDS)[1] and the indexes.

Credit derivatives enable the isolation and transfer of credit risk between two parties. They are bilateral financial contracts which allow credit risk to be isolated from the other risks of a financial instrument, such as interest rate risk, and passed from one party to another party. Aside from the ability to isolate credit risk, other reasons for the use of credit derivatives include:

- Asset replication/diversification
- Leverage
- Regulatory capital efficiencies
- Yield enhancement
- Hedging needs
- Liquidity
- Relative value opportunities

We begin this chapter with a brief introduction to CDS on specific corporate issuers, discussing what they are, who uses the market, and why. We then discuss the CDS indexes, and examine factors such as how they perform relative to other assets.

---

[1] Notice the use of CDS rather than CDSs for credit default swaps. According to an anonymous UBS desk analyst in response to a *60 Minutes* report on credit default swaps, "'CDS' is a plural noun, like grain, rice, and sand. You don't say, 'I love having brown 'rices' with my Moo Goo Gai Pan.'"

WHAT ARE CREDIT DEFAULT SWAPS?

The typical analogy used for CDS is an insurance contract. When you buy insurance, you are buying financial protection against a specified event. For example, a homeowner buys earthquake or flood insurance to "hedge" against a catastrophic event. CDS can be considered a policy used to "hedge" against corporate default.

That said, there are important differences between CDS and insurance contracts. For example, can you imagine a homeowner buying flood protection that pays out in the event of a flood impacting a neighbor's home rather than his or her own? Or how about a homeowner buying protection on a neighbor's house that is worth five, six, or seven times the notional amount of his or her neighbor's home?

It is difficult to envision these things in the context of the insurance market, but these are certainly components of the CDS market. For example, in theory CDS buyers can purchase an unlimited amount of contracts on an underlying reference entity (although if risk managers are doing their jobs, this would not occur). As such, CDS is a way to not only hedge risk, but also a way to take risk—and levered risk at that. Moreover, because homeowners do not necessarily mark-to-market flood insurance that they may have purchased on their (or their neighbor's) house, it cannot be used to protect against other assets being damaged in the event of bad weather (e.g., a boat docked in a nearby lake). But CDS is typically marked-to-market, and as such it can be used for purposes other than to protect against a default by a particular issuer. For example, it can be used to hedge against the mark-to-market risk of an equity option position.

Contract Details and Mechanics

The absolute basic components of a credit default swap are a credit protection buyer, a credit protection seller, a reference obligor, and reference obligations.

In a credit default swap, the *credit protection buyer* (or simply protection buyer) purchases credit protection from the *credit protection seller* (or simply protection seller) in a dollar-amount size referred to as the *notional amount* on a *reference obligor*. Potentially,

FIGURE 7.1 Basic Mechanics of a CDS Contract

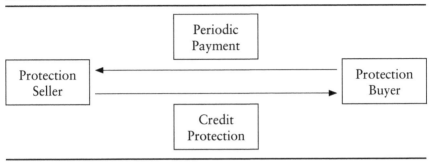

any actual or potential issuer in the debt markets, including corporations, sovereign governments, municipal governments, or supranationals, may be a reference obligor. Typically, the protection buyer pays the protection seller a fee based on a number of basis points per annum times the notional amount. These payments are paid by the protection buyer for the life of the swap (which is either maturity or a credit event). Figure 7.1 highlights these flows.

In a typical CDS, the protection buyer pays for the protection premium over several settlement dates rather than upfront, usually quarterly. In the case of quarterly payments, the payment is computed as follows:

Quarterly swap premium payment = Notional amount swap rate (in decimal form)
× Actual number of days in quarter ÷ 360

A reference obligor credit event, should it occur, triggers a payment from the protection seller to the protection buyer. (We will define a "credit event" later.) With respect to the payment from the protection seller to the protection buyer, the payment depends on whether there is physical or cash settlement. After the payment is made the contract is cancelled.

In *physical settlement,* illustrated in Figure 7.2, the protection buyer selects a reference obligation of the reference obligor and delivers it to the protection seller. Usually, any senior unsecured (or any secured) obligation of the reference obligor is a qualified reference obligation. The protection buyer can deliver a par amount of a reference obligation equal to the notional amount of the CDS. The protection seller must then pay the protection buyer par for the reference

FIGURE 7.2   Following Credit Event: Physical Settlement

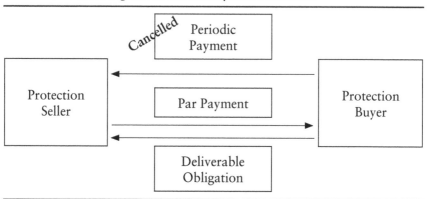

obligation. The key point here is that after a credit event, reference obligations will most likely trade at a value that is less than par. As such, CDS owners can deliver something worth less than par and receive par for it. After a credit event, as the owner of the reference obligations, the protection seller is free to take whatever steps he or she thinks best to recover the maximum value possible, including working out or selling the assets. If reference obligations have different market values, the protection buyer has what is referred to as the *cheapest-to-deliver option*. This is the choice of finding and delivering the least expensive reference obligation to the protection seller in exchange for par.[2]

In the case of *cash settlement*, the difference between the reference obligation's par value and its market value is paid in cash by the protection seller to the protection buyer. The value of the reference obligation is determined in the market by a specified mark-to-market auction process. This arrangement is illustrated in Figure 7.3.

Credit Events

The essential part of a credit default swap is the specific circumstances considered to be *credit events*. The triggering of a credit event is what causes the protection seller to make a protection payment to the protection buyer. ISDA defines six possible credit events that attempt

---

[2] This option is similar to the delivery option granted to the short in a Treasury bond and note futures contract.

FIGURE 7.3   Following Credit Event: Cash Settlement

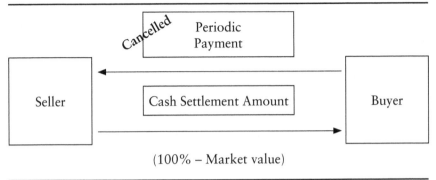

to capture every type of situation that could cause the credit quality of the reference entity to deteriorate:

1. Bankruptcy
2. Failure to pay
3. Obligation default
4. Obligation acceleration
5. Repudiation and moratorium
6. Restructuring

The broader the definition of a credit event, the easier it becomes for a protection payment to be triggered. But the market consensus over the years has been to exclude some credit events and to tighten the definitions for the rest. Parties now generally agree to exclude obligation default and obligation acceleration in nonemerging market corporate CDS. The logic is that these situations do not always rise to the severity intended to trigger a protection payment. And if the situation of the underlying credit is severe, failure to pay will follow shortly anyway.

Similarly, the bankruptcy definition has been tightened. In the 1999 ISDA definitions, the bankruptcy definition contained the phrase "action in furtherance of bankruptcy." In practice, the market discovered this phrase to be vague. If, for example, a debtor under financial stress hires an attorney to help it understand the bankruptcy process, does that mere consultation qualify as an "action in furtherance of bankruptcy"? This ambiguity was resolved when the phrase was stricken from the bankruptcy definition.

Because repudiation and moratorium are only applicable to sovereign credits, this leaves three remaining credit events common in most corporate underlying CDS: bankruptcy, failure to pay, and restructuring. "Bankruptcy" is the voluntary or involuntary filing of bankruptcy. "Failure to pay" is the failure of the reference obligor to make principal or interest payments on one or more of its obligations. "Restructuring" has been the focus of a great deal of concern and debate.

The Restructuring Debate

Restructuring refers to relaxing the terms of a debtor's loan or bond obligations to take into account the debtor's weakened credit situation. Debt maturities might be extended, coupons lowered, principal reduced, or debt seniority might even be reduced. Restructuring debt is seen as a less disruptive and less costly alternative to the bankruptcy process. While it definitely inflicts a credit loss, the issue in the CDS market is whether, and how, restructuring should be included as a credit event capable of triggering a protection payment.

Restructuring as a credit event is a concern to credit protection sellers. One reason is that it can give the protection buyer an unintended "cheapest-to-deliver" option. When a credit is in bankruptcy, all same-seniority debt trade similarly, regardless of coupon or maturity. This is because the bankruptcy court is apt to treat all debt of the same seniority identically with respect to the distribution of cash or new securities from the bankrupt estate. But this is not the case in a restructuring, where the coupon and maturity of certain obligations issued by the reference entity may remain unaffected by the restructuring. The buyer of protection could find it economically advantageous to search out the cheapest trading debt to purchase and deliver to the protection seller in exchange for par.

Another concern about restructuring is the possible manipulation of the process by bank lenders that have bought credit protection that includes restructuring. The issue is that if a bank controls the restructuring process, and has purchased protection that covers restructuring, the bank has no economic incentive to limit the diminution of the restructured loan. Such a bank could oversee the restructuring of its loan, allow its terms to be slashed, present that loan to the protection seller for a payment of par, and even provide separate new funding to the troubled credit at a higher point in its new capital structure.

On the other side of the issue have been banks, chiefly in Europe, that view restructuring as a legitimate way to work out a problem loan, and thus desire credit protection to cover this eventuality. The regulators of these banks have been reluctant to give capital relief for credit protection that excludes restructuring risk.

Different approaches have been implemented to address the concerns of both protection sellers and protection buyers. There are four standard ISDA definitions dealing with restructuring: "restructuring," "modified restructuring," "modified–modified restructuring," and the elimination of restructuring entirely. Modified restructuring and modified–modified restructuring limit the maturity of deliverable reference obligations in different ways, thus constraining a protection buyer's cheapest-to-deliver option.

Understanding the Economic Positions of the Counterparties

The protection buyer is said to be "short" the credit risk of the reference obligor while the protection seller is said to be "long" the credit risk of the reference obligor. To understand why, consider first what happens when an investor sells credit protection on a reference obligor. The investor receives the swap premium and if there is no credit event, the swap premium is received over the life of the CDS contract. In many ways, this is economically equivalent to the investor buying a bond of the reference obligor (assuming no counter-party risk, liquidity differences, etc.) Instead of receiving coupon interest, the investor receives the swap premium payment. If there is a credit event, then the investor under the terms of the CDS must make a payment to the credit protection buyer. This is equivalent to a loss that would be realized if the investor purchased the bond. Hence, in many ways selling credit protection via a single-name CDS is economically equivalent to a long position in the reference obligor.

Suppose, instead, that an investor wants to short the bonds of a reference obligor. Shorting a bond involves making payments to another party (the security lender) and then if the investor is correct and the bond's price declines, the investor can purchase the bond at a lower price (i.e., realize a gain). That is precisely what occurs when single-name CDS is purchased: the investor makes a payment (the swap premium) and realizes a gain if a credit event occurs. Hence, buying credit protection via a single-name CDS is economically equivalent to shorting (again, given a few assumptions).

WHO USES PROTECTION, AND FOR WHAT?

Traditionally, banks have been the most active buyers and sellers of credit derivative products. However, that could change given the changes in the hedge fund industry. In 2008, hedge funds made up nearly 31% of the market (verse a downward trending 40% by the banks). Table 7.1 shows the shift in the market of buyers and sellers of credit derivative products looking back to the year 2000.

When the products of the credit derivatives market are observed, single-name CDS outstanding and full index trades alone made up more than 50% of outstandings in 2006 (see Figure 7.4). Although the market share of single-name CDS is expected to decline slightly, they still serve as a key product for the investors in the market, in terms of establishing and hedging risk positions as well as serving as building blocks for synthetic structures such as bespoke collateralized loan obligations (CLOs). Bespoke CLOs consist of customized portfolios chosen by the end investor.

GROWTH OF THE MARKET

The CDS market has grown tremendously since 1996 in terms of both trading volume and product evolution. As can be seen in Figure 7.5, the notional amount of outstanding CDS rose from $20 billion in 1996 to over $54 trillion through the first half of 2008. In terms of product evolution, the market has developed from one that was characterized by highly idiosyncratic contracts taking a great deal of time to negotiate into a standardized product traded in a liquid market offering competitive quotations on single-name instruments and indexes of credits.

TABLE 7.1 Buyers and Sellers of Credit Derivative Products

Type	Buyers 2000	2002	2004	2006	2008 (est.)	Sellers 2000	2002	2004	2006	2008 (est.)	Purpose
Banks—Trading activities	81%	73%	67%	39%	36%	63%	55%	54%	35%	33%	Hedging, investments, regulatory
Banks—Loan portfolio				20%	18%				9%	7%	
Hedge funds	3%	12%	16%	28%	28%	5%	5%	15%	32%	31%	Speculation, carry, hedging
Pension funds	1%	1%	3%	2%	3%	3%	2%	4%	4%	5%	Investment, fee's, collateral enhancement
Corporates	6%	4%	3%	2%	3%	3%	2%	2%	1%	2%	Hedging, yield enhancement
Monoline insurers			2%	2%	2%		21%	10%	8%	8%	
Reinsurers	7%	3%	3%	2%	2%	23%		7%	4%	4%	Investment, speculation
Other insurance companies		3%	2%	2%	2%		12%	3%	5%	6%	
Mutual funds	1%	2%	3%	2%	3%	2%	3%	4%	3%	3%	Investment, fee's, collateral enhancement
Other	1%	2%	1%	1%	2%	1%	0%	1%	1%	1%	

Data for this table obtained from the British Bankers' Association, *Credit Derivatives Report 2006*.

FIGURE 7.4   Distribution of Credit Derivatives Products Globally

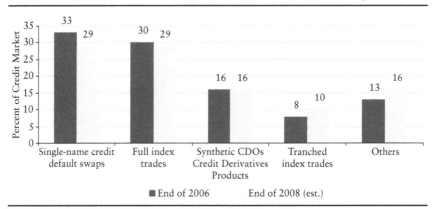

Data for this figure obtained from the British Bankers' Association, *Credit Derivatives Report 2006*.

The growth of the CDS market can partly be attributed to the International Swaps and Derivatives Association's (ISDA) creation of credit derivatives definitions in 1999 (revised in 2003) discussed earlier. ISDA not only eliminated documentation inconsistencies and provided a common negotiating language for all market participants, but also designed a confirmation template that organizes the defined terms into a short, easily understandable, and comparable document. The orderly settlement of the Argentina, Enron, Fannie Mae, Freddie Mac, Lehman Brothers, and WorldCom credit events based on standard ISDA documentation added considerably to the credibility of the documentation and to the credit derivative products as well.

MARKING-TO-MARKET: SDV01

We noted earlier that one difference between CDS and insurance contracts was, in some cases, marking-to-market. At this stage, we quickly review spread DV01 (SDV01), or the dollar value of a one basis point change in spread. That is, given some notional amount a single basis point change will have some amount of impact on an investor's portfolio or trading position. Importantly, SDV01 is not constant; it increases or decreases depending on spread level. For example, the SDV01 of CDS that is at 50 basis points will be higher than the SDV01 of a CDS at 100 basis points.

FIGURE 7.5 Credit Default Swap Growth

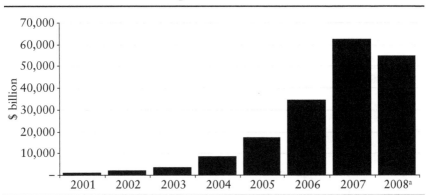

[a] 2008 figure represents 1H08.
Note: As of November 20, 2008.
Data for this figure obtained from ISDA.

One easy way to visualize this is using an extreme hypothetical case. First, consider a spread movement for an issuer with a spread of only 1 bp. If the spread moves from 1 bp to 2 bp, it is a big deal because the probability of default for this issuer has essentially doubled (see Figure 7.6). As such, the change in price will be fairly large—a standard five-year CDS that pays a 1 bp coupon will fall from par to 99.50 when its spread widens 1 bp (to 2 bps). But for an entity that is trading much wider, say 3,000 bp, a 1 bp change spread will not likely move the needle in terms of implied default—the market is already pricing in a likely default (see Figure 7.7). In relative terms, CDS is little changed (price falls from par to $99.98). The key point here is that the sensitivity to spread change decreases as the probability of default increases.

If an investor buys five-year protection on $10 million notional for 50 bps on Company X, he or she is signing up to pay $50,000 per year (or $12,500 per quarter) for the protection.[3] Let's assume the SDV01 is around $4,500 for $10 million in notional. If the CDS spread widens to 60 bp the next day, the investor has made approximately $45,000 in mark-to-market profit and loss (P&L), which can be realized (minus transaction costs) if he or she unwinds the trade.

[3] As explained earlier, the amount in each quarter will vary depending on the number of days in the quarter.

FIGURE 7.6 Implied Probability of Default Changes Significantly when Spread Moves from 1 to 2 bp

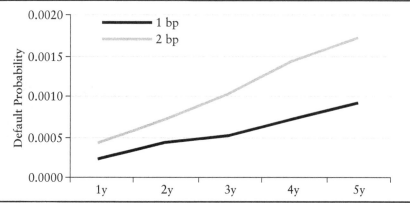

Data for this figure obtained from Bloomberg.

FIGURE 7.7 Implied Probability of Default Does Not Change Meaningfully when Spread Moves from 3,000 to 3,001 bp

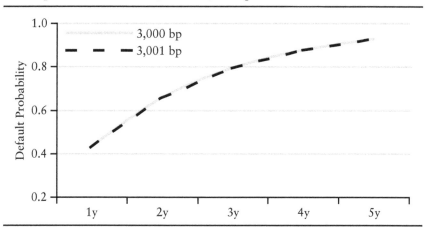

Data for this figure obtained from Bloomberg.

CREDIT DEFAULT SWAPS INDEXES

Pre-defined single-name CDS contracts are also grouped by broad market segments. The three most common are CDS for high-grade corporate bonds (index denoted by CDX.IG), high-yield corporate bonds (index denoted by CDX.HY) and loans (index denoted by LCDX), and help market participants with a number of requirements. The core buyers and sellers of CDX indexes have been index arbitrager players, correlation desks, bank portfolios and proprietary trading desks, and credit hedge funds. Increasingly, greater participation by equity and macrohedge funds has been observed. They are looking for the following from CDX indexes.

- *Barometer of market sentiment.* Credit indexes are averages of a universe of single-name CDS contracts, and provide a snapshot of the market's risk appetite in the same way that the S&P 500 equity index provides a snapshot of equity trading markets. Note that although there are many similarities between the CDX indexes and equity indexes, some major differences still exist as highlighted in Table 7.2.
- *Hedging tool.* Because of the relatively large trading volume and favorable liquidity provided by both the CDX.HY and LCDX indexes, a number of investors use the products to tactically alter portfolio exposures.
- *Arbitrage and relative value positioning.* One of the more challenging endeavors that many long/short investors face is funding short positions; Companies A, B, and C may be high beta and face more fundamental pressures than the average company in the market, but how to pay for shorts and limit mark-to-market risk? Many use the indexes in this regard.

TABLE 7.2 Differences between Credit and Equity Indexes

	Credit Indexes	S&P 500
Weighting	Equally weighted	Market cap weighted
Additions/Deletions	Roll to a new series every six months	Changes are made as needed
	Determined by a consortium of dealers	Determined by S&P
Index Calculations	Index level driven by demand/supply	Float adjusted market cap/divisor

Data for this table obtained from UBS and Markit Group Limited.

- *Capital structure positioning.* Market participants have increasingly been using the CDX.HY and LCDX indexes in combination with other broad market assets, such as the various equity indexes, oil, etc., in order to express specific broad market views (e.g., credit crunch will hurt equities more than loans).

The mechanics of a CDS index are slightly different from that of a single-name CDS. A summary of the North American high-grade and high-yield indexes and the European high-grade index is provided in Table 7.3.

For these contracts, there is a swap premium that is paid periodically. If a credit event occurs, the swap premium payment ceases in the case of a single-name CDS (but paid up to the credit event date) and the contract is terminated. In contrast, for an index, the swap payment continues to be made by the credit protection buyer. However, the amount of the quarterly swap premium payment is reduced. This is because the notional amount is reduced as result of a credit event for the reference obligor.

These broad indexes are available in maturities from one to 10 years, with the greatest liquidity at 5-, 10-, and, 7-year maturities. A new index series is created every six months. At that time, the specific composition of credits in each new series is determined and a new premium level determined for each maturity. Premiums on indexes are exchanged once a quarter on or about the twentieth day of March, June, September, and December. Each name in an index is equally weighted in the indexes. For the North American indexes, only bankruptcy and failure to pay are credit events even though modified restructuring is commonly a credit event in the North American market. For the European indexes, bankruptcy, failure to pay, and modified-modified restructuring are credit events.

What's in An Average? A Look at the CDX.HY

Table 7.4 lists CDX.HY and LCDX spread levels and their 52-week range as of the end of November 2008. What's interesting, though, is not just the average spread per se, but the distribution of constituent spread levels. Note that distributions are by no means constant. Figures 7.8 and 7.9 highlight spread distributions of the CDX.HY series

TABLE 7.3 Summary of CDX Indexes: North America and Europe

	North America Investment Grade Index	North America High Yield Index	Europe Index
Main Index Name	CDX NA IG	CDX NA HY	iTraxx Europe
Main Index Composition	125 corporate names	100 corporate names	125 corporate names
Subindexes	Five Industries: Consumer, Energy, Financials, Industrials, and Technology/Media/Telecom High Volatility	BB rated B rated High Beta	9 Industries: Autos, Consumer, Consumer Cyclicals, Consumer Noncyclicals, Energy, Senior Financials, Subordinate Financials, Industrials, and Technology/Media/Telecom Largest Corporates Lower Rated (aka Crossover) High Volatility

Data for this table obtained from UBS and Markit Group Limited.

TABLE 7.4   Actively Traded Leveraged Finance Indexes in the United States

Index	Spread (bp)	52-week Range (bp)
CDX.HY11 Index	1,394	460–1,394
LCDX10 Index	1,271	299–1,271

Note: As of November 19, 2008.
Data for this table obtained from Markit Group Limited.

FIGURE 7.8   CDX HY10 Spread Distribution, June 15, 2007

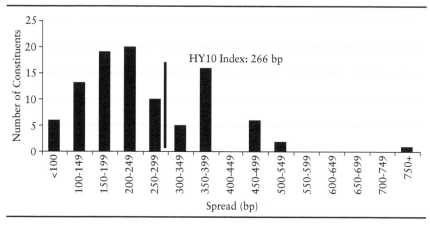

Data for this figure obtained from Markit Group Limited.

FIGURE 7.9   CDX HY11 Spread Distribution, October 10, 2008

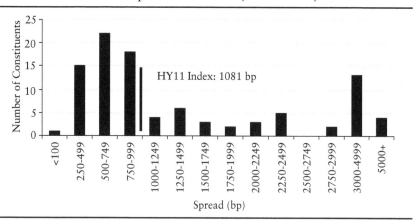

Data for this figure obtained from Markit Group Limited.

10 and series 11 constituents in June 2007 (more or less the end of the bull market) and October 2008 (bear market in full force).

During this period the spread for the CDX.HY index widened by almost 800 bp, but also note how the distribution evolved. In 2007 (see Figure 7.8), the distribution was more or less normal and the range of spreads was fairly tight around the average (almost all issue were trading in the 100 to 600 bp range. In 2008 (see Figure 7.9), though, the distribution has a fat tail—more than 15 issuers are trading at spread levels over 3,000 bp—and the range is very wide.

What does this mean? Well, for starters it could be a sign that risk aversion remains acute, with investors demanding particularly high compensation for exposure to any "risky" name. And it could be a sign that less traditional market participants, such as distressed investors, may become more active participants as return potential meets their higher un-levered hurdle rates.

The key point here is that it is not just the average that matters when assessing market conditions and opportunities, but the composition of the average.

CONTRASTING THE LCDX AND CDX INDEXES

What differentiates the LCDX from other synthetic corporate debt indexes such as CDX.HY is that it references a collection of loan CDS (i.e., any/all outstanding senior secured bank debt of the reference issuer). Table 7.5 illustrates that LCDX is quite comparable to the CDX.HY index. Both indexes reference the same number of credits (albeit secured loans versus unsecured bonds), offer unfunded exposure, quote on price rather than spread, and follow similar coupon payment mechanics.

Two important differences, however, exist between LCDX and CDX: the recovery assumption and the cancellation of LCDS. First, *recovery* simply reflects the difference in valuations of secured and unsecured debt in the event of bankruptcy. As a first lien instrument, loans typically enjoy a higher recovery rate than unsecured debt in the event of default. Although realized recovery estimates vary (anywhere from 50 to 80%), Markit Partners currently assumes 65% recovery for its published price/spread calculations, as opposed to 40% for CDX.HY. Second, *cancellation* describes a situation where

TABLE 7.5   CDX.HY and LCDX Characteristics

	LCDX	CDX.HY
Launch date	5/22/2007	3/27/07 (Series 8)
Constituents	100 equal weight 1st lien LCDS	100 equal weight HY CDS
Roll dates	Semiannual: April 3 and October 3	Semiannual: March 27 and September 26
Coupon	Paid quarterly	Paid quarterly
Coupon payments	Quarterly: Mar–Jun–Sep–Dec 20	Quarterly: Mar–Jun–Sep–Dec 20
Cancellability	Cancellable if all 1st lien secured debt is called; index notional is reduced by 1% following cancellation	NA; Index notional reduced by 1% only if default occurs
Credit event	Bankruptcy or failure to pay debt	Bankruptcy or failure to pay debt
Recovery rate	65% (75% before February 28, 2008)	40%
Quotation	Price	Price

Data for this table obtained from Markit Group Limited.

a firm repays all of its outstanding first lien loans without issuing new first lien debt, perhaps due to an asset sale, an upgrade to investment-grade status, and so on. In this case, the LCDS is cancelled after 30 days if no debt substitute is found. The original index notional is reduced by 1%.

BETA: A STUDY OF MOVEMENT

How do CDS move relative to other assets? We examined relative movements in a number of different ways over their brief existence . Our three key findings are summarized below:

1. *Single-name CDS versus cash.* Although, in many ways cash bonds and CDS for a specific issuer are similar economic exposures, they are not identical. In Figures 7.10, 7.11, and 7.12, we

present the spread difference between benchmark cash bonds and CDS for Cardinal Health, Kinder Morgan, and Autozone, respectively. Spread movements tracked fairly closely for the first portion of the period (January 2006 to early November 2008), but cash bonds dramatically underperformed toward the end of that period. There are a number of reasons for this, including more expensive financing costs for cash bonds in the wake of the credit crunch, Wall Street's balance sheet constraints, and so on. We discuss these factors in more detail in the next section.

2. *Synthetic indexes versus cash markets.* Much like the spread difference between cash and CDS at the single-name level, the difference between cash and synthetic can be meaningful at the broad market level as well (see Figures 7.13 and 7.14). The funding and balance sheet issues highlighted above play a role, but other asset specific factors are critical as well. For example, brokers hedging their loan commitments during this period largely took place via the indexes. For reference, we also present relative spread movements of the CDX.HY and LCDX indexes in Figure 7.15. As might be expected, the correlation between the two is by no means 1.

FIGURE 7.10 Cardinal Health Bond vs. CDS

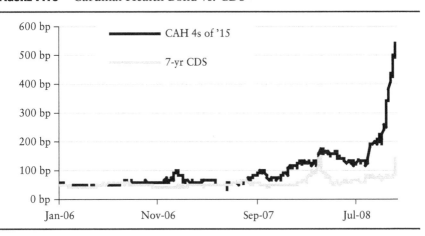

Note: As of November 4, 2008.
Data for this figure obtained from UBS and Markit Group Limited.

FIGURE 7.11   Kinder Morgan Bond vs. CDS

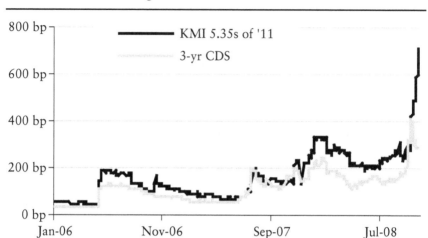

Note: As of November 4, 2008.
Data for this figure obtained from UBS and Markit Group Limited.

FIGURE 7.12   Autozone Bond vs. CDS

Note: As of November 4, 2008.
Data for this figure obtained from UBS and Markit Group Limited.

FIGURE 7.13 Historical Difference in Cash Bond and CDX Spreads

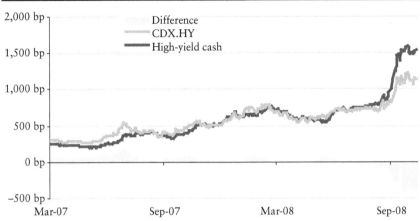

Note: As of November 7, 2008.
Data for this figure obtained from Markit Group Limited and *Yield Book*.

FIGURE 7.14 Historical Difference in Cash Loan and LCDX Spreads

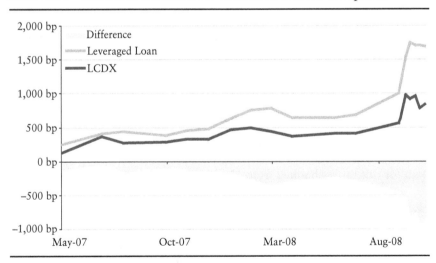

Note: As of November 7, 2008.
Data for this figure obtained from Markit Group Limited and *Yield Book*.

FIGURE 7.15   Historical Difference in Synthetic Market Indexes

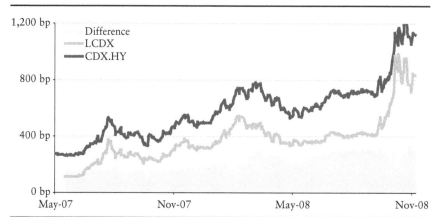

Note: As of November 10, 2008.
Data for this figure obtained from Markit Group Limited.

TABLE 7.6   Betas of the Broad Market Indexes, September 2007 to
September 2008

	Cash Bond	Cash Loan	CDX.HY	LCDX	Average
Beta	1.00	0.75	1.28	0.97	1.00
R-squared	0.82	0.91	0.87	0.93	1.00
Beta in Bull Markets	0.79	0.71	1.70	0.79[a]	1.00
Beta in Bear Markets	1.41	0.92	0.74	1.05[a]	1.00

[a] From June 2007 to September 2008 in order to take the early summer
hedging into account.
Data for this table obtained from Markit Group Limited and *Yield Book*.

3. *Stability of beta.* We also compared price moves (as opposed to
   spread changes) of the cash bond and loan markets and the CDX.
   HY and LCDX indexes to the average price move in the overall leveraged finance space from September 2007 to September
   2008 (see Table 7.6). The results are more or less inline with
   what might be expected. The bond market exhibited a higher

beta[4] than the loan space, and synthetics had a higher beta than the cash markets. But one important point is that assets exhibited meaningfully different betas during bull and bear markets. The CDX.HY index has had a higher beta in tightening environments than in widening ones, and LCDX exhibited the opposite tendency. Technical conditions have obviously contributed to this dynamic. For example, many banks and brokers hedged committed LBO financing and loan portfolios as market prices were under pressure, and to a large extent, LCDX was the hedge vehicle of choice. These short positions were not necessarily unwound when the market tone firmed, but rather when deals were placed. Bottom line is that there was less impetus for short-covering rallies in LCDX.

SUMMARY

Despite the recent growth and popularity of the synthetic market, it is still a relatively young area of the overall corporate credit world. While participation in the market will likely continue, whether it be to express a view on a corporate issuer, hedge a portfolio of risk assets, or used as a measurement of confidence in a corporate issuer or market, the manner in which we trade these instruments is likely to evolve in the coming years. At the time of writing, financial broker/dealers and government officials are working toward moving the market from an over-the-counter market to an exchange-traded market.

The synthetic market is likely here to stay and will likely only grow in importance and popularity in the future as credit and equity markets converge and these instruments become intertwined in their trading strategies. As such, the study and understanding of the basics of these instruments are as important as understanding the basics of bonds and loans in the cash market.

---

[4] Beta is estimated from a simple linear regression model where the explanatory (independent) variable is the broad-based index and the dependent variable is an individual member of that index.

8
Index Tranches

In the previous chapter, we introduced the synthetic markets, with a focus on credit default swaps and the credit indexes. This chapter takes a closer look at the credit and loan indexes (CDX and LCDX, respectively) and the unique feature of "tranching."[1] This means that the cash flows for the overall index can be divided among holders of different portions of total credit risk, which are referred to as *index tranches*.

The chapter is divided into two parts. In the first part we discuss the basic mechanics of the tranche market. The second part will focus on the LCDX tranche market and the special features of LCDX tranches (such as high recoveries and cancellation events). In addition, we will evaluate whether synthetic tranches are interchangeable with cash tranches and identify some of the similarities and differences.

BASIC MECHANICS OF THE TRANCHE MARKET

The basic building block of an index tranche is a static index portfolio. The most widely traded index tranches are based on the standard credit default swap (i.e., CDS) indexes that we described in the previous chapter: CDX (IG, HY, LCDX) and iTraxx (Main). These indexes are typically equal-weighted static portfolios. CDX.HY and LCDX contain 100 names in their portfolios, while iTraxx Main and CDX.IG contain 125 names.

As we learned in the previous chapter, the indexes provide investors with a tool to efficiently and effectively hedge their corporate

---

[1] We would like to thank David Kim and George Attokkaran, the primary authors of this chapter, for their help and contributions.

bond exposure or to express views on the overall corporate credit market. Going short index protection expresses a bearish credit view which profits if bonds or loans in the portfolio default. Conversely, going long index protection expresses a bullish view. Indexes are typically reissued twice a year to ensure their constituents reflect benchmark issuers in the current environment and standard maturities. This process is often referred to as "the roll."

Tranche Conventions

Index tranches redistribute the expected losses due to anticipated defaults in the index portfolio across a capital structure and allow investors to take more targeted loss exposure. A tranche is typically described in terms of its position in the capital structure (equity, mezzanine, senior, etc.) as shown in Figure 8.1. The attachment indicates how much subordination, or cushion, the tranche enjoys. The *de-*

FIGURE 8.1   Index Tranching: An Example with the CDX.IG Index[a]

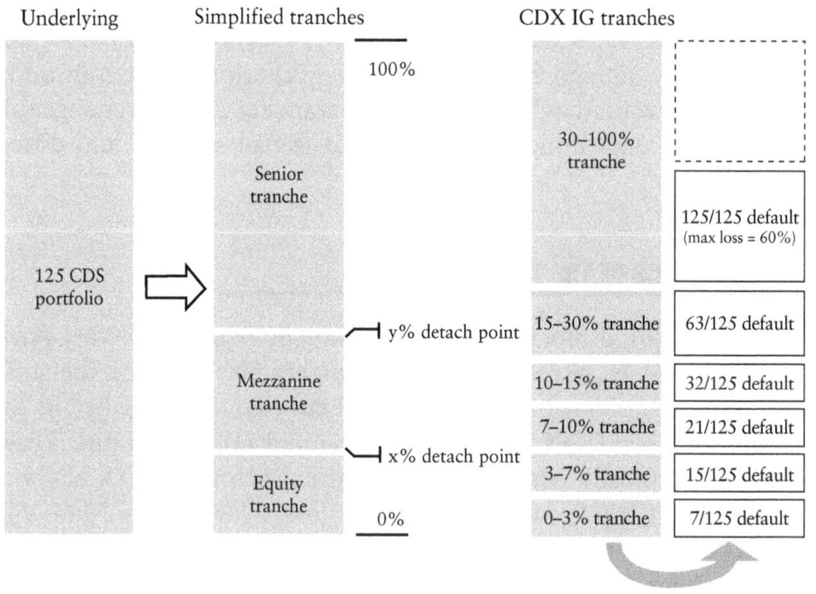

[a] Graphic not to scale, number of defaults assumes an average 40% recovery. Data for this figure obtained from UBS.

tachment point determines the thickness of the tranche. These conventions are described in terms of percentage loss. For example, the 0–3% equity tranche of the CDX.IG index is exposed to the first 3% of losses. If one member of the CDX.IG index defaults, the equity tranche loses 16% of its notional value.

As Figure 8.1 illustrates, approximately seven defaults are needed to wipe out the CDX.IG equity tranche. Given a 40% recovery assumption, the maximum theoretical loss for the portfolio is 60%. In other words, a 60–100% tranche should offer zero spread assuming 40% recovery. Tranches are quoted as a running spread (like a regular credit default swap (CDS)), points upfront, or some combination. For example, the CDX.IG equity tranche is quoted in points upfront and 500 basis points running while the other CDX.IG tranches are quoted in running spread only.

Naming conventions follow the CDO cash market. Starting from the bottom of the capital structure (with regard to CDX.IG), the "first loss piece" is the equity tranche. The 3–7% or "second loss piece" is the junior mezzanine (the 10Y 3–7% is a special case as it can be considered a first loss piece; it is sometimes called the "orphan tranche"). The 7–10% is the senior mezzanine. The 10–15% and 15–30% are senior tranches. The 30–100% is the super-senior tranche.

Why Tranche?

A primary motivation for the tranche market during 2003–2006 was the spread-ratings arbitrage—rated tranches offered higher spread than similarly rated corporate bonds. Rating agencies used historical simulations (using historical defaults and historical default correlation) to determine the ratings of tranches. In the CDS market, investors demand a premium over historical values to take on default risk. Synthetic tranches allowed investors to capture this premium for a given rating. Figure 8.2 shows the difference between the spreads implied by historical defaults and those implied by market spread.

A single synthetic tranche (a tranche based on CDS rather than cash bonds), unlike a cash CDO, does not require the issuance of the entire capital structure. The investor still enjoys the benefits of subordination, can take spread risk, and gain leverage in a nonrecourse format. Even though the investor is leveraged in spread terms, he cannot lose more than the notional amount placed at risk.

FIGURE 8.2 Difference Between the Spreads Implied by Historical Defaults and Those Implied by Market Spread

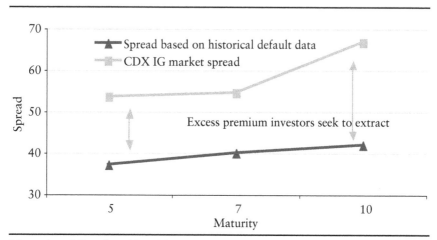

Note: As of October 19, 2007.
Data for this figure obtained from UBS and Markit Group Limited.

Think in Terms of Expected Loss

The key concept for understanding the tranches is "expected loss." This concept can provide substantial insight into how tranche pricing works, regardless of whether a tranche is based on a standard index or a bespoke (customized) portfolio. For a single-name CDS, the spread approximately equals the product of the default probability and loss-given-default (or one minus the recovery rate with the standard recovery assumption being 40% for CDS and 65% for LCDS). Using the standard recovery assumption and the market-observable spread, one can solve for an implied default rate.

This simple formula highlights the relationship between spread and "expected loss," or the probability-weighted value of the loss. For this reason, many often use "spread" and "expected loss" interchangeably. If spreads widen, the expected loss must also increase. The fundamental relationship between expected loss and spread is clear when discussing the profit and loss of a CDS contract.

Using an insurance analogy, the value of a stream of insurance premium payments should equal the expected loss of an event (again, the probability of the event occurring multiplied by the magnitude of the loss should the event occur).[2] For example, assume insurance contracts can be traded readily. Two parties enter an insurance contract on Day 1. On Day 2, the market determines that the likelihood of the insured event has increased. The insurance buyer has enjoyed a marked-to-market (MTM) profit since the contract has increased in value. The insurance seller has lost money because the premium payments he is receiving no longer compensate him adequately for the risk he is taking (expected loss has increased).

This intuition holds true for a CDS contract. If the market believes default risk is increasing for a given credit, spreads widen and protection buyers make a MTM gain.

Expected Loss Snapshot

- Default probability $\approx$ Spread /(1 − Recovery rate)
- Expected loss = Spread × Risky duration[3]
- Portfolio expected loss $\approx$ Average of constituent expected losses

This logic extends to the standard indexes. Just as in single-name CDS, the index spread implies an expected loss for the portfolio of credits. If the index spread increases, the expected loss of the aggregate portfolio has increased.

Expected loss (EL) reflects the mean number of defaults anticipated by the market, but does not say anything about the loss distribution around that mean. The mean could be achieved by a barbell-like distribution or a more centered distribution. Implied correlation attempts to capture this information.

---

[2] This is the heart of what is called *risk-neutral pricing*. In reality, insurers may demand a premium above the risk-neutral price to protect themselves and provide additional cushion. Insurers of flood or fire risk will likely use historical data to determine the chances of an event occurring. In contrast, the implied volatility market and CDS market mostly reflect what investors think the future stock volatility or default risk will be for a given firm.

[3] *Risky duration*, or *RiskyDV01*, represents how much a CDS changes in dollar value for a one basis point change in the CDS spread. RiskyDV01, spread duration, and risky duration are often used interchangeably. Higher spread names have lower RiskyDV01 since they are more likely to default (future cash flows are less likely to occur).

Correlation Reflects Risk Allocation

Implied correlation reflects the market's view of default: Will defaults occur in a binary fashion (no one defaults or everyone defaults) or a more bell-curve fashion (defaults occur independently)? We address this in detail in Chapter 13. Correlation reflects how portfolio loss is being allocated across the tranches and does not necessarily imply changes in the expected, or average, loss of the portfolio. In other words, the spread level of the underlying index does not necessarily need to change for the tranche value to change.

One way to understand correlation is to think in terms of idiosyncratic and systemic risk. If the market believes systemic risk is rising (e.g., the banking system is in trouble), correlation is likely to increase. The reason is that a credit crunch is likely to produce forced selling, difficult refinancing, and other unexpected problems. This type of risk is distinct from idiosyncratic risks that may only impact a single company or subsector. Changing perceptions of idiosyncratic and systemic risk impact tranche investors because they influence how index expected loss is allocated across the tranches (reflected in dealer pricing).

The important thing to remember is that changing perceptions of risk can affect tranche pricing without any change in index spread. The sum of the loss in each of the tranches must equal the expected loss of the underlying portfolio to avoid arbitrage (see Table 8.1). As such, we could consider tranches the equivalent of CDS on discrete portions of the portfolio's expected loss. The twist comes when the amount of loss in each tranche changes even when there is no change in the total expected loss/average spread of the portfolio. Remember, loss is conserved. If the index spread stays constant (i.e., the loss implied by the portfolio does not change), a decrease in loss for one tranche must result in an increase in loss elsewhere in the capital structure. As such, changes in correlation do not necessarily mean the total expected loss has changed.

Consider two extreme loss distributions: 100% and 0% correlation (see Figure 8.3). Remember, both distributions share the same expected loss. In the 0% correlation case, the loss distribution implies that defaults are independent. In this case, equity carries the most risk because it is the first-loss piece. On the other hand, the super-

TABLE 8.1 Hypothetical CDX IG Tranche Pricing Illustrates the Conservation of Loss

Tranche	Notional ($)	Price	Expected Loss (% of tranche notional)	Expected Loss (% of $10mm)
0–3%	300,000	41.50 bp	63.8%	1.71%
3–7%	400,000	229 bp	15.0%	0.41%
7–10%	300,000	73 bp	4.0%	0.10%
10–15%	500,000	34 bp	3.0%	0.08%
15–30%	1,500,000	17 bp	4.0%	0.12%
30–100%	7,000,000	8 bp	10.0%	0.26%
Total risk	10,000,000	—	100.0%	2.68%
CDX IG	10,000,000	60 bp	—	2.68%

Data for this table obtained from UBS.

FIGURE 8.3 Two Extreme Loss Distributions: 100% and 0%

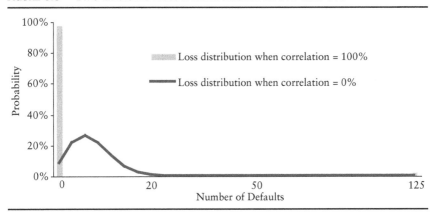

Data for this figure obtained from UBS.

senior tranche is completely protected since there is very little chance enough credits will default to wipe out all subordinate tranches.

In the 100% correlation case, the loss distribution implies a binary outcome—a good chance that no credits will default and a small chance that the entire portfolio will default. This case benefits the equity tranche since there is a chance it will never suffer a loss, particularly when compared to the 0% correlation case. The super-senior tranche, however, suffers since there is now some chance all the credits will default where there was none before. These two extreme examples define the limits of the implied loss distribution, but pricing can obviously take the correlation anywhere between 0% and 100%.

While the basic correlation intuition is as previously described, certain mathematical inconveniences led to the development of *base correlation*. Base correlation essentially treats nonequity tranches as the difference between two equity tranches of differing thickness. For example, the loss implied for a 3–7% mezzanine tranche is equal to the difference between the loss implied by a 0–7% tranche and the loss implied by a 0–3% tranche. Using this logic, one can bootstrap base correlations from market-observed tranche pricing to generate an upward sloping *correlation skew* (Figure 8.4).

The bottom-line: tranches are essentially CDS contracts on discrete portions of a portfolio's loss distribution. The difference in tranche value is dependent not only on the index spread but also perceptions of correlation. Figure 8.5 shows the factors that influence CDX index and tranche pricing.

FIGURE 8.4 Base Correlation Results in an Upward Sloping CDX IG Correlation Curve

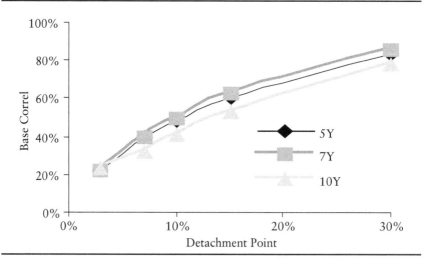

Data for this figure obtained from UBS.

FIGURE 8.5 A Schematic of the Factors that Influence CDX Index and Tranche Pricing

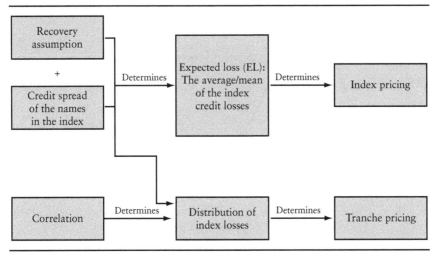

Informtation for this figure obtained from UBS.

Comparing Market Implied Correlations and Historical Correlations

The "Monte Carlo bootstrapped historical loss distribution" in Figure 8.6 represents the loss distribution generated by realized default rates with an added premium for short-term spread volatility and transaction costs. The Gaussian Copula distribution represents our best attempt to fit a loss distribution to the historical distribution using a flat implied correlation curve. Using our understanding of expected loss, market prices on September 10, 2007 imply a relatively large amount of loss probability in the senior mezzanine and senior tranches. This difference is visible in the tranche pricing. As Figure 8.6 indicates, the "fair" pricing of the iTraxx Main tranches using realized default probabilities differs greatly from the pricing witnessed in the market on September 10, 2007.

Understanding Tranche Sensitivities in an Option Context

Delta, in a correlation market context, describes how much the value of a tranche changes in basis points for a one basis point change in the value of the underlying index. Practically speaking, delta indicates

FIGURE 8.6 iTraxx Loss Distribution—Comparing Historical versus Market Implied Distributions

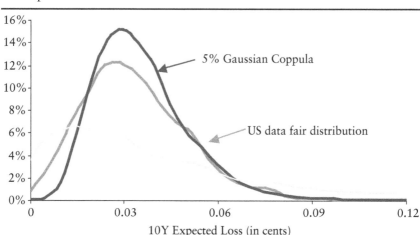

Data for this figure obtained from UBS.

how much index the investor must buy or sell to immunize a given tranche position against small movements in the index spread. As such, delta is an indicator of tranche leverage *vis-à-vis* the underlying index. Delta is important because it helps index tranche traders maintain market-neutral positions as they typically want to take views on implied correlation, not the underlying index itself.

Tranches can be considered options on the index loss. For instance, buying protection on the IG 0–3% tranche is essentially buying a "call spread" on the index loss, with the investor long a call option at 0% and short a call option at 3%. Similarly, buying protection on the IG 3–7% tranche is like buying a call option with a 3% strike and selling a call option with a strike of 7%.

A call spread's sensitivity to the underlying index's expected loss is the greatest when the index expected loss is in the middle of the strike of the two tranches. For example, the IG 3–7% tranche has the highest delta when the index expected loss is around 5%. As the index expected loss moves away from 5%, in either direction, the delta falls. At extremely low or high expected losses (well below 3% or well above 7%), the delta approaches zero. An index with high expected loss suggests the 3–7% tranche will be wiped out, hence providing the maximum possible return for the protection buyer. This maximum gain is capped at the protection notional amount and does not change for small changes in the index expected loss. Conversely, at very low spreads, the 3–7% tranche will probably remain unscathed, leaving the protection buyer with a zero return.

The key point here is that tranches with strikes flanking the index expected loss should have the highest delta relative to other tranches. Deltas for tranches further away from the index expected loss are lower than tranches closer to the index expected loss.

LOAN TRANCHES

The key assumptions of the LCDX are:

- Recovery (65% for LCDX as compared to 40% for indexes in the unsecured markets, such as CDX.HY).
- Cancellation (LCDS is cancelled when the referenced first lien loans are repaid and no substitutes can be found within 30 days).

The assumed recovery rate is similar to the long-term average rate (about 70%), but can vary from period to period. For example, the seniority of first lien loans and technical factors can drive recoveries much higher (or lower) than 65%. Although the LCDS recovery rate is greater than the 40% typically used for CDS, it does not pose any technical hurdles as it simply reduces expected loss given a default. The recovery rate, however, does have a significant impact on the number of defaults each tranche can withstand before the tranche notional is wiped out (see Figure 8.7).

Cancellation is more interesting and problematic as it impacts duration and risk allocation across the tranche capital structure. Cancellation impacts the duration and convexity of individual LCDS. Unlike CDX names, where lower spreads typically correspond to longer durations, cancellation can potentially shorten the duration of LCDS. Cancellation reduces duration, or DV01. Assuming lower spread names are more likely to cancel due to a rating upgrade, cancellation may reduce the weight of lower spread names in the LCDX index, relative to the CDX.HY index (and CDX.IG), and impacts the theoretical price of the index. This negative convexity exposes inves-

FIGURE 8.7   Higher Recovery in the LCDX Results in Lower Expected Loss

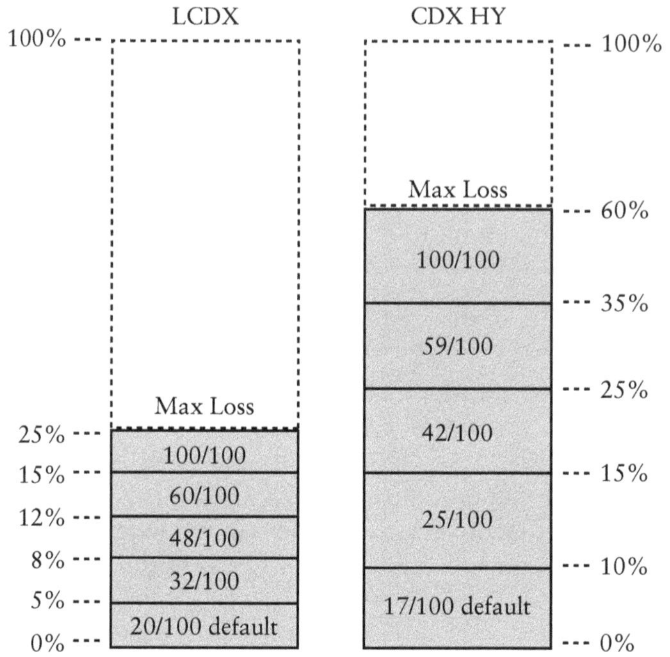

Note: Not drawn to scale.
Data for this figure obtained from UBS.

tors to the "double-whammy" of a decline in index price after a cancellation (since the remaining population of credits will be skewed toward higher spreads) and lower coupon due to the reduction in notional. Furthermore, an appropriate cancellation rate is difficult to estimate given the lack of reliable historical data.

Although cancellation can be triggered by a ratings upgrade, there are other reasons why a company may decide to call its first lien debt. For example, Advanced Micro Devices (AMD) called its loans and refinanced in the convertible market for reasons that had nothing to do with a ratings upgrade. M&A (mergers and acquisitions) activity or asset sales can also trigger early repayment of loans, as covenants typically require the meeting of maintenance standards. While there are many reasons why corporations choose to repay loans, many may also choose to maintain their revolvers (which qualify as first lien)

TABLE 8.2 Rescaling Tranches: Default versus Cancellation Scenarios

Tranche	1 Default	1 Cancellation
5%	4.4%	5.1%
8%	7.5%	8.1%
12%	11.5%	12.1%
15%	14.5%	15.2%
100%	100.0%	100.0%

Data for this table obtained from UBS.

as a relatively inexpensive option on future liquidity. Countrywide's draw-down of its revolvers ($11.5 billion) in late 2007 points to the potential value of this option.

Cancellation benefits the junior tranches at the expense of the senior tranches since cancelled LCDS results in a write-down of super-senior notional. Table 8.2 illustrates, through a simple rescaling exercise, how cancellation might affect the LCDX tranches. In the usual default scenario, defaults are realized from the bottom of the capital structure upwards. Assuming one default, we see that a rescaling of the existing tranches to 100% produces smaller subordinate tranches while the super senior remains protected (a negative result for equity tranche investors). Cancellation, as noted, works from the super senior tranche *down*. More specifically, cancelled LCDS results in amortization of the senior tranche (to 15–99% from 15–100%). As seen in Table 8.2, one cancellation results in larger subordinate tranche thicknesses relative to the super-senior tranche (a negative result for the senior tranches).

Cancellation's Impact on LCDX9 Tranche Risk

In an attempt to quantify the impact of cancellation on tranche risk, we assume prepayments are uncorrelated with defaults. Some argue cancellation is more likely for low spread names, as they have better access to capital. Prepayments in the LCDX8 by relatively high spread names, however, suggest our assumption is at least reasonable.

Cancellation has the following effects on the underlying LCDX index:

- *Reduced Expected Loss.* For a given spread level, prepayments cause a reduction in the index expected loss because they reduce the future size of the portfolio for which protection is being provided. As prepaying entities have no possibility of default (and hence do not contribute to index expected loss), the reduction in average portfolio size results in a reduction in index expected loss.
- *Reduced Risky Duration.* As mentioned previously, risky duration (average duration adjusting for defaults) or (DV01) of the index equals the index expected loss divided by the index spread, the reduction in expected loss results in a reduction of the index DV01.

Cancellation impacts tranche risk as follows:

- *The super-senior DV01 is reduced while other tranche DV01s remain roughly the same.* Since prepayments result in a reduction of super-senior principal, the super-senior tranche logically bears the brunt of the reduction in DV01. Table 8.3 highlights the changes in DV01 and expected loss for the LCDX tranches given different prepayment scenarios.
- *Reduction in tranche delta senior to the at-the-money (ATM) point and an increase in tranche delta junior to the ATM point.* Table 8.4 describes the effect of changing prepayment rates on the hedge ratios, or deltas, of the respective tranches. ATM expected loss is defined as the index expected loss. Increasing cancellation rates reduces ATM expected loss, making tranches junior to the ATM

TABLE 8.3 DV01 for LCDX9 Tranches vs. Annualized Prepayment Rates (LCDX9 5Y)

Tranche	0%	1%	2%	3%	4%
0–5%	2.23	2.22	2.22	2.22	2.22
5–8%	3.27	3.27	3.27	3.27	3.26
8–12%	3.82	3.82	3.82	3.81	3.81
12–15%	4.00	4.01	4.02	4.03	4.03
SS	3.64	3.55	3.47	3.38	3.30
LCDX9	3.61	3.53	3.46	3.38	3.31

Data for this table obtained from UBS.

TABLE 8.4 Hedge Ratios for LCDX9 Tranches vs. Annualized Prepayment Rates (LCDX9 5Y)

Tranches	0%	1%	2%	3%	4%
0–5%	1.78	1.82	1.86	1.91	1.96
5–8%	2.84	2.91	2.99	3.07	3.15
8–12%	3.21	3.36	3.49	3.61	3.71
12–15%	2.07	1.82	1.69	1.70	1.89
Super senior	0.64	0.64	0.63	0.62	0.61

Data for this table obtained from UBS.

expected loss more "in-the-money." This increases the tranche delta at the expense of tranches senior to the ATM point.

SUMMARY

Index tranches can be an effective means to hedge a portfolio, enhance returns, or take outright positions on specific areas of the market. However, they are one of the more complex areas of the corporate credit markets and require market participants to have a solid understanding of the basic dynamics of the corporate credit and loan indexes (CDX and LCDX) and the concepts of "expected loss" and correlation. As such, the purpose of this chapter is to convey the intuition behind synthetic tranches and the language typically associated with this market.

Four

How to Trade the Leveraged Finance Market

9

Recessions and Returns

A question commonly asked by investors in the leveraged finance market is the extent of their exposure during an economic downturn. The answer is usually dependent on whether an investor expects that the economic downtown will be fairly short and shallow or whether it will be deep and protracted. In most cases, investors should be poised to add exposure if the former is true but trim risk positions if the latter appears more likely.

In this chapter, we assess return prospects during economic downtowns. In order to do so, we examine the relationship between economic growth and valuations during the previous five recessionary periods in the United States prior to the 2007 setback: (1) November 1973 to March 1975; (2) January 1980 to July 1980; (3) July 1981 to November 1982; (4) July 1990 to March 1991; and, (5) March 2001 to November 2001. Specifically, we considered each setback in distinct parts:

1. A pre-setback period, which is defined as the six months preceding the actual recession.
2. The actual recessionary period.
3. A post-setback period, which is defined as the six months following the official conclusion of each recession.

In addition to looking at the performance at the broad market level, we study the performance at the sector level and across ratings categories.

BROAD MARKET PERFORMANCE

In Table 9.1, we present the cumulative total return and excess return of five-year Treasuries, high-grade, high-yield, and equity markets. The following findings are noteworthy:

- *For investors that care about total returns.* For investors with a total return objective, we found that each of the four markets we assessed performed worse on a cumulative total return basis in the period leading up to the recession than in the recession itself! For example, the average cumulative return of the high-yield bond was 1.74% in the six months leading up to prior recessions, while the average total return during actual setback periods was 2.85% (i.e., outperformance of 1.1%). Again, we found similar results in the Treasury, high-grade, and equity markets.
- *For those that care about excess returns.* The credit market appears to be somewhat less forward-looking when excess returns are considered. For example, the high-grade market generated about the same performance before and during setback periods, and high-yield underperformed modestly during downturns. It is important to note, however, that due to data limitations, results reflect *approximate* excess returns (i.e., excess returns are calculated at the asset class level rather than maturity matching individual securities). As such, we put more weight on our total return findings and a bit less on excess return findings.
- *Being too late can be just as bad as being too early.* In the six-month period following the recessions studied, the high-yield bond market returned an average of 7.2% and excess returns in the high-yield market were significant (3.0%). The natural tendency, in our view, is to wait until the fundamental backdrop is clearly on the mend before adding exposure, but as we have seen in the past, the high-yield market will gap tighter. For a two-week period starting at the end of 2008 through the beginning of 2009, the high-yield cash index tightened by almost 500 basis point. It simply may not be possible to build positions that benefit from future improvements in the economy at attractive valuations if one waits too long.

TABLE 9.1 Total Returns: Before, during, and after Setback Periods

	No. of Months	Cumulative Total Return				Excess Return[a]	
		5Y Treasury	HG	HY	Equity	HG	HY
Six-Month Prerecession							
Period 1 May-73 to Oct-73	6	—	—	—	1.23%	—	—
Period 2 Jul-79 to Dec-79	6	—	—	—	4.89%	—	—
Period 3 Jan-81 to Jun-81	6	0.91%	-0.81%	—	-3.35%	-1.72%	—
Period 4 Jan-90 to Jun-90	6	1.84%	3.13%	0.91%	1.31%	1.28%	-0.93%
Period 5 Sep-00 to Feb-01	6	7.65%	7.87%	2.57%	-18.30%	0.22%	-5.08%
Average	6	3.47%	3.40%	1.74%	-2.84%	-0.07%	-3.01%
Recessionary Period							
Period 1 Nov-73 to Mar-75	17	—	—	—	-23.02%	—	—
Period 2 Jan-80 to Jul-80	7	10.47%	5.82%	—	12.72%	-4.64%	—
Period 3 Jul-81 to Nov-82	17	31.17%	35.71%	—	5.59%	4.55%	—
Period 4 Jul-90 to Mar-91	9	8.21%	8.06%	5.41%	4.80%	-0.15%	-2.80%
Period 5 Mar-01 to Nov-01	9	6.32%	7.27%	0.29%	-8.10%	0.95%	-6.03%
Average	12	14.04%	14.22%	2.85%	-1.60%	0.18%	-4.42%

TABLE 9.1 (continued)

| | No. of Months | Cumulative Total Return | | | | Excess Return[a] | |
		5Y Treasury	HG	HY	Equity	HG	HY
Six-Month Postrecession							
Period 1 Apr-75 to Sep-75	6	—	—	—	0.61%	—	—
Period 2 Aug-80 to Jan-81	6	-2.90%	-5.24%	—	6.48%	-2.34%	—
Period 3 Dec-82 to May-83	6	4.39%	8.43%	—	17.22%	4.04%	—
Period 4 Apr-91 to Sep-91	6	6.98%	8.00%	11.92%	3.37%	1.02%	4.94%
Period 5 Dec-01 to May-02	6	1.39%	1.50%	2.46%	-6.35%	0.11%	1.08%
Average	6	2.46%	3.17%	7.19%	4.27%	0.71%	3.01%

[a] Excess Return defined as total return less five-year Treasury total return.
Data for this table obtained from UBS, Markit Group Limited, and *Yield Book*.

SECTOR PERFORMANCE

With regard to sector performance, we compared the performance of high-yield bonds in more cyclical and less-cyclical sectors before, during, and after recent downturns (see Table 9.2). Our more-cyclical basket is composed of assets in the Airline, Automobile, Building Products, Chemical, and Retail sectors. Our less-cyclical portfolio is comprised of issuers in the Consumer Products, Cable/Media, Energy, Healthcare, and Utility industries. Note that due to data limitations, we can only use the 2000–2001 experience as a reference point.

As most would expect, we found that less-cyclical sectors outperformed their more-cyclical counterparts heading into and during recessions, and lagged when exiting setback periods. What was surprising, in our view, was the extent by which performance differed. For example, in total return terms, less-cyclical issuers outperformed more-cyclical names by an average of 9.9% heading into the March 2001 to November 2001 recession, and outdistanced more-cyclical credits by 11.2% during the previous setback. In the post-setback period, underperformance was almost 7.5%.

And when looking at specific sectors, differences can be even more dramatic. Consider the Auto sector relative to the Health Care space. In the prerecession period the sectors generated total returns of –20.2% and 11.5%, respectively (difference of 31.7%). During the March 2001 to November 2001 recession, the Auto sector returned –5.9% while the Health Care sector returned 12.6% (a difference of 18.5%), and exiting that recession Auto outperformed by 11.3%.

The key point is that sector selection is critical during economic turning points.

PERFORMANCE BY RATING

In Table 9.3, we present total returns and spread changes for double-Bs, single-Bs, and triple-Cs before, during, and after the last two recessions (data limitations did not allow for a review of additional setbacks).

We found, for lack of a better phrase, mixed results. For example, triple-Cs generated an average return of 2.9% during prerecession periods, versus 4.7% during recessions. Returns jumped sharply

TABLE 9.2 Difference between More-Cyclical and Less-Cyclical Assets

Six-Month Prerecession (Sep-00 to Feb-01)

More Cyclical		vs.	Less Cyclical		Difference[a]
Sector	Total Return		Sector	Total Return	Avg. Total Return
Airlines	5.75%		Consumer Products	4.13%	
Automobiles	−20.22%		Cable/Media	5.48%	
Building Products	0.87%		Energy	8.09%	
Chemicals	0.15%		Health Care	11.49%	
Retail Stores	1.75%		Utilities	8.50%	
Average	−2.34%		Average	7.54%	9.88%

Recessionary Period (Mar-01 to Nov-01)

More Cyclical		vs.	Less Cyclical		Difference[a]
Sector	Total Return		Sector	Total Return	Avg. Total Return
Airlines	−24.41%		Cable/Media	2.35%	
Automobiles	−5.92%		Consumer Products	16.91%	
Building Products	11.00%		Energy	8.24%	
Chemicals	−3.42%		Health Care	12.55%	
Retail Stores	14.79%		Utilities	7.90%	
Average	−1.59%		Average	9.59%	11.18%

Six-Month Postrecession (Dec-01 to May-02)

More Cyclical		vs.	Less Cyclical		Difference[a]
Sector	Total Return		Sector	Total Return	Avg. Total Return
Airlines	10.61%		Cable/Media	−4.37%	
Automobiles	15.12%		Consumer Products	9.75%	
Building Products	9.06%		Energy	3.81%	
Chemicals	7.05%		Health Care	3.81%	
Retail Stores	2.76%		Utilities	−5.48%	
Average	8.92%		Average	1.51%	−7.41%

[a] Difference calculated by subtracting cyclical from noncyclical.
Data for this table obtained from UBS, Bloomberg, Markit, and *Yield Book*.

TABLE 9.3 Performance across the Ratings Spectrum

		No. of Months	Total Return (%)			Change in Spread (bp)		
			BB	B	CCC	BB	B	CCC
(A) Six-Month Prerecession								
Period 1	Jan-90 to Jun-90	6	7.92	9.69	13.97	—	—	—
Period 2	Sep-00 to Feb-01	6	5.91	1.69	-8.12	+39	+141	+255
	Average	6	6.92	5.69	2.92	+39	+141	+255
(B) Recessionary Period								
Period 1	Jul-90 to Mar-91	9	5.34	7.77	8.50	-76	-236	-187
Period 2	Mar-01 to Nov-01	9	7.27	-5.09	0.98	+4	-87	+932
	Average	9	6.30	1.34	4.74	-36	-161	+372
(C) Six-Month Postrecession								
Period 1	Apr-91 to Sep-91	6	8.83	13.06	22.92	+0	-87	-74
Period 2	Dec-01 to May-02	6	3.44	1.80	2.50	+154	-57	-995
	Average	6	6.13	7.43	12.71	+77	-72	-535

Data for this table obtained from UBS, Bloomberg, Lehman HY Index, Markit Group Limited, and *Yield Book*.

in the six months after setbacks ended (12.7%). These results suggest that the market may be forward-looking at the ratings level.

However, single-Bs lagged during setback periods relative to prerecession periods. And double-Bs generated essentially the same return before, during, and after downturns (around 6.5%). Bottom line: Our findings are inconclusive.

SUMMARY

In this chapter, we examined the total return performance of the high-yield market during the five recessions (dating back to the early 1970s through 2001). We deconstruct each of the setbacks into three distinct parts: (1) pre-setback period, which is defined as the six months preceding the actual recession; (2) actual recessionary period; and (3) post-setback period, which is defined as the six months following the conclusion of each downturn.

Based on an assessment of total return performance at the broad market level, high-yield bond investors appear to be forward-looking (as well as Treasury, high-grade, and equity investors). These markets performed worse on a cumulative total return basis in the period leading up to the average recession than in the recession itself. Results were mixed when considering excess returns.

As most would expect, less-cyclical sectors outperformed their more-cyclical counterparts heading into and during recessions, and lagged exiting setback periods. What was surprising was the extent of the performance differences.

At the ratings level, we found mixed results. Triple-Cs generated an average return of 2.9% in prerecession periods, versus 4.7% during actual recessions. The opposite held true among single-Bs (outperformance heading into setback period), and double-Bs generated essentially the same return before, during, and after downturns.

10

Framework for the Credit Analysis of Corporate Debt

In this chapter, we provide a framework for the analysis of corporate debt, explaining how credit assessments are more than just the traditional review of financial ratios and leverage metrics.

APPROACHES TO CREDIT ANALYSIS

At one time, when interest rates were stable and investors purchased debt instruments with the purpose of holding them to maturity, the major focus of credit analysis for corporate debt was almost exclusively on the likelihood that the corporation would not make the scheduled interest and principal payments. The analysis primarily involved the calculation of a series of ratios (e.g., fixed charge coverage, leverage, and cash flow to total debt) that were associated with debt instruments. This one-dimensional approach ignored fluctuations in the market value of the debt instruments because changes in interest rates were minimal, and fluctuations attributable to credit changes of the obligor were mitigated by the fact that the investor had no intention of selling the instrument prior to its maturity date.

During the past three decades, the approach to the analysis of corporate debt instruments changed due to the fact that the motivation for acquiring debt instruments changed dramatically. Specifically, an increasing number of institutional investors actively trade them with the purpose of generating an attractive returns attributable to changes in interest rates, or in absolute or relative credit quality or spread. The second dimension of corporate credit analysis addresses this motivation for acquiring positions in debt instruments.

More specifically, it addresses questions such as: the probability of a change in credit quality that will impact the value of a corporate debt instrument.

In contrast to the earlier, one-dimensional approach that focused primarily on the analysis of ratios associated with corporate debt, a second approach deals with ratios associated with debt instruments as well as tools generally associated with common stock analysis: profitability trends, such as return on equity, operating margins, and asset turnover. Although both the one-dimensional approach and this second approach—a two-dimensional approach—address the issue of default or credit risk, the second approach provides a better framework given the two motivations for investing in debt instruments: security of interest and principal payments (i.e., default risk) and improvement (or deterioration) of credit risk during the life of the debt instrument (changes in ratings and credit spreads). This two-dimensional approach closes the gap between what was once viewed as two separate frameworks for security analysis: common stock analysis and corporate credit analysis. This view of the role of common stock analysis is often espoused by high-yield bond managers. As one such manager notes:

> Using an equity approach, or at least considering the hybrid nature of high-yield debt, can either validate or contradict the results of traditional credit analysis, causing the analyst to dig further.[1]

He further states:

> For those who invest in high-yield bonds, whether issued by public or private companies, dynamic, equity-oriented analysis is invaluable. If analysts think about whether they would want to buy a particular high-yield company's stock and what will happen to the future equity value of that company, they have a useful approach because, as equity values go up, so does the equity cushion beneath the company's debt. All else

---

[1] Steven E. Esser, "High-Yield Analysis: The Equity Perspective," in Ashwinpaul C. Sondi (ed.), *Credit Analysis of Nontraditional Debt Securities* (Charlottesville, VA: Association for Investment and Research, 1995): 47.

being equal, the bonds then become better credits and should go up in value relative to competing bond investments.[2]

Adding to the arsenal of tools for the analysis of corporate credit has been the development of options theory. Today corporate debt analysis and option theory are viewed as complementary frameworks as option-based credit risk modeling has increased in popularity since the turn of the century. This approach to credit risk modeling, referred to as a *structural model*, view default as some type of option by the equity owners on the assets of the company, and that the option is triggered (i.e., the corporation defaults) when the market value of the corporation's assets declines below a certain point.[3] The practical implication of option theory for corporate debt analysis is that the perceptions of both the common stock and debt markets should be compared before an investor renders a credit view.

For those investors who take the position that the common equity market offers a higher level of efficiency than the debt market, particular attention should be paid to the common equity price of the company being analyzed. Potential opportunities arise in situations in which the two markets are judged to have significantly different values. Here is an example of how this sort of framework would have been helpful in the early 1980s where the focus was primarily on one-dimensional analysis. In early 1981, the market-to-book values of the major chemical companies ranged from 0.77 to 2.15. The bond ratings of these same companies ranged from Baa/BBB to Aaa/AAA. Neither the range of the market-to-book values nor the bond ratings are the important points here. Rather, it is the fact that although there was some correlation between the market/book ratios and bond ratings, there were instances in which there was little or no correlation. Based on an options theory, more of a relationship between the two would be expected. When the relative valuation of the bond (as measured by its rating) is compared to the common stock valuation (as measured by its market/book), one or both markets may be incorrectly valuing the major chemical companies. Given the empirical evidence that bond rating changes generally lag behind

---

[2] Ibid., 54.
[3] Because of this feature, structural models are also known as *firm-value models*.

market moves, it is likely in this case that the bond rating was too high for the financial profile of the chemical companies at that time.

There is a major benefit to an institutional investor of monitoring common stock price movements. Typically, institutional investors hold a large number of names in their credit portfolio. Watching stock movements of those companies is an efficient way of monitoring those holdings. Unusual movements in the stock price may be indicators of future favorable or unfavorable information and would suggest a further inquiry as to why. For example, sometimes a sharp run-up in the price of a stock may indicate an acquisition. Typically, acquisitions benefit common stockholders of the acquired company because of the premium paid for the stock by the acquirer.

However, the effect of an acquisition on debt holders varies from transaction to transaction. In a favorable scenario, the issuer of the bond is acquired by a higher-rated entity. For example, in 1997, double-A rated Boeing Company acquired single-A rated McDonnell Douglas Corporation. In an unfavorable scenario, the issuer of the bond is either acquired or merged with a lower-rated entity, and its ratings are lowered. For example, this was the case with the debt of triple-B rated Ohio Edison after it merged with Centerior Energy and its double-B+ rated Cleveland Electric Illuminating and double-B rated Toledo Edison operating subsidiaries. In a more recent example, in September 2008, single-A rated U.S. Smokeless Tobacco Inc. (UST Inc.), the largest manufacturer and distributor of snuff and chewing tobacco in the United States, was put on Negative Watch by Moody's and S&P following triple-B rated Altria Group Inc.'s announced plans to acquire the company. Altria is the largest cigarette company in the United States.

Moreover, monitoring option prices can have the same benefit. An important measure derived from option prices is implied volatility. Substantial changes in implied volatility can provide information about the future for an issuer's fundamental profile as well as performance prospects. For example, consider the implied volatility of Ford Motor Company's call options (Figure 10.1) during 2005. We see a spike in April, which happened about one month before the company was downgraded to high yield from investment grade by S&P. In addition, a similar spike occurred in October, ahead of the company being put on Watch Negative. Similar to the relationship of

FIGURE 10.1 Implied Volatility of Ford Motor Company on a Daily Basis in 2005

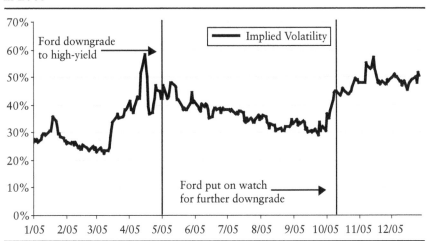

Note: Implied volatility is measured in annualized standard deviations. Data for this figure obtained from Bloomberg.

market-to-book value and bond ratings discussed previously, a spike in implied volatility of a company can indicate that the fundamentals could be likely to change in the future.

Implied volatility can also be viewed on a broad market level. One of the broadest means for monitoring this is through the Volatility Index (the VIX—Figure 10.2). The VIX measures market expectations of near-term volatility conveyed by equity index option prices. It is based on S&P 500 Index option prices and incorporates information from the volatility "skew" by using a range of strike prices (verse at-the-money series). Since the VIX is based on real-time option prices, it reflects investors' consensus view of future stock market volatility. A rise in the VIX may very well be a signal of deteriorating fundamental prospects in the future.

Consider the Moody's default rate as a proxy for the credit quality of the overall market. Note that the VIX traded relatively in line with the trend in default rates from January 2005 through the end of January 2007. At that point, the VIX Index began to trend higher, but it wasn't until December 2007 that corporate default rates started to turn higher.

FIGURE 10.2 The VIX Index vs. High-Yield Defaults

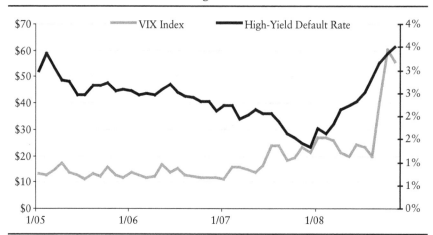

Note: Data as of November 28, 2008.
Data for this figure obtained from Bloomberg and Moody's.

With regard to the VIX and valuations, in Figure 10.3 we plot daily observations of spreads for the broad high-yield market and the VIX. We find that these two series track very closely over time. Unfortunately there is not much of a lead or a lag, which means that one probably could not use one series to predict movements in the other. What this relationship could be used for, though, is to validate current levels. For example, high-yield spreads at the end of 2008 were five standard deviations above average. Was this proper, or was the market a "screaming" buy? Based on where the VIX was at that point, one could conclude that extreme valuations were probably warranted. One market confirmed the other.

INDUSTRY CONSIDERATIONS

A first step in analyzing a corporate bond is to gain some familiarity with the industry. Although there are numerous industry considerations, the following six areas are the primary focus of a typical credit analysis to assess a company's prospects:

- Economic cyclicality
- Growth prospects

FIGURE 10.3 The VIX vs. the High-Yield Corporate Cash Index since 2000[a]

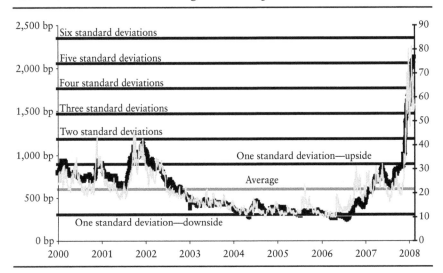

[a] Data taken from January 1, 2000 through December 15, 2008.
Data for this figure obtained from Bloomberg and *Yield Book*.

- Research and development expenses
- Competition
- Sources of supply
- Degree of regulation
- Labor

Economic Cyclicality

The industry's economic cyclicality is the initial factor that one should investigate in reviewing an industry. Does the industry closely follow gross domestic product (GDP) growth or is it recession resistant? Some industries may be somewhat dependent on general economic growth but be more sensitive to demographic changes. In general, however, the earnings of few industries correlate perfectly with one economic statistic. Not only are industries sensitive to many economic variables, but often various segments within a company or an industry move countercyclically or at least with different lags in relation to the general economy. On a company level, the growth in earnings per share (EPS) of a company should be measured against the growth trend of its industry. Attention should be paid to reasons why there may be major deviations from the industry trend. We discuss company-specific considerations in greater detail later in this chapter.

Growth Prospects

Related to economic cyclicality is an industry's growth prospects. Is the growth of the industry projected to increase and be maintained at a high level or is growth expected to decline? Each growth scenario has implications for a company. In the case of a fast-growth industry, how much capacity is needed to meet demand, and how will this capacity be financed? In the case of slow-growth industries, is there a movement toward diversification or consolidation within the industry? A company operating within a fast-growing industry often has a better potential for credit improvement than does a company whose industry's growth prospects are mature or below average. However, barriers to entry and the sustainability of growth must be considered along with the growth prospects for an industry. If an industry is growing rapidly, many new participants may enter the business, causing oversupply of product, declining profit margins, and possible bankruptcies.

Research and Development Expenses

Related to an industry's growth prospects are the research and development (R&D) expenditures required to maintain or expand market position. Evaluation of R&D expenditures is further complicated by the direction of technology. Successful companies not only must spend an adequate amount of resources on development, but management also must be correct in their assessment of the direction of the industry. Deployment of significant amounts of capital may not prevent a decline in credit quality if the capital is misdirected.

Competition

Competition is based on a variety of factors that depend on the industry. Although most competition is based on quality and price, competition is also derived from other factors. Increasingly, all forms of competition are waged on an international basis and are affected by fluctuations in relative currency values. Companies that fare well are those that compete successfully on a global basis and concentrate on the regions with the highest potential for growth. Consumers are largely indifferent to the country of origin of a product as long as the product is of high quality and reasonably priced. Competition within an industry relates directly to the market structure of an industry and has implications for pricing flexibility.

Sources of Supply

The market structure of an industry and its competitive forces have a direct impact on the sources of supply of major production components. A company that is not self-sufficient in its factors of production, but is sufficiently powerful in its industry to pass along increased costs, is in an enviable position.

Labor

The labor situation of an industry should also be analyzed in order to answer the following questions:

- Is the industry heavily unionized?
- What level of flexibility does management have to reduce the labor force?
- When do the current contracts expire, and what is the likelihood of timely settlements?

The labor situation is also important in nonunionized companies, particularly those whose labor situation is tight and should be analyzed to address the following questions:

- What has been the turnover of professionals and management in the firm?
- What is the probability of a firm's employees, such as highly skilled engineers, being hired by competing firms?
- What is the likelihood of union activity in nonunionized companies?

The more labor intensive an industry, the more significance the labor situation assumes.

FINANCIAL ANALYSIS

Having achieved an understanding of an industry, the investor can then proceed with a financial analysis. This analysis should include the following:

1. Analysis of traditional ratio analysis for debt instruments.
2. Analysis of the components of a company's return on equity.
3. Analysis of nonfinancial factors such as management and foreign exposure and includes an analysis of the indenture.

Traditional Ratio Analysis

The following ratios are commonly used in credit analysis and will be discussed in detail below:

- Pretax interest coverage ratios
- Leverage ratios
- Cash flow ratios
- Net assets ratios
- Liquidity ratios

These selected ratios are the ratios with the widest degree of applicability. In analyzing a particular industry, however, other ratios assume significance and should be considered.

In addition to the above ratios, other factors that an investor should consider within the realm of traditional debt analysis are intangibles, unfunded pension liabilities, and age and condition of plant and equipment.

Pretax Interest Coverage Ratios

The *pretax interest coverage* measures the number of times interest charges are covered on a pretax basis. This ratio is calculated by dividing pretax income plus interest charges by total interest charges.

The higher the coverage figure, the safer the credit. If interest coverage is less than 1×, the company must borrow or use cash flow or proceeds from the sale of assets to meet its interest payments. Once pretax interest coverage and fixed charge coverage are calculated, it is necessary to analyze the ratios' absolute levels and the numbers relative to those of the industry.

Generally, published coverage figures are pretax as opposed to after-tax because interest payments are a pretax expense. Although the pretax interest coverage ratio is useful, its value depends on the company's other fixed obligations. For example, if a company has other significant fixed obligations, such as rents or leases, a more appropriate coverage figure would include these other fixed obligations.

Leverage Ratios

Leverage can be defined in several ways. The most common definition of *leverage* is long-term debt as a percent of total capitalization. The higher the level of debt, the higher the percentage of operating income that must be used to meet fixed obligations. If a company is highly leveraged, an investor also should look at its margin of safety. The *margin of safety* is defined as the percentage by which operating income could decline and still be sufficient to allow the company to meet its fixed obligations. Typically leverage is calculated using the company's capitalization structure as stated in the most recent balance sheet. In its simplest form, leverage can be considered a measure of risk.

One of the most common ways to measure leverage is with the total debt to EBITDA (earnings before depreciation, interest and taxes) ratio. This ratio is calculated by adding short-term and long-term borrowings and dividing by the trailing 12-month EBITDA. For companies that do not have historical data available, pro forma (projected) ratios are often calculated.

The nature of the debt itself should be analyzed, including the maturity structure. For example, the investor would want to look at what percentage of debt is coming due within the coming years because this debt may need to be refinanced. It also involves looking at how much of the debt is fixed and how much is floating.

Because a company's bank lines typically represent a major portion of a company's total debt, an investor must analyze these lines closely in order to determine the flexibility afforded to the company. The lines should be evaluated in terms of undrawn capacity as well as security interests granted and whether the line contains a "material adverse change" (MAC) clause under which the line could be withdrawn. For example, a company that has drawn down its bank lines completely and is in jeopardy of activating its MAC clause may have trouble refinancing any debt. In a similar manner, undrawn lines should be evaluated in terms of their capacity to replace commercial paper, if needed.

Cash Flow Ratios

An important ratio is cash flow as a percent of total debt. *Cash flow* is often defined as net income from continuing operations plus depreciation, depletion, amortization, and deferred taxes. In calculating cashflow for credit analysis, the investor also should subtract non-cash contributions from subsidiaries. Basically, an investor should be concerned with cash from operations. Any extraordinary sources or uses of funds should be excluded when determining the overall trend of cash-flow coverage. Cash dividends from subsidiaries also should be questioned in terms of their appropriateness (too high or too low relative to the subsidiary's earnings) and also in terms of the parent's control over the upstreaming of dividends. If there is a legal limit to the upstreamed dividends, an investor must look at how close the current level of dividends is to the limit.

Net Asset Ratios

Another significant ratio is net assets to total debt. In analyzing this aspect of a bond's quality, consideration should be given to the liquidation value of the assets. Liquidation value will often differ dramatically from the value stated on the balance sheet. In addition to the asset's market value, some consideration should also be given to the liquidity of the assets. A company with a high percentage of its assets in cash and marketable securities is in a much stronger asset position than a company whose primary assets are illiquid real estate, for example.

Liquidity Ratios

Another measure that is important in assessing the financial strength of a company involves the strength and liquidity of its working capital.

Working capital, defined as the difference between current assets and current liabilities, is viewed as a primary measure of a company's financial flexibility. Other such liquidity measures include:

- *Current ratio,* which is current assets divided by current liabilities.
- The *"acid" test,* which is the sum of cash, marketable securities, and receivables divided by current liabilities.

The stronger the company's liquidity measures, the better it can weather a downturn in business and cash flow.

Analysis of the Components of Return on Equity

After an examination of traditional ratios is complete, the two-dimension approach calls for analysis of both a company's earnings growth and historical *return on equity* (ROE). The analysis is vital in determining credit quality because it gives investors the necessary insights into the components of ROE and indications of the sources of future growth. Equity investors devote a major portion of their time examining the components of ROE, and their work should be recognized as valuable resource material.

ROE is calculated as follows:

$$ROE = \frac{\text{Net income}}{\text{Stockholders' equity}}$$

A basic approach to the examination of the components of ROE breaks down ROE into four principal components:[4]

- Pretax margins = Net income/Sales

---

[4] This framework for analyzing ROE was first suggested more than 30 years ago in a popular investment textbook at the time: Jerome B. Cohen, Edward D. Zinbarg, and Arthur Zeikel, *Investment Analysis and Portfolio Management* (Homewood, IL: Richard D. Irwin, 1977).

- Asset turnover = Sales/Assets
- Leverage = Asset/Stockholders' equity
- 1 – Tax rate

These four components together equal net income/stockholders' equity, or ROE as shown below:

$$\text{ROE} = \text{Net income/Stockholders' equity}$$
$$= (\text{Net income/Sales}) \times (\text{Sales/Assets})$$
$$\times (\text{Assets/Stockholders' equity}) \times (1 - \text{Tax rate})$$

Ideally, an investor should investigate the changes in these four components of ROE through at least one business cycle. The changes of each component should be compared with the trends of the same components for the industry, and deviations from industry standards should be further analyzed. For example, perhaps two companies have similar ROEs, but one company is employing a higher level of leverage to achieve its results, whereas the other company has a higher asset-turnover rate. Since the degree of leverage is largely a management decision, an investor should focus on asset turnover. Why have sales for the former company turned down? Is this downturn a result of a general economic slowdown in the industry, or is it that assets have been expanded rapidly, and the company is in the process of absorbing these new assets? Conversely, a relatively high rise in the asset turnover rate may indicate a need for more capital. If this is the case, how will the company finance this growth, and what effect will the financing have on the firm's embedded cost of capital?

Similar components of ROE for all companies in a particular industry will deviate. These deviations from industry norms typically reflect differences in management philosophy. For example, one company may emphasize asset turnover, and another company in the same industry may emphasize profit margin. As in any financial analysis, the trend of the components is as important as the absolute levels.

A general idea of the types of ratios expected for a particular rating classification can be obtained from rating agencies. For example, a median of key ratios by rating category is available from Standard & Poor's or Moody's. In using these published ratios, an investor should note that their suitability may be limited because (1) industry standards vary considerably and (2) typically major adjustments must be made to the financial statements to make them comparable with the financial statements of other companies.

Nonfinancial Factors

After the analysis of traditional credit ratios and the earnings growth and ROE are completed, an investor should consider several nonfinancial factors that might modify the evaluation of the company. This involves an analysis of:

- Degree of foreign exposure
- Quality of management
- Covenants

Degree of Foreign Exposure

A company's annual report will provide information about the amount of foreign exposure. It is not always clear what the exposure is to specific countries. This is because the breakdown on foreign exposure in annual reports is typically by broad geographic areas rather that concentration by country. Obviously, foreign exposure results in foreign exchange risk. Management policy for the controlling of this risk should be understood.

Quality of Management

Unlike the analysis of financial factors, evaluating the quality of management is extremely difficult. Equity analysts of institutional investors will do this by spending time with management, if possible. A company led by one person who is approaching retirement and has made no plan for succession or a company that has had numerous changes of management and philosophy would be of concern to an investor.

In discussing the quality of management in assigning credit ratings, Moody's states the following:

> Although difficult to quantify, management quality is one of the most important factors supporting an issuer's credit

strength. When the unexpected occurs, it is a management's ability to react appropriately that will sustain the company's performance.[5]

The following factors are studied by Moody's in an attempt to assess the quality of management quality and understand the business strategies and policies formulated by management:

- Strategic direction
- Financial philosophy
- Conservatism
- Track record
- Succession planning
- Control systems

Moreover, in recent years, investors have also focused on a company's corporate governance and the role of the board of directors. The rules of governance are set forth in the corporate bylaws which define the rights and obligations of officers, members of the board of directors, and shareholders.

Analysis of Covenants

In many lending agreements, there are provisions that impose restrictions upon the activities of management or require management to take certain actions. These provisions, referred to as *covenants*, function as safeguards for the lender. Covenants establish rules for several important areas of operation for corporate management. In bonds, the covenants are contained in the indenture and summarized in the prospectus for its bond offering.

As one high-yield portfolio manager notes:

Covenants provide insight into a company's strategy. As part of the credit process, one must read covenants within the context of the corporate strategy. It is not sufficient to hire a lawyer to review the covenants because a lawyer might miss the critical factors necessary to make the appropriate decision.

[5] Moody's Investors Services: Global Credit Research, "Industrial Company Rating Methodology" (July 1998): 6.

Also, loopholes in covenants often provide clues about the intentions of management teams.[6]

Covenants fall into two general categories: affirmative and negative covenants. Covenants that require the borrower to take certain actions are referred to as *affirmative covenants*. Examples would include the maintenance of insurance, the payment of taxes, and the conducting of its business in the ordinary course so as to preserve its business and goodwill. Covenants that set forth restrictions on what management actions management may not take are referred to as *negative covenants* or *restrictive covenants*. Common negative covenants include various limitations on the company's ability to incur debt since unrestricted borrowing can be highly detrimental to the bondholders. The two most common tests are the maintenance test and the debt incurrence test. The *maintenance test* requires the borrower's ratio of earnings available for interest or fixed charges to be at least a certain minimum figure on each required reporting date for a certain preceding period. When the company wishes to borrow additional amounts, the *debt incurrence test* applies. In order to take on additional debt, the required interest or fixed charge coverage adjusted for the new debt must be at a certain minimum level for the required period prior to the financing. There could also be *cash flow tests* (or *cash flow requirements*) and *working capital maintenance provisions*.

What Causes Ratios to Change?

Given how important financial ratios are to determining a company's credit quality (and valuation), it is important to consider what variables may cause them to change, for better or worse. The economy? The cost of inputs such as fuel for airlines or steel for automakers? We looked at the relationship between leverage metrics and various economic factors, including the relationship between GDP growth and debt/EBITDA. Next we discuss this relationship for three specific companies: (1) Chesapeake Energy, (2) KB Home, and (3) Harrah's.

---

[6] Robert Levine, "Unique Factors in Managing High-Yield Bond Portfolios," in Frank K. Reilly (ed.), *High-Yield Bonds: Analysis and Risk Assessment* (Charlottesville, VA: Association for Investment Management and Research, 1990): 35.

We find that GDP can be an important driver of this leverage met-ric—but many other factors can be important drivers as well. The key point is that an investor should use a broad and dynamic set of tools when assessing potential changes in a company's credit quality.

Chesapeake Energy: Three Periods of Leverage

Chesapeake Energy is a producer of oil and natural gas. According to Bloomberg, the company's operations are focused on developmental drilling and producing property acquisitions in onshore natural gas-producing areas. Figure 10.4 shows three distinct periods in Chesa-peake Energy's leverage history: declining leverage (1998 through mid-2003), more or less steady leverage (mid-2003 through mid-2006), and rising and falling leverage (mid-2006 through the end of 2008).

Within the first period, Chesapeake's leverage ratio dropped by almost four turns (from about 6.0× to about 2.0×), in part benefiting from fairly robust economic growth in the late 1990s. What is inter-esting, though, is that the debt/EBITDA ratio continued to decline even after GDP growth slowed sharply in 2000–2001. Here the key

FIGURE 10.4   Chesapeake Energy: Three Periods of Leverage, 1998–2008

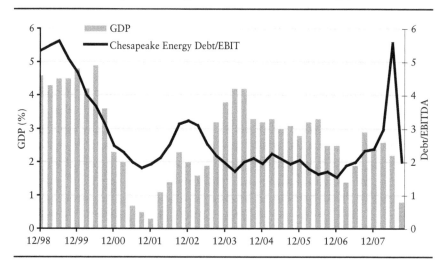

Note: As of September 30, 2008.
Data for this figure obtained from Bloomberg.

point is that GDP, among the many other variables that exert influence on a companies leverage profile, has a lagging effect.

The other interesting period is the most recent period (2006 to 2008), when leverage both increased sharply and declined dramatically. Why the rise? Chesapeake was able to take advantage of its low cost of debt capital and acquire attractive assets. Why the decline? In part because Chesapeake was able to sell equity stakes in these attractive assets to other industry participants at high valuations. The key point is that in the most recent period, company-specific actions may have had as big an influence on its leverage metrics as the overall economy.

KB Home: Leverage Ratio Makes a Roundtrip

Figure 10.5 illustrates the connection between debt/EBITDA during the 1990–2008 period for KB Home, a homebuilder that primarily builds single-family homes targeted toward first-time and move-up buyers. In general, there seems to be some connection between this company's leverage and economic growth, but there are noteworthy exceptions. For example, during the weak economic growth period of 2000–2002, leverage was virtually unchanged.

FIGURE 10.5   KB Home: Leverage Ratio Makes a Roundtrip

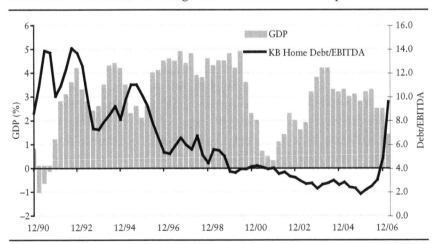

Note: As of March 31, 2007.
Data for this figure obtained from Bloomberg.

FIGURE 10.6   KB Home: Leverage Ratio vs. Home Price Change

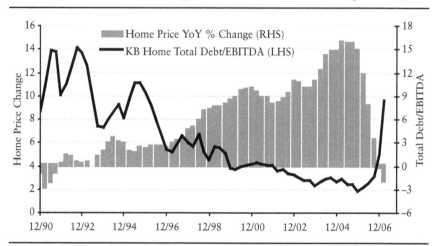

Note: As of September 30, 2008.
Data for this figure obtained from Bloomberg.

And the leverage multiples carried at different points in time is not entirely consistent with GDP growth. During the 1996–1999 period, GDP grew at an average rate of 4.5% and KB Home carried a leverage ratio on average of 6×. During the 2003–2006 period, GDP growth averaged 3% but the company's leverage had fallen to less than 3×, on average.

As might be expected, it is not just economic growth per se that drives a typical homebuilder's leverage profile, but the "health" of the housing market plays a critical role as well. Economic conditions certainly influence the housing market, but so do factors such as the value of the dollar verse other currencies, immigration trends, birth rates, and the like. To illustrate, in Figure 10.6 we present the relationship between year-over-year (YoY) changes in home prices and KB Home's debt/EBITDA ratio. Note that the correlation exceeds 0.70 (as of September 30, 2008).

Harrah's: The Impact of a Leveraged Buy-Out

We next examine the relationship between leverage and GDP growth for Harrah's, a large gaming company with operations primarily in

FIGURE 10.7 Harrah's Co.: LBO Action

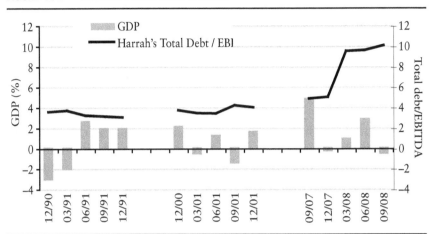

Note: As of December 16, 2008.
Data for this figure obtained from Bloomberg.

the United States and the United Kingdom. According to Bloomberg, operations include land-based casinos, casino clubs, and riverboats, among others.

With regard to the relationship between GDP growth and debt/ EBITDA for Harrah's, we focus on the relationship during three periods of economic weakness: 1990–1991, 2000–2001, and 2007–2008. (See Figure 10.7.) The gaming industry had been thought by many analysts to be fairly resilient to soft economic conditions, and this is consistent with what we observed in the 1990–1991 and 2000– 2001 recessions. Harrah's Debt/EBITDA ratios were little changed throughout both periods (hovering at about 4×).

How about the more recent downturn in 2007–2008? Something very different occurred, with leverage rising sharply to the low double digits. The reason in large part is due to the company's leveraged buy-out (LBO) by private equity firms Texas Pacific Group (TPG) and Apollo Group. The private equity firms levered up the company to pay for the acquisition, which pushed the leverage ratio to about 10× from 4.9× prior to the acquisition.

QUANTITATIVE MODELS

Beginning in the mid 1960s, several academics proposed statistical models for forecasting corporate bankruptcy using only historical financial data. The statistical models that these researchers proposed were *univariate analysis, multiple discriminant analysis,* and *logit regression analysis.* For example, univariate analysis involved comparing key accounting ratios with industry or sector norms at a given point in time.[7] A superior statistical model, multiple discriminant analysis, was used by Altman to forecast bankruptcy propensity.[8] Critics of multiple discriminant analysis pointed out that certain assumptions needed to estimate the model were typically not satisfied in the real world and proposed an alternative statistical technique called logit regression analysis.[9]

Attacks on all of these statistical models that rely on historical financial ratios have been discussed in the literature. For example, a leading high-yield corporate credit analyst remarks:

> [Q]uantitative models tend to classify as troubled credits not only most of the companies that eventually default, but also many that do not default. Often, firms that fall into financial peril bring in new management and are revitalized without ever failing in their debt service.

He also notes that "companies can default for reasons that a model based on reported financials cannot pick up."[10]

Moreover, these statistical models ignore information contained in market information such as market price and volatility. To overcome this drawback, credit risk models applying the capital structural

---

[7] William Beaver, "Financial Ratios as Predictors of Failure," *Empirical Research in Accounting: Selected Studies*, supplement to *Journal of Accounting Research* 4, no. 3 (1966): 71–111.

[8] See Edward I. Altman, "Financial Ratios, Discriminant Analysis, and the Prediction of Corporate Bankruptcy," *Journal of Finance* 23, no. 4 (1968): 589–609.

[9] James S. Ohlson, "Financial Ratios and the Probabilistic Prediction of Bankruptcy," *Journal of Accounting Research* 18, no. 1 (1980): 109–131.

[10] Martin Fridson, *Financial Statement Analysis* 2nd ed. (Hoboken, NJ: John Wiley & Sons): 195.

model proposed in option theory by Black and Cox[11] and Merton[12] to predict default have been proposed.[13]

SUMMARY

This chapter emphasized a framework for analyzing corporate debt instruments. The approaches to credit analysis go beyond the traditional ratio analysis, utilizing the tools of equity analysis and option theory. This is particularly true in the case of evaluating high-yield borrowers.

[11] Fischer Black and Jonathan Cox, "Valuing Corporate Securities: Some Effects of Bond Indenture Provisions," *Journal of Finance* 31, no. 2 (1976): 351–367.
[12] Robert C. Merton, "The Pricing Of Corporate Debt: The Risk Structure of Interest Rates," *Journal of Finance* 29, no. 2 (1974): 449–470.
[13] Peter Crosbie and Jeff Bohn, "Modeling Default Risk," Moody's KMV White Paper, December 2003.

11

Trading the Basis

There are several ways in which valuations in the cash markets are linked to those in the synthetic markets. One straightforward way is simply a reference point. Suppose an investor wanted to take exposure to the high-yield bond market, for example. Moreover, suppose the investor could earn a spread of 1,500 basis points by buying a broad portfolio of cash bonds, or a spread of 500 basis points via the a credit default swap index (CDX.HY). Where is the incremental dollar going to be allocated?

Incremental capital will probably be deployed in the cash market, working to compress the valuation difference between the two. Or the investor may be inclined to take an even more aggressive position and establish a basis package; that is, the investor would go long high-yield cash bonds combined with a short CDX.HY position. This more aggressive position will have a more dramatic impact on compressing relative valuations.

In general, basis packages are the purchase (or sale) of specific exposure in the cash market and the simultaneous sale (or purchase) of the same risk in the synthetic market, ideally at two different prices.

Theoretically, assets with a similar risk profile should move more-or-less in tandem in the cash and synthetic markets (e.g., bonds and credit default swaps for the same company). But they do not at all times. In this chapter, we discuss reasons why, and how to take advantage. We begin by providing a basic template for market participants to assess *negative basis package* value in the single-name space. Specific conclusions are not entirely transferable to more complex basis packages, but general conclusions are appropriate. We then consider a more complex package. Specifically, we begin by reviewing the basic basis package (par bond paired with similar maturity CDS). We consider both spread and "other" sources of value and cost. We then build upon the basic model and review sources of positive and negative convexity. Finally, we present a complex basis package—loan only CDX (LCDX) tranches paired with a cash collateralized loan obligation (CLO) position—and evaluate risks and return prospects in various scenarios.

THE BASIC BASIS PACKAGE

Basis packages are the purchase (or sale) of specific credit exposure in the cash market and the simultaneous sale (or purchase) of the same risk in the synthetic market, ideally at two different prices. Specifically, in the single-name space the basis can be defined as

$$\text{Basis} = \text{CDS spread} - \text{Cash bond spread}$$

There are two basic basis strategies:

- A *negative basis package strategy* (buy bond/buy protection) is typically motivated by a low spread in the CDS market relative to a comparable cash bond spread (i.e., an attempt to earn a riskless return by buying and selling the same credit in different markets).
- A *positive basis package strategy* (sell bond/sell protection) is the opposite—an attempt to take advantage of a fairly high CDS spread relative to the cash market.

The most common approach to gauging basis package relative value is a comparison of London Interbank Offered Rate (LIBOR) spreads, but total return is ultimately what matters. In this regard, the larger the spread pickup the better, but other factors can be equally important.

CONSTRUCTING THE BASIC PACKAGE

To begin, we focus on two basic factors for basis package relative value:

▪ What cash market spread is most comparable to a CDS premium?
▪ What is an appropriate cash/default swap hedge ratio?

In the examples in this section, we use the cash bonds of a hypothetical issuer, Company A. Specifically, we use the 7.65s of '08 and five-year Company A CDS. The cash bonds are trading at 164 basis points (Z-spread) and the five-year CDS at 175 basis points.

What Exactly Is the Spread?

Given that credit default swaps and cash bonds are different instruments, what spread can be used to link the two to make meaningful relative value assessments?

Default swap spreads are periodic payments or premiums that an investor (credit protection seller) receives for taking credit risk. These premiums reflect the views of market participants about the likelihood of a credit event, the timing of cash flows, recovery rates given a credit event, discount rates, and so forth.

A corporate bond's price also reflects the clearing level for default prospects, recovery rates, etc. However, a given bond price often translates into meaningfully different LIBOR spreads, depending on the calculation methodology chosen (asset swap margin, interpolated spread, zero-volatility spread, and so forth). Since the LIBOR spread for any given bond price can vary, the choice of which LIBOR spread to compare to a CDS premium can potentially have a meaningful impact on basis package results.

Although there is no perfect cash bond spread to use, as a rule of thumb most believe that zero-volatility spread or simply Z-spread is the most appropriate measure as it is a discount rate that provides meaningful information about the likelihood of default and loss severity in the event of a default over the life of the bond. That said, total return is ultimately what matters. In our view, the focus should be on total return prospects in order to assess the impact of factors such as roll, amortization of premium or discount, funding advantage or disadvantage, and so forth. But a key component of total return potential depends on how investors decide to balance cash market and CDS exposures when initiating the package. More specifically, what is the right hedge ratio?

Hedging Economic Exposure

Importantly, there is no perfect cash/default hedge for all investors across all investment horizons and in all market environments. In general, the hedge ratio can be approached in three ways, and each has its pros and cons:

1. *Delta neutral.* Duration-weighted packages are relatively immune to modest changes in spreads, but if unadjusted over time can leave investors exposed to extreme credit scenarios. This method is most appropriate for cash bonds trading on a spread basis for mark-to-market investors, particularly for issues with durations notably different from CDS hedging instrument. Although we are focused on same maturity cash/CDS positions at this stage, delta neutral hedges can create large jump-to-default advantages or disadvantages.

2. *Dollars-at-risk.* Dollar-weighted packages can be constructed by either matching CDS exposure to cash bond dollar price (i.e., 10% less CDS for bond at $90) or risk in a potential scenario. For example, assuming a 40% recovery, a bond at $90 would stand to lose $50 in a default scenario; this loss could be offset by a purchase of about 85% CDS protection (difference between par and recovery multiplied by 85% equals approximately $50). This approach is usually most appropriate for names susceptible to near-term credit events.

3. *Par/par.* Par-weighted packages (e.g., buy $10 million notional cash bonds versus $10 million default protection) are simple and easily maintained over time, but could result in risk in the event of fairly small changes in spread and extreme credit scenarios. This method is most appropriate for issues trading near par for investors with longer investment horizons.

To illustrate the impact of hedge ratio choice (see Table 11.1), consider three Company A basis packages that employ these different hedge styles during the March 2003 to June 2003 period. In late March or early April, assume that Company A's spreads widened sharply due to a lost lawsuit and threatened bankruptcy. In late March, the 7.65s of '08 traded at 164 basis points and five-year protection was 175 basis points. By early April, this issue traded as wide

TABLE 11.1 Basis Package Results Given Various Hedging Strategies: Company A 7.65s of '08 vs. Five-Year Protection, March 2003 through June 2003

Hedge Type	Detail	Hedge Ratio (% of bond par value)	Bond ASM and CDS Premium						Result		
			3/26/03		6/23/03						
			7.65s of 2008	Five-year CDS	7.65s of 2008	Five-year CDS		7.65s of 2008	Five-year CDS	Estimated Basis Package Change[a]
Delta-neutral	Bond DV01/ CDS DV01	112%	164 bp	175 bp	242 bp	220 bp		+78 bp	+45 bp	−1.43%
Dollars-at-risk	Bond price/100	113%	164 bp	175 bp	242 bp	220 bp		+78 bp	+45 bp	−1.42%
Par/par	Par/100	100%	164 bp	175 bp	242 bp	220 bp		+78 bp	+45 bp	−1.63%

[a] Beginning period DV01 times spread change.

Note: Assume no hedge adjustments made during holding period, $10 million par cash position. Data for this table obtained from UBS.

as 470 basis points and protection reached 500 basis points, before partially recovering in the following months.

In Table 11.1, note that the price action during this three-month period was extremely volatile, and at the end of our investment horizon, bonds widened more than the credit default swaps. That said, although all three negative basis packages suffered losses during this period, performance varied significantly—by as much as 21 basis points—depending on the hedge style. Note that the lowest spread package at the beginning of the investment horizon (dollars-at-risk, give 33 basis points) turned out to be the best performer, and the highest spread package (par/par, give 11 basis points) was the worst performer.

MOVING AWAY FROM THE BASIC MODEL

Although spread is the most straight-forward way of assessing basis package value, there are a number of other factors that contribute to return prospects. Below we review four:

1. Cost of financing
2. Counterparty risk
3. Liquidity
4. "Cheapest" options

The Cost of Financing

In the examples used here, we assume a par priced five-year floater and five-year CDS for a hypothetical issuer (Company B). The initial spread for the Company B floating rate note is assumed to be LIBOR + 110 basis points, with their CDS trading at 100 basis points. Our focus is to assess how sensitive negative basis package spread pickups are to changes in financing conditions.

With credit conditions tightening (at the time the examples were created), assume the following:

- General collateral rates widened 65 basis points to 75 basis points.

■ Spreads to general collateral rose from about 10 basis points to 25 to 30 basis points for the average high-grade credit and from 12 to 35 basis points for the typical high-yield credit.

■ Collateral requirements rose from 10% to 15–20% in the high-grade space and moved from a 15–20% range to a 30–35% range in the high-yield space.

To put these changes into perspective and holding all else equal, we assessed how much wider negative basis package pickups should be given these changes. Specifically, in Table 11.2 we provide a return on capital template and calculate the return on capital employed using the terms that were available in "liquid" times (bond spread of LIBOR plus 110 bp, financing cost of LIBOR plus 8 bp, 90% available to be financed). We find that the return on capital was 5.6%.

In Table 11.3 we calculate what bond spread is required given a "credit crunch" environment (LIBOR + 30 basis points financing and 85% financing available) in order to equate the package's return on capital to that available in "liquid" times. All else being equal, we find that a basis package pickup of 21 basis points is needed to generate the same return as what was previously available. Spread pickup has to more than double!

Leveraged investors should be indifferent between a basis point pickup in spread or in financing since total return or return on capital deployed is the objective for most market participants.

To summarize, the appropriate reference point for a negative basis package is not necessarily spread pickup, but spread pickup plus or minus any financing advantage or disadvantage. All else being equal, most investors should be indifferent to spread advantage or financing advantage.

From Whom Is Protection Being Purchased?

Many market participants have expressed concern about counterparty risk. As such, some investors view higher spread pickups for negative basis packages as compensation for this type of risk. The bankruptcy filing by Lehman Brothers and the failing of AIG brought this issue to the forefront of investors' minds at the time they occurred.

TABLE 11.2 Return on Capital for a Typical Positive Carry Negative Basis Package Based on Available Financing During "Liquid" Times

	Bond			+	CDS		=	Basis Package Net	
Description	LIBOR Spread	LIBOR	Total		Description	Spread		Description	Result
Interest income	110	530	640		Interest expense	100		Spread pick	10
–									
Cost of finance	8	538	542						
Percent financed			90%						
Net cost of finance			484.2						
=									
Net interest income			155.8		Net interest cost	100		Net income	55.8
Equity employed			10%		Posted collateral	0%		Capital used	10%
								Return on capital	5.6%

Data for this table obtained from UBS.

TABLE 11.3 Given the New Circumstances, Negative Basis Package Spread Pickup Required to Generate a Return on Capital Equal to What Had Been Available in "Liquid" Times

	Bond			+	CDS		=	Basis Package Net	
Description	LIBOR Spread	LIBOR	Total		Description	Spread		Description	Result
Interest income	121	590	711		Interest expense	100		Spread pick	21
−									
Cost of finance	30	590	620						
Percent financed			85%						
Net cost of finance			527						
=									
Net interest income			184		Net interest cost	100		Net income	84
Equity employed			15%		Posted collateral	0%		Capital used	15%
								Return on capital	5.6%

Data for this table obtained from UBS.

The following example delves into this issue and walks through how market participants should account for this sort of risk in basis packages. Specifically, if Company B defaults will the counterparty to Company B CDS (Broker A) be around to provide compensation? The basis package example used here involves hypothetical broker (Broker A) and hypothetical issuer (Company B). The hypothetical five-year par bond trades at LIBOR + 110 basis points, five-year CDS trades at 100 basis points, Broker A trades at 40 basis points. Our focus in this illustration is how susceptible negative basis packages are to broker–counterparty risk.

Although counterparty risk is an important consideration in general, in the context of negative basis packages, the biggest risk is not Broker A defaulting, but the joint probability of Broker A and Company B defaulting. Consider our negative basis package performance in the following scenarios:

- *No default by Broker A or Company B.* The basis package holder can collect the spread advantage for the holding period (i.e., clip coupon).
- *Broker A defaults, no default by Company B.* The basis package holder can sell Company B bond (albeit potentially at a loss). Net loss in this scenario will likely be limited to the difference between bond purchase price and financing costs, and the combination of bond sales price, and interest earned during holding period.
- *Company B defaults, no default by Broker A.* Collect on CDS purchase to offset loss on bond.
- *Broker A and Company B default.* In this scenario the negative basis package holder would lose on the bond purchase and would likely receive only a portion of the claim on Broker A in court. What is the probability of joint default?

To assess the probability of joint default we make a conservative assumption, in that we view spreads as entirely compensation for credit risk (i.e., investors receive no compensation for illiquidity, etc.). As noted previously, Broker A CDS was initially trading at 40 basis points, but let's assume it widened to 130 basis points. Company B CDS is still trading at 100 basis points.

FIGURE 11.1 Implied Probability of Default Probability of Joint Default with Broker A CDS Spread at 40 bp

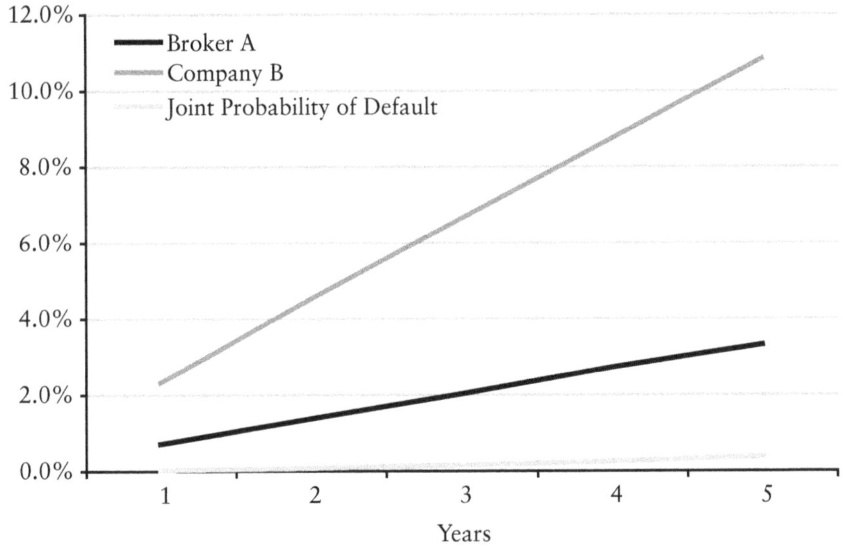

Data for this figure obtained from UBS.

Figures 11.1 and 11.2 show that the probability of Broker A default rises sharply as spreads increase (from about 3% in the first year to more than 8% over five years), but the joint probability of default with Company B is little changed (up less than 1%).

We summarize this illustration as follows: Counterparty risk is more of a concern for individual CDS trades than it is for basis packages. By and large, a basis package shifts the risk from the probability of a counterparty defaulting to the joint probability of a counterparty and issuer defaulting.

Liquidity Considerations

The liquidity available in the credit markets has evolved over the years, moving from an environment where select cash benchmarks were most actively traded and used as tools to take market views to one in which the CDX indexes are most liquid, followed by single-name CDS (albeit far more so in the high-grade sector than the high-yield sector), with cash bonds typically the least actively traded.

FIGURE 11.2   Implied Probability of Default Probability of Joint Default with Broker A CDS Spread at 130 bps

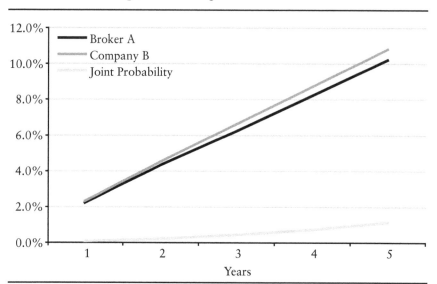

Data for this figure obtained from UBS.

The credit derivatives market is able, in many cases, to provide comparable or better liquidity because a credit default swap effectively concentrates broad investment interests (loans, bonds of various maturities, currencies) into a few trading vehicles. This is the same as in futures markets, where trading interest across many issues (i.e., the deliverable universe) is consolidated into a few contracts.

However, there are three characteristics that can cause deviations from "average" liquidity, in our view:

1. *Away from the benchmark names and tenor (five-years), bid–ask spreads tend to widen sharply.* For example, in 2007 the bid–ask spread for Fannie Mae protection was 10 basis points in the three-year sector, narrowed to 3 basis points in the more actively traded five-year, and widened back out to 10 basis points in the 10-year tenor.
2. *CDS liquidity tends to be market directional.* In reviewing the UBS database for all issuers with at least one U.S. dollar bond outstanding, a Moody's rating of C or better, at least one year

to maturity, and with an issue size of $500 million or more, we found that the correlation between the average credit default spread for this universe and the average CDS bid–ask spread over time is 0.89, with liquidity diminishing during setbacks and increasing amid rallies. Strong demand for protection in a bear market (in part due to the "fixed" cost for a short position) can result in wide spread pickups for negative basis packages.

3. *In select cases liquidity can vary on a name-specific basis, since there are no "measures" of short or long positions.* For example, in the cash market, heightened shorting interest in a particular name will often be apparent via repo market tightness. In addition, cash market positions are balance sheet items that can, to some extent, be monitored. In the CDS market there is no such information about exposures, and by extension, liquidity can be more sporadic.

"Cheapest" Options

Given a credit event, protection buyers have an option to deliver the cheapest form of exposure to protection sellers that meets specified criteria, although the value of this option has diminished over time due to changes in CDS protocol. That said, protection buyers still are able to select the most efficient hedge ex post facto. Valuations can vary meaningfully, not only leading up to, but in the wake of a credit event.

To illustrate, we consider a point in time when defaults were commonplace (2002) and focus on the WorldCom bankruptcy. In late April 2002, WorldCom was downgraded and the firm's chief executive officer resigned. In early May 2002, WorldCom's credit rating was cut to junk. In late June of that same year, WorldCom stated that it misreported $3.9 billion in expenses, and lenders notified the company that it had defaulted on two senior unsecured credit facilities. WorldCom sought Chapter 11 protection on July 21.

Even with signals of a credit event building, bonds did not perfectly converge around a dollar price pre- or postbankruptcy; the '04s, '11s, and '28s, for example, diverged by as much as five points in the weeks following the bankruptcy announcement (see Figure 11.3). The tendency for prices to not always converge uniformly given a credit event—especially for issuers with multibillion dollar cap struc-

FIGURE 11.3 Price Levels for Select WorldCom Bonds, April 2002 to August 2002

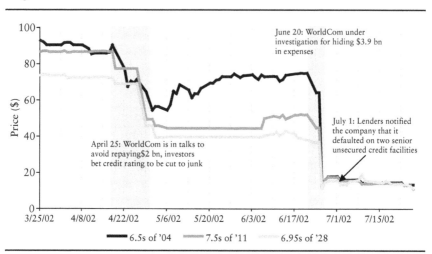

Data for this figure obtained from UBS.

tures—creates value for protection owners. In addition, spread volatility itself, absent any default, can also create opportunities to buy "cheap" economic exposure that can be offset with a standard hedge (CDS). This feature has value even absent a credit event.

To illustrate, we return to the hypothetical Company A example introduced earlier. Although all bonds declined in value in the wake of the lawsuit, all did not move in tandem or fall by the same magnitude. In particular, the 4s of '07 (denominated in Swiss francs) fell more significantly in percentage terms than similar maturity, USD-denominated issues despite having a lower price prior to the event.

Consider the impact of this price action on a hypothetical negative basis package (7.5s of '09; for simplicity, par/par hedge via five-year CDS). Assume that this package was established in mid-March, before litigation results weighed on the market. In the wake of the lawsuit this investor would have the option to either (1) maintain status quo by holding the 7.5s of '09, or (2) substitute a cheaper cash position within the existing package (i.e., capture value via a hedged position). Specifically, the holder could have swapped the hedged '09s for the 4s of '07 to shorten maturity, take out dollars, and pick up spread—again, enhancing value via a hedged position.

The second choice would clearly have an advantageous impact on package performance. Table 11.4 shows that the spread pickup (via 4s of '07) was 396 basis points in early April, but compressed to 87 basis points by mid-December, or more than 300 basis points of tightening. Conversely, the pickup via 7.5s of '09 tightened a relatively modest 176 basis points.

The opportunity to select the "cheapest" form of credit risk and neutralize this exposure with a generic hedge can be valuable, as it enables upside via a hedged position.

The key point is that the "cheapest" option can still benefit negative basis package holders, as investors have the ability to deliver the cheapest issue given a credit event and take advantage of price action otherwise.

ADDING POSITIVE CONVEXITY

Basis packages can provide positive convexity, by which we mean more upside potential across a broader range of scenarios than downside. From the perspective of a negative basis package holder, positive convexity can come from a variety of sources (e.g., change of control language or long duration). In this section, we examine the impact of two sources in particular—excess duration (longer maturity bond than CDS) and subpar dollar price bonds—on performance prospects in various scenarios.

In the example in this section, we use the cash bond of hypothetical Company D 7.25s of '11 paired with five-year protection during the 2002 period. We will examine how long maturity, low dollar price cash bonds paired with CDS can enhance returns, even absent a change in the yield curve.

As noted above, two common sources of positive convexity are maturity mismatches (longer maturity for cash, shorter for CDS) and low dollar price bonds. These sources exhibit positive convexity for reasons including:

- *Longer duration.* A cash bond position that has a relatively long duration is likely to outperform its shorter-duration hedge (such as five-year CDS) if risk premiums decline. If risk premiums rise sharply, bonds across the maturity spectrum tend to trade based

TABLE 11.4 Company A Basis Performance: Cash Bond Price/Spread vs. Five-Year Protection, April 2003 to December 2003

	April 4, 2003				December 8, 2003				Package P&L
Issue	Price	ASM (bp)	Five-Year Protection (bp)	Pickup (bp)	Price	ASM (bp)	Five-Year Protection (bp)	Pickup (bp)	Price
7.65s of '08 (USD)	104.5	337	350	−13	110.44	169	155	+14	5.94
7.5s of '09 (USD)	89.0	569	350	+219	108.24	198	155	+43	19.24
4s of '07 (CHF)	77.5	746	350	+396	99.15	242	155	+87	21.65

Data for these tables obtained from UBS.

on dollar price rather than duration; this is particularly true for lower-rated and lower-dollar price bonds. As such, longer duration may not weigh as significantly on performance in a spread widening environment as it helps during a tightening environment.

- *Dollar price*. Because CDS is a "par" instrument and cash bonds—even high quality cash bonds—can trade at significant discounts to par, negative basis packages can enable significant advantages due to fewer dollars at risk. Consider, for example, a package consisting of a generic bond trading at $80 and a Z-spread of 500 basis points and CDS that is trading at 500 basis points. This package will be well positioned to outperform. A par/par hedged package, for example, will be overhedged in a severe downward move or a default scenario, as bonds will decline from $80 and approach expected recovery, while CDS will move from $100 to expected recovery.

- *Jump to default*. Because delta-neutral curve trades (long maturity cash, shorter CDS) are notionally mismatched, investors that delta hedge will benefit as the possibility of default increases.

- *CDS is relatively "easy" to short*. Due to the ability to lock-in a cost of financing for a long period of time (i.e., five years), CDS represents an easy short that can encounter more pressure than the cash market in spread widening scenarios (although not always).

Scenario Analysis

Given the factors outlined in the previous section, we reviewed a negative basis package comprised of Company D 7.25s of '11 and five-year CDS across a variety of spread scenarios and assuming a par/par hedge during the 2002 period. Figures 11.4 through 11.6 display spread changes and price returns for this basis package under these different scenarios, and the total return for the overall package. (Note that scenarios reflect "instantaneous" shocks; roll-down/reinvestment not considered.) We find:

- *Spread-tightening scenario*. Cash and CDS spreads are likely to move about the same because the spread duration of the 7.25s of

FIGURE 11.4 Spread Scenarios for Company D 7.25s of '11, Five-Year Protection

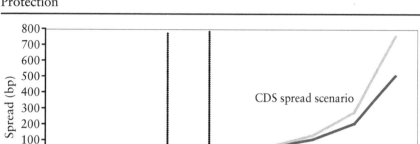

Data for these figures obtained from UBS.

FIGURE 11.5 P&L for Company D 7.25s of '11 and Five-Year CDS under Various Scenarios

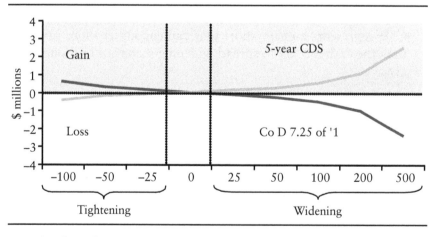

Data for these figures obtained from UBS.

FIGURE 11.6 P&L for Combination of Company D 7.25s of '11 and Five-Year Protection

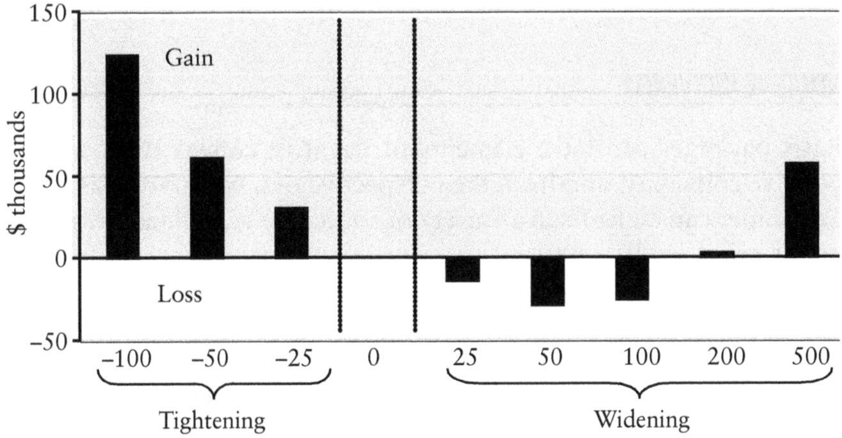

Data for these figures obtained from UBS.

'11 is higher (5.4 versus 4.3), the price return is significantly higher as well.

- *Unchanged spread scenario.* In an unchanged spread scenario, the key driver of performance is the net spread pickup/give-up provided by the basis package. Since the spreads of the '11s and five-year protection are about the same (164 basis points for bond, 171 basis points for protection), the total return for the package is approximately zero.
- *Modest spread-widening scenario.* A key risk for maturity–mismatched basis packages occurs when credit spreads edge wider, but do not move far enough to offset duration differences. This is a particular challenge for near or above par bonds.
- *Severe spread-widening scenario.* During severe downturns, CDS spreads widen significantly more than cash market spreads (even after adjusting for dollars-at-risk differences). During the 2002 period Company D credit default swap spreads widened 33% more than cash bond spreads. Using this experience as a baseline, the basis package generated positive total returns in our severe widening scenario.

To summarize, holding the yield curve steady, negative basis packages comprised of cash bonds that have longer maturities and lower dollar prices can exhibit positive convexity in a wide variety of scenarios.

NEGATIVE CONVEXITY

Basis packages can have elements of negative convexity as well as positive convexity, and from the perspective of a negative basis package holder can come from a variety of sources (e.g., call features, high dollar price, etc.).

For example, loans can usually be repaid or refinanced (i.e., coupon flexed down) prior to maturity without restriction (although this is unlikely in certain credit environments). In the context of a negative basis package, this creates a problem—how much spread pickup can an investor be expected to earn if the loan spread level and timing is not fixed? Unfortunately, basis packages comprised of cash securities that have "call" features cannot be fully adjusted for, but only accounted for.

To illustrate and with a focus on refinancing risk, we use an example from the loan market. Early in the summer of 2007, the average cash market loan spread for a LCDX index constituent was 206 basis points, while the LCDX index spread was about 145 basis points. At first blush this 60+ basis point difference may have appeared to represent an attractive negative basis opportunity (buy cash constituents, short the index), but as noted above, refinancing risk must first be accounted for.

In this regard, we adjust constituents' nominal loan spreads for the negative impact of potential refinancing via three-step process:

Step 1: Estimate the probability of a refinancing. Historical data provided by S&P shows that, on average, loans have a 40% probability of being refinanced. Even during "bearish" market environments, refinancing potential can be meaningful.
Step 2: Estimate the impact of a refinancing. S&P data show that, on average, coupon step-downs have amounted to 58 basis points.
Step 3: Discount to nominal spread. Given the above data (and assuming five-year maturity, one step-down during life of loan),

we find that on average a LCDX constituent's spread should be reduced by about 40 basis points to account for refinancing potential.

After adjusting for this refinancing risk, the average cash market loan spread is 166 basis points and provides a far more modest pickup (around 20 basis points) relative to the LCDX index spread.

There are three key points here to keep in mind:

1. Although we have made an adjustment to nominal spreads for refinancing risk at this stage, it is important to note that we have only adjusted for this risk on average and it is not fully "hedged." Index constituents may refinance faster or slower than historical norms or any other modelling assumptions that we have made. Model results cannot fully hedge this risk, only account for it.
2. Although we have focused on refinancing risk in this example, conclusions can be extended to negatively convex cash securities in general. For example, a callable bond may be used in a negative basis package based on an option-adjusted spread or a spread-to-worst, but again, there remains a risk that model assumptions will not come to fruition.
3. Refinancing risk is very much dependent on the market environment. There is not great risk of a refinancing in a tight credit environment such as 2008.

To summarize, basis packages in some markets are susceptible to negative convexity. Negative convexity must be adjusted for, but because adjustments are model-driven, risk probably cannot be fully hedged.

A MORE COMPLEX BASIS PACKAGE

The basis template outlined in the previous section is fairly straightforward. Market participants often look to establish more complex packages in an effort to capture favorable payoff profiles in a majority of market scenarios. Next we assess a fairly complex basis package, a triple-B CLO tranche hedged with LCDX tranches.

Cash CLOs Paired with LCDX Tranches

Assume an investor is long a triple-B CLO tranche and is looking to hedge (i.e., create a basis package). Investors interested in hedging long CLO triple-B exposure have considered buying LCDX9 12–15% protection in the past, given its estimated A– (S&P) rating. In a spread widening environment, this hedge works relatively well as the short synthetic hedge will likely outperform. In a spread tightening scenario, however, investors have expressed concern that the synthetic product rallies faster than the cash product, generating MTM losses. This occurred in April 2007 as cash CLO spreads remained wide (albeit in a wide range) while LCDX9 12–15% spreads tightened considerably. The mark-to-market impact of correlation also adds a twist which complicates the synthetic hedge proposition.

Given these concerns, an ideal CLO hedge would generate a positive return when the market widens, no return when the market tightens, and offer little exposure to correlation risk (changes in price due to changes in market implied correlation). The following analysis attempts to construct such a position out of the LCDX tranches.

The trade is buy $4.5 million five-year LCDX9 12–15% protection and sell $3.4 million five-year 8–12% protection. When the LCDX index implies an expected loss of about 12%, the LCDX 8–12% is at-the-money. By buying 12–15% protection and selling 8–12% protection, we hope to take advantage of a net positive gamma (convexity) position.

Using a standard model (Gaussian copula) and calibration, we evaluated the trade by applying upward and downward multiplicative shocks to the underlying spreads. Although potential dispersion effects are ignored, shocks can increase or decrease spread dispersion. Figures 11.7 and 11.8 provide the return profile of the trade computed. We compare the trade to 1× delta equivalent hedging alternatives using the 12–15% tranche and the LCDX9 index. The trade appears to outperform equivalent hedges using bought index protection or bought 12–15% tranche protection. The trade also exhibits relatively flat performance in index tightening scenarios and offers positively skewed performance during index widening.

Figures 11.9 illustrates the historical performance of the trade since the inception of the LCDX9 Index. As suggested, the position generated profits when the index widened but yielded relatively flat

FIGURE 11.7 Trade Return Profile Compared to Equivalent Hedges (1×
delta) Using LCDX9 Index and LCDX9 12–15% Tranche (percentage
points)

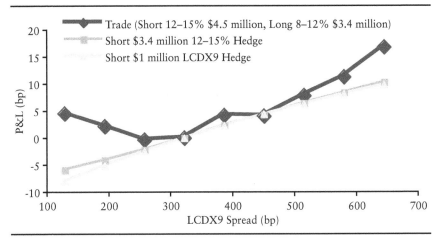

Data for these figures obtained from UBS.

FIGURE 11.8 Trade Return Profile Broken Down into its Component Parts
(percentage points)

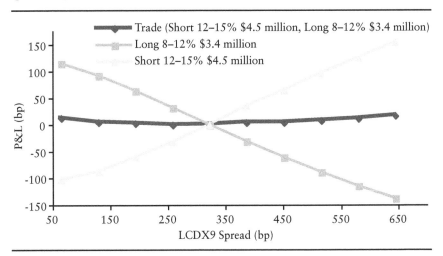

Data for these figures obtained from UBS.

FIGURE 11.9   Trade Historical Performance vs. LCDX9 Index Levels (basis points)

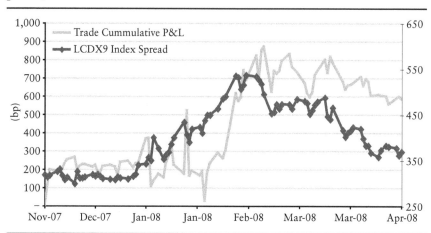

Data for these figures obtained from UBS.

returns when the index tightened. This suggests the position can help hedge CLO exposure.

Risk vs. Return

The trade's return profile is generated by the 12–15% tranche gaining delta when the index widens as the 8–12% tranche loses delta. In other words, as the index widens, the 8–12% tranche moves further out-of-the-money as the 12–15% tranche moves deeper into-the-money. Some of the trade's key risks are as follows:

- *Carry and theta.* The trade has positive carry and a significant positive theta (time decay) of 184 basis points, as the long 8–12% tranche decays at a faster rate than the 12–15% tranche.
- *Jump to default.* The trade exhibits negative exposure to the risk of a median name defaulting. Wide name "jump to defaults" are largely priced into the tranches.
- *Correlation level and slope sensitivity.* The net exposure of the trade to parallel movements in the base correlation curve is relatively small; the position, however, is negatively exposed to a steepening of the correlation curve. Given that the LCDX9 base

correlation curve is already steep, this is a risk we are comfortable taking.

HEDGE RATIOS FOR CLO HEDGING

It is important to find a trade notional that provides roughly the same performance as $1 million of the LCDX9 index. Tables 11.5 and 11.6 compare the performance of various hedges. It turns out, $4.5 million of the trade offers similar performance as, for example, $1

TABLE 11.5   Risk Table for Trade: Buy $4 million Protection LCDX9 12–15% and Sell $3 million Protection LCDX9 8–12% Protection

	LCDX9 8–12%	LCDX9 12–15%	Trade[b]
Weight[a]	0.75	(1.00)	
Leverage (measured in delta)	3.2	2.5	–0.1
ATM (basis points)	721	434	
Median JTD (basis points)	(142)	(79)	(28)
Correl01 (attachment) basis points	(100)	(158)	
Correl01 (detachment) basis points	128	187	
Correl01 (parallel)	28	29	(7)
Slope01	50	93	(56)
Carry (basis points) ($3 million)	180	139	28
Roll down (basis points) ($3 million)	457	161	186
Theta (basis points) ($3 million)	637	300	215
DV01 (basis points)	4.13	4.35	
Gamma Down P&L (20% fall in index spread) (basis points)	9.4	7.2	(0.0)
Gamma Up P&L (20% rise in index spread) (basis points)	(9.1)	(7.8)	0.9

[a] Positive weight implies selling tranche protection and negative weight implies buying protection.

[b] The values in the Trade column are calculated by subtracting the trade-weighted figures of each leg of the trade from each other. For example, in the Leverage row, $(0.75) \times 3.2 - (1.00) \times 2.5 = -0.1$.

Data for these figures obtained from UBS.

TABLE 11.6   Comparing Various Hedges, 1× Delta Equivalents

	Trade (short 12–15% $4.5 mm, long 8–12% $3.4 mm)	Short $0.3 mm 12–15%	Short $1 mm LCDX9
Equivalent values	–4.5	–0.3	–1
$3 million carry (basis points)	125	–36	–81
JTD (basis points)	–125	24	39
Return basis points (20% wider index)	4.15	2.34	2.27
Return basis points (20% tighter index)	–0.35	–2.15	–2.45
Return basis points (40% wider index)	4.03	4.3	4.38
Return basis points (40% tighter index)	2.12	–4.07	–5.1

Data for these figures obtained from UBS.

million of the LCDX9 index or $0.3 million of LCDX9 12–15% in a spread widening scenario. Empirical analysis suggests a hedge ratio of around 1:3 (CLO paper to trade notional) is appropriate.

The position we describe above enjoys positive carry, at the cost of jump-to-default and correlation slope exposure, and offers the asymmetric return profile of our "ideal" hedge. Although investors will need to find ways to "certify" CLO pricing, either through their own fundamental research or through some other channel, we believe the LCDX tranches can provide an effective hedge against mark-to-market CLO movements.

SUMMARY

The basis provides a reference point for the valuation of assets between the cash and synthetic markets. Market participants can use the basis for a number of purposes, ranging from informational to actual arbitrage trading. It is important to understand that there are a number of dynamics that can influence the basis, including technical and market conditions.

The basis package is a widely used trading strategy by credit investors. Investors buy and sell the same security in different markets, taking advantage of any discrepancies that may exist in pricing.

We will see another detailed basis packages in the next chapter, which focuses on specific trading opportunities in the leveraged finance market.

12

How Much Should You Get Paid to Take Risk?

In this chapter, we look at trading strategies in the leveraged finance market. Specifically, we describe the following four key risks and and consider ways to determine how much investors should be paid to take these risks:

- Single-name credit risk or compensation for exposure to a particular issuer.
- Curve risk or compensation for long/short contributions on the same issuer's credit curve.
- Basis risk or compensation for long/short combinations expressed in the cash and synthetic markets.
- Capital structure risk or compensation for long/short combinations among different liabilities of the same issuer.

SINGLE-NAME CREDIT RISK

Single-name credit picking is a critical component of investing in the corporate market in general, and certainly in the leveraged finance space. In this regard, a deep understanding of company fundamentals is needed when making investment decisions, but not at the expense of a reference point by which to assess the relationship between company fundamentals and valuations.

In this section, we focus on evaluating a cash bond issued by Company N. Note that Company N had been covered by UBS credit analysts (coverage since dropped), and we draw upon work done by these analysts as it captures key considerations that investors may want to take into account when assessing single-name credit risk.

This company was initially recommended with a buy rating across the structure. The credit team highlighted a specific issue as providing a particularly attractive way to take the issuer risk (see Table 12.1). In particular, a two-pronged approach was used in this investment recommendation: a detailed fundamental assessment and technical/relative value analysis. What follows is a closer look at these concepts and how the analysts incorporated them.

Fundamental Credit Analysis

Fundamental credit analysis in its most basic form asks two questions:

1. What is the default risk of the issue?
2. What is the likelihood of a change in credit quality over the life of the bond?

Financial ratios are critical to answering these questions. For example, in order to determine what the risk of default might be, an analyst might consider using interest coverage, leverage, and cash-flow-to-total-debt ratios. Chapter 10 provides a more detailed discussion.

In determining how the credit quality might change over time, the analyst would use ratios such as profitability trends for the issuer and the industry, including return on equity, operating margins, and asset turnover. Putting this general template into practice with our example of Company N, we look at the following analysis/comment done by the analysts:

> We believe the company is making steady progress with its re-structuring program and is on track to realize $250 million in run rate savings by the end of the year. [Company N's] adjusted EBITDA margin of 18.7% in 3Q07 was the highest in four quarters, and we believe there is room for improvement to the low to mid-20% range in the next 12 months.

TABLE 12.1 Capitalization Table for Company N

	Agency Rating	Book Value ($ bn)	Debt Issue Characteristics						Leverage Multiples		
			Price	Coupon	Yield-to-Worst	Spread-to-Worst	Call Date	Call	Last 12 Months	2007	2008
Revolver & other		(65)									
US$ Secured FRN due 2013 (L+275)	Ba3/BB–	1,117	83.50	7.01%	9.88%	NA	10/15/2008	$102.00			
Euro Secured FRN due 2013 (E+275)	Ba3/BB+	1,000	82.00	7.33%	11.43%	NA	2/8/2008	$102.00			
US$ 7.875% Secured note due 2014	Ba3/BB–	746	82.00	7.88%	11.8%	869	10/15/210	$103.94	3.9×	3.9×	3.5×
Euro 8.625% Senior note due 2015	B3/B–	525	76.50	8.63%	13.64%	841	10/15/2011	$104.31			
US$ 9.5% Senior note due 2015	B3/B–	909	88.25	9.50%	11.86%	795	10/15/2011	$104.75	5.9×	5.9×	5.3×
Total debt		4,232									
Cash		681									
Net debt		3,551								4.9×	4.9×	4.4×

Data for this table obtained from UBS.

With $681 million of cash on the balance sheet and additional proceeds due from pending asset sales, [Company N's] liquidity is strong. During the last 12 months, the company has announced several actions, including exiting joint ventures, shutting down the facility and the sale of underperforming business, which we estimate will generate about $500–600 million in total proceeds.

[Company N] is transitioning to an asset-light strategy to increase manufacturing flexibility and reduce the amount of capital invested in fixed assets. Management estimates that about 15% of total manufacturing was outsourced during Q3 and plans to grow that figure to around 30–40% in coming years. We estimate that capex will amount to about 7% of revenue in 2008, which is down significantly from 13% in 2004.

So a solid company from a fundamental perspective (at least at the time of the analyst's publication). But should an investor buy it? If so, which issue should the investor buy? Why?

Technicals/Relative Value

Complimenting fundamental analysis is *relative value analysis*, or a way to make sure that the relationship between valuations and fundamentals is appropriate. Company N may be a wonderfully sound entity, but if an equally risky entity (example: Company Y) offers far more compensation, why invest in Company N?

Relative value analysis usually includes "ratio" analysis of a different sort. Rather than focusing on, for example, leverage in and of itself, the focal point becomes compensation for leverage. This effort often involves comparing the balance between valuations and fundamentals for one issuer to other issuers or assets. This analysis can be used to show the attractiveness (unattractiveness) of one issuer verse its peers or a broad market, or in the creation of a long or short strategy. The following comments from the analyst illustrate the use of relative value:

We prefer the Company N secured notes to the Company Y secured notes and point out that the Company N 7.875% notes trade about 5 points lower than Company Y's 7.5% notes. Despite the recent pullback in the Company Y senior notes, we still prefer the [Company N] senior notes at similar leverage. We believe the fundamental outlook for [Company N] has turned a corner and will continue to steadily improve throughout 2008. [See Table 12.2 for reference.]

On the other hand, we believe uncertainty surrounding [Company Y's business segment], especially with regard to [a competitor's] multivendor component sourcing strategy and floundering market share, will weigh on the credit for some time.

The bottom line is that when making investment decisions in the leveraged finance space, never lose sight of the fundamentals. That said, fundamentals are not an island, and should never be considered in isolation.

CURVE RISK

Building on the single-name fundamental analysis from our first trade example, investors can also express their opinion about an issuer through the use of credit curves. Because curve trades are typically long/short packages on the same company—duration weighted—they are not a "bet" on a company's credit spreads per se. Rather, curve trades express a view on the relative performance of different maturities. For example, if one was uncertain about near-term market direction but expected a credit to begin aggressively deleveraging at some point in the future, a curve flattener might be considered (buy short maturity credit default swap (CDS), sell long maturity CDS), particularly if it involved carry positive. Conversely, if a company's near-term liquidity prospects were firm, but leverage was expected to rise over time, a curve steepener might be appropriate (sell near-term protection, buy long-maturity CDS).

Table 12.3 shows three curve flattener examples. Note that because curves are so steep (80 basis points on average), duration-neutral packages can be implemented and investors can still earn positive carry (22 basis points on average). But there is another important element of return to consider: roll-down.

TABLE 12.2 Company N US$ Secured Notes vs. Company Y Term Loan

| | | | O/S | UBS | Agency | | January 28, 2008 | | |
Issuer	Coupon	Maturity	($ mm)	Rating	Ratings	Bid ($)	YTW	LTM	2008E
Company Y	7.5%	12/1/2013	3,491	Sell	Ba1/BB	87.00	10.3%	4.0x	3.7x
Company N	7.875%	10/15/2014	1,026	Buy	Ba3/BB–	82.00	11.8%	3.9x	3.5x

Data for this table obtained from UBS, Bloomberg, Company reports.

TABLE 12.3 CDS Curve Trade: Sell Five-Year Protection/Buy Three-Year Protection to Enhance Spread and Roll Potential

| | LONG | | | SHORT | | | Duration-Weighted Results | | |
| | Sell Five-year CDS | | | Buy Three-year CDS | | | | | |
Issuer	Current Spread	Roll per Year	Duration	Current Spread	Roll per Year	Duration	Spread Pickup	Roll Pickup	Breakeven Steepening
Company A	121	31	4.2	60	19	2.8	31	12	21
Company B	204	41	4.1	128	22	2.7	10	19	22
Company C	235	58	4.0	163	49	2.7	24	9	16
Average	187	43	4.1	117	30	2.7	22	13	20

Note: Calculations assume steepening in the two- or four-year curve.
Data for this table obtained from UBS.

Roll-down refers to the price appreciation that can occur due to the aging of positions. For example, if a company's five-year CDS is trading at a spread of 150 basis points and its four-year protection is trading at 100 basis points, as the five-year becomes a four-year issue over time it could hypothetically tighten 50 basis points. For the examples highlighted in Table 12.3, the five-year space enables roll-down of 43 basis points per year on average, relative to only 30 basis points in the three-year tenor.

As a result, duration-neutral packages for these issuers offer positive carry and attractive total return potential in a wide variety of scenarios. In particular:

- *Neutral spread environment.* In an environment in which spreads hover near current levels, these positions are well positioned to benefit from spread pickups (22 basis points on average) and roll advantages (13 basis points).
- *Spread tightening.* Although most spread curves may be biased to steepen in a tightening environment, the trades highlighted in Table 12.3 have already steepened sharply and at current levels "breakevens" are very high (average of 22 basis points). Note that in a tighter spread environment, curve steepening for these examples would most likely be the result of the three-year position tightening (as opposed to the five-year drifting wider). This means that, on average, the three-year positions would have to tighten almost 20% before the highlighted swaps begin to lose money, and this assumes that the five-year positions do not tighten at all.
- *Spread widening.* Although there are exceptions (such as an LBO), spread widening tends to result in curve flattening, particularly if the overall market is repricing. Also note that in extreme bearish scenarios (points upfront), these positions are likely to outperform due to the notional mismatch required to neutralize duration (i.e., it requires selling less five-year protection relative to the amount of thre-year protection purchased).

The bottom line is that curve positioning can be a key source of return, stemming not just from spread pickups but also from factors such as roll-down and jump-to-default.

BASIS RISK

In the first two trades (single-name and curve) we stayed in the same market. The single-name trade focused on positioning in the cash market, the curve package assessed relative positioning in the CDS market. Typically, basis trades combine cash and synthetic positions into a single package. (We covered the basics of basis packages and walked through a few examples of how to construct packages in Chapter 11.)

As explained in Chapter 11, theoretically, assets with a similar risk profile should move more-or-less in tandem in the cash and synthetic markets (e.g. bonds and CDS for the same company). But they do not. Basis packages can offer attractive value, as we highlight in the following example.

Basis Package Illustration

As we mentioned in the previous chapter, a simple "negative basis" package strategy (buy bond/buy protection) is typically motivated by a relatively low spread in the CDS market relative to the comparable cash bond spread. Here, we look at a slightly more complex basis package using First Data Company (FDC).

The trade idea is to:

- Buy FDC 9.875s of 2015 at $68 (spread: 1,466 basis points).
- Buy seven-year CDS at 707 basis points.
- Buy Total System Services (TSS) May 2009 put option contracts ($10 strike).

The rationale for this trade idea is as follows: a "no cost" position that appears inexpensive to comparables and is well positioned to provide asymmetric payoff profiles in a number of scenarios.

Background on First Data Company

FDC provides electronic commerce solutions. The company offers a variety of processing solutions, including credit, debit, check, and pre-paid payments, along with value-added information and internet based services. In September 2007, it was acquired by KKR & Co. in a leverage buyout (LBO) deal worth $27.5 billion.

At the end of 2008, First Data's bonds traded at a fairly low dollar price. However, the company did exhibit a number of positive factors. These factors included the company's position as the market leader in payment processing. This function had a long-term secular growth story based on shifting consumers' spending habits (from traditional cash and check payments to electronic payments). The company also had $2 billion in available liquidity (as of June 2008), limited debt coming due in the near-term, and was free cash flow positive.

The company did have some negatives—yields in the high teens are not offered for no reason. FDC was highly leveraged to consumer use of credit and debit cards, and at the time of this trade idea the economy was in a recession. Should consumers materially constrain spending (personal consumption expenditures turned negative in September 2008), it could significantly impact earnings in the near- to medium-term. And in a financial sense, the company was also highly levered (approximately 9× as of June 2008).

So why put this package on? We see a meaningful likelihood that this basis trade could have an asymmetric payoff profile, particularly with the tweaks to the "basic" package. Consider the impact of several package characteristics on performance prospects, and assume a par/par hedge:

1. *Carry is attractive.* The difference between the income provided by the 9.875s of 2015 and the cost of CDS is fairly large (see Figure 12.1). If one uses Z-spread as a proxy for income, the difference is 705 basis points (1,408 basis points less 703 basis points). But Z-spread is not "cash" per se. If the dollar price of the cash bond does not accrete towards par over an investor's holding period, that money will not actually be received. But this is not a problem with this particular basis package, as the coupon income provided by the cash bond is more than enough to pay for CDS (988 basis points versus 703 basis points).

2. *Basis looks cheap to comparables.* FDC is a large, heavily levered LBO deal. Where does the basis for some other heavily levered

FIGURE 12.1   FDC 9.875s of 2015 Have Underperformed the CDS since Birth

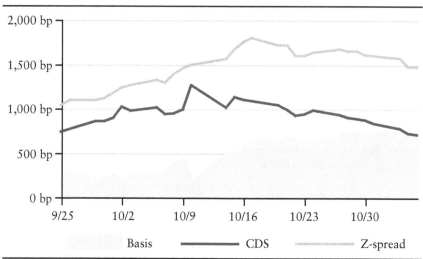

Basis ———— CDS ········ Z-spread

Note: As of November 7, 2008
Data for this figure obtained from UBS.

TABLE 12.4   FDC Looks Cheap to Comparables

	FDC	TPORT
Cash bond (basis points)	1,408	2,520
7-year CDS (basis points)	703	2,542
Difference (basis points)	705	–22

Note: As of November 7, 2008
Data for this figure obtained from UBS.

LBO deals trade? Meaningfully tighter than the FDC package trade (see Table 12.4).

3. *Dollars-at-risk.* While we do not expect a "worst case" fundamental scenario to unfold for FDC, it is a heavily levered company. Does this position suffer if there is a default? Not really—in fact, because bonds are trading at such a low dollar price, a credit event could be a best profit and loss (P&L) outcome. We could expect both the bond and CDS to trade at recovery levels, but the bonds have a lot less room to fall (assuming recovery of 40%, bonds could fall 28 points while CDS could decline 60 points).

FIGURE 12.2 FDC Cash Bond Price and TSS Equity Price Have a Correlation of 83%

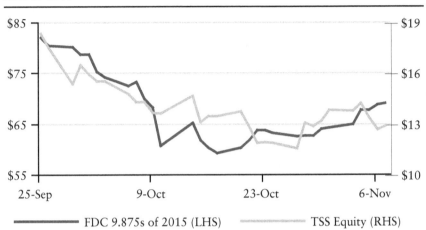

Note: As of November 7, 2008

Data for this figure obtained from UBS.

4. *Room-to-run.* The cash bonds also appear to have more upside in a bullish market environment as well, in part because the starting spread level is so much wider than CDS (investors tend to reach for spread in bullish environments), and the bonds can appreciate much further before they become par constrained.

5. *Just-in-case.* But, for technical reasons, bonds can certainly underperform CDS. (See Figure 12.1.) How can you protect against it, especially over a prolonged period? We could, for example, buy equity put options on a publicly traded company that is in the same general business, such as Total System Services (TSS). TSS is an information technology processor of credit, debit, commercial, and private-label cards. The correlation between FDC 9.875s and TSS equity is fairly high (83%, see Figure 12.2). One could use extra coupon income being generated by this package to purchase more than 2,000 May '09 contracts ($10 strike).

It is important to realize that basis packages may not be for everyone, but perhaps that is why opportunities exist. Well-thought-out packages can provide attractive results in a wide range of investment scenarios.

CAPITAL STRUCTURE RISK

With so many tools currently available to take risk (e.g., bonds, loans, CDS, LCDS, etc.), many investors now take advantage of relative value opportunities within a single company's capital structure. For example, the term loan for a particular company may offer higher risk-adjusted return prospects than the senior unsecured bonds for the same name. For instance, on October 21, 2008 the Community Health 8.875s of 2015 issue was trading almost $5 over the term loan Bs. Or perhaps short-maturity CDS for a company may be cheap relative to equity put options for the same company, providing an opportunity to implement a long/short package that has an asymmetric payoff profile. A recent example would be KB Home, which had both equity options and CDS levels align to enable a positive P&L under numerous scenarios.

Such trades, referred to as *capital structure trades*, are typically packages of long/short positions in a specific company executed in different markets (e.g., long loan, short bond; long equity, short bond, etc.). Capital structure packages usually have elements of the first three risks discussed in this chapter. For example, consider a bond/equity capital structure package—can the maturity of both be determined? If not, there may be curve risk. Capital structure trades can offer tremendous value, but because there are so many moving parts, the risk can be very high as well. For some of the more complex capital structure packages, scenario analysis can be very helpful.

Next we walk though two capital structure risk examples.

Illustration 1: Compensation for Subordination—How Much Should You Get?

One of the key concerns that investors face is whether or not compensation for being in one portion of a company's capital structure is fair relative to another part. What is the proper compensation for subordination?

Are there any rules-of-thumb that investors may use on a regular basis? To answer this question, we posed the following question to a particular sales, trading, and credit team: "If you were to use the average credit that you cover or trade as a reference point, how much extra compensation would you expect to receive for rotating into a sector comp with 1× more leverage?" With one exception, responses were in the 50 to 100 basis point range.

It should be noted that in our survey, the initial response of everyone on the credit team was that the amount of extra compensation for moving down in quality depends on the leverage starting point. That is, if the rotation is from a name that is 1× levered into one that has two turns of leverage, compensation should be less than for a 5× to 6× rotation. In essence, survey participants believe that the relationship between spreads and leverage is (or should be) exponential, not linear.

This expectation may be realistic, but it is not entirely consistent with reality. Our study shows that for the bulk of the investment universe the spread–leverage relationship is more-or-less linear (see Figure 12.3), at least in the market environment at the time of the study. This suggests that our survey participants should see good relative value opportunities—either highly leveraged names are too richly valued, or names with modest leverage are too cheap.

We attempt to better understand senior/subordinate relationships by examining data points in the loan market. In particular, we examined 70+ benchmark issuers in June 2008 and grouped the credits

FIGURE 12.3 Incremental Compensation for Leverage in the Bond Market

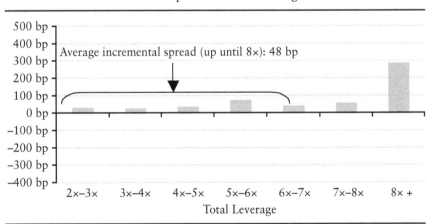

Note: As of June 26, 2008. Total leverage for the issuer and median spread per leverage bucket used.
Data for this figure obtained from UBS and *Yield Book*.

FIGURE 12.4   Relationship between Spread and Incremental Leverage in the Loan Market

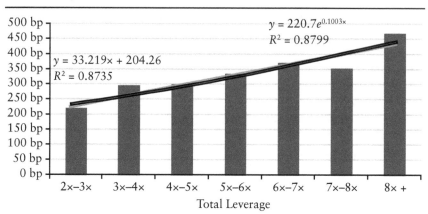

Note: As of June 27, 2008. Linear and exponential equations based on the best-fit lines.

Data for this figure obtained from UBS, Bloomberg and *Yield Book*.

into eight categories based on total leverage. The first bucket is comprised of names with leverage in the 2× to 3× range (e.g., TRW Automotive), and the last bucket had names with eight or more turns of leverage (e.g., First Data Company). The groupings between these two end-points are separated by one turn of incremental leverage.

We estimated two regressions (one linear, one exponential) and found the following:

- *Nice fit.* Both approaches had fairly good fits, with *R*-squares of 87% and 88%, respectively (see Figure 12.4).
- *Still the same.* And there was little difference between the two different approaches with regard to predicted spread levels for the bulk of the universe (see Figure 12.5).
- *What's it worth?* Based on the linear approach, each unit of incremental leverage is worth 33 basis points.

How to Take Advantage?

In terms of trading opportunities, in Figure 12.6 and Table 12.5 we present names that were favored by the team of credit analysts in our

FIGURE 12.5 Expected Compensation for Various Leverage Ratios, Using Linear and Exponential Equations in the Loan Market

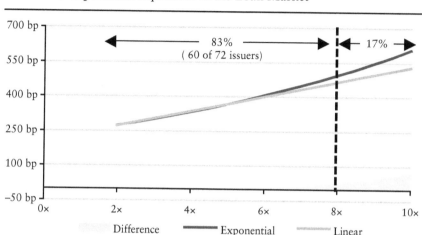

Note: As of June 27, 2008. Linear and exponential equations based on the best-fit lines.

Data for this figure obtained from UBS, Bloomberg, and *Yield Book*.

FIGURE 12.6 Compensation for Leverage Can Vary Meaningfully in the Loan Market

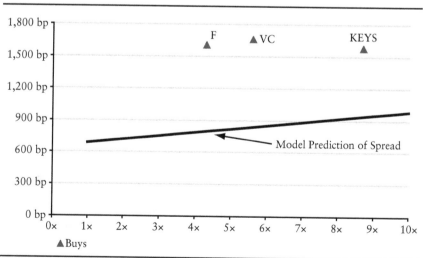

Note: As of October 13, 2008. Linear equation based on the best-fit line.

Data for this figure obtained from UBS, Bloomberg, and Markit.

TABLE 12.5 Picks in the Loan Market

Issuer	Coupon	Maturity	Spread	Total Leverage
Ford TLB	300	12/15/2013	1605	4.3×
Keystone Auto	350	1/12/2012	1579	8.7×
Visteon TLB	300	6/13/2013	1660	5.6×

Note: As of October 13, 2008.
Data for this figure obtained from UBS, Bloomberg, and Markit.

study (as of July 31, 2008) and offer more compensation per turn of leverage than predicted by our analysis.

Illustration 2: Incorporating Equity Options

In normal times, the risk associated with capital structure packages can be daunting. What if the equity (bond) market is subject to a short squeeze, but the bond (equity) market is not? What if a company announces a more (less) shareholder-friendly policy than consensus expectations? What if the cost of borrow rises sharply for a particular bond (equity) issue, but not for the corresponding equity (bond)? A capital structure package may make perfect sense in the context of valuations and fundamentals, but typically there are many technical factors that can cause disconnects.

There are times that are anything but normal, such as in 2008, which provided opportunities to effectively earn positive carry and register positive performance in a wide variety of bullish and bearish scenarios.

Consider a Company P package consisting of the purchase of six-month CDS protection and the sale of equity put options (six-month tenor). In particular, buy $10 million notional CDS protection and sell 10,000 six-month put options with a strike price of $5. CDS costs 3 points upfront and 500 basis points running for a total cost of $550,000, and selling options generates income of $1.1 per contract, or $1.1 million for position size of 10,000 contracts, resulting in positive carry of $550,000 (see Table 12.6). Note that the stock of Company P is trading at $7.14.

Next, we outline performance in various scenarios.

TABLE 12.6 Capital Structure Trade: Buy CDS, Sell Put

Action	Issue	Price	Size	Inflow/ Outflow
Sell	6-mo, $5 strike	$1.10	10,000 contracts	$1,100,000
Buy	6-mo CDS	3 pts, 500 bp	$10,000,000	($550,000)
Net				+$550,000

Note: Sell 10,000 contracts at $1.1 million (receive this amount), buy $10 illion notional protection at 3 points. and 500 running (pay $550,000 positive "carry" of $55,000. No option commission/fees included.

TABLE 12.7 Scenario 1: Status Quo Payoff Profile

Position	Issue	Size	Price Horizon End	P&L
Long	6-mo, $5 strike	10,000 contracts	0%	$1,100,000
Short	6-mo CDS	$10,000,000	0%	($550,000)
Net				+$550,000

Note: Both contracts "expire" at zero, package benefits from carry of $550,000. No option commission and fees included.

Scenario 1: Status Quo. If nothing happens, both puts and CDS "expire" in about six months, so net return is $550,000 (see Table 12.7).

Scenario 2: Severe Pressure On Company. Suppose the company encounters severe credit pressure (default). And assume a very low recovery for equity holders (0%), and an average recovery for bond holders (40%). Even with these very aggressive assumptions, the package would still perform well (see Table 12.8). The loss on the put position would total $5 million ([Strike price of $5 – Stock price of $0] × Contract size of 100 × 10,000 contracts), but the gain on CDS would be $6 million ($10 million par – $4 million recovery). In addition, carry would also be favourable, particularly if the default occurred early in the holding period (only pay 500 basis points running until default, already pocket option premium).

TABLE 12.8　Scenario 2: Severe Pressure on the Company Leading to Default

Position	Issue	Size	Recovery	P&L
Long	6-mo, $5 strike	10,000 contracts	0%	($5,000,000)
Short	6-mo CDS	$10,000,000	40%	$6,000,000
Carry				$550,000
Net				+$1,550,000

Note: Difference between strike price ($5) and recovery ($0) results in loss of $5 million; offset by gain of $6 million in CDS (difference between notional $10 million and recovery of $4 million). No option commission and fees included.

TABLE 12.9　Scenario 3: Basis Risk (bond rally, option static)

Position	Issue	Size	Assumed Change	P&L
Long	6-mo, $5 strike	10,000 contracts	0%	—
Short	6-mo CDS	$10,000,000	−1000 bp	($442,000)
Carry				$550,000
Net				+$108,000

Note: Even in disconnect scenarios, positive carry provides significant cushion; for example, if spreads rally 1,000 basis points and equity is unchanged, net return would still be positive. No option commission and fees included.

> *Scenario 3: Basis risk.* Almost all package trades have some element of basis risk. In the context of a bond/equity package, for example, what if there was a sharp rally in spreads and an unchanged put price due to a modestly dilutive equity injection (see Table 12.9)? Basis risk in this Company P package is mitigated in part by (1) a high breakeven due to positive carry, (2) a meaningfully out-of-the money put option, and (3) a short time horizon; spread compression has a modest impact on price. Also noteworthy is that at the time of this package trade, CDS and puts have been tracking closely (see Figure 12.7).

FIGURE 12.7   Company P CDS vs. Put Option

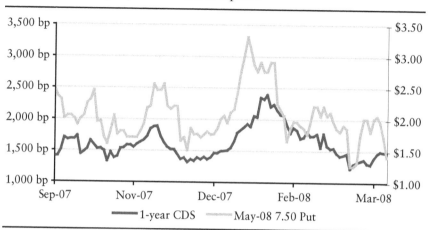

Data for this figure obtained from Bloomberg.

Although the package appears attractive in most scenarios, it is important to note that risk still exists. For example, if the company were to raise equity capital that was massively dilutive, shares would likely fall and spreads could hold steady or rally.

SUMMARY

All investments have risk. The major issue that market participants have is ascertaining, particularly in times of volatility, how much compensation they should receive for taking that risk. In the first eleven chapters of this book, we provided the basics of the corporate credit markets. Chapter 12 puts these basics into practice by illustrating different trade strategies within the leveraged finance markets.

Specifically, we developed templates for four kinds of common risk elements in the leveraged finance market. We first provided a framework for assessing the risk and reward for taking exposure to a single credit. We then moved on to curve risk, where the risk is not necessarily a movement in the absolute spread values of a particular company per se, but instead the relationship of spreads across the maturity profile of a corporate issuer. Next, we focused on basis risk, which combined exposures from both the cash and synthetic markets. Finally, we addressed capital structure risk, which is a review of compensation for exposure to different segments of an issuer's balance sheet.

Default Correlation

13

Default Correlation

The Basics

Default correlation measures whether credit risky assets are more likely to default together or separately. For example, default correlation answers the following question: If 10 bonds each have a 10% probability of default, does that mean: (1) One and only one is definitely going to default? Or (2) is there a 10% chance *all* of them will default and a 90% chance *none* of them are going to default? If the answer is "in between," where in between?

Default correlation is essential to understanding the risk of credit portfolios and is the subject of this chapter. Along with *default probability* and *loss in the event of default*, default correlation determines the credit risk of a portfolio.

In this chapter, we look closely at the definition of default correlation and discuss its drivers. We then provide pictorial representations of default probability and default correlation and present mathematical formulas relating default correlation to default probability. The difficulty of the problem becomes evident when we show that pairwise default correlations are not sufficient to understand the behavior of a credit risky portfolio and introduce "higher orders of default correlation." In the next chapter, we continue our discussion of default correlations where we cover empirical results and problems related to default correlation, as well as our opinion on proposed solutions to the problem of incorporating default correlation into credit analysis.

DEFAULT CORRELATION DEFINED

Default correlation is the phenomenon that the likelihood of one obligor defaulting on its debt is affected by whether or not another obligor has defaulted on its debts. A simple example of this is if one firm is the creditor of another: If Credit A defaults on its obligations to Credit B, we think it is more likely that Credit B will be unable to pay its own obligations. This is an example of *positive* default correlation. The default of one credit makes it *more* likely the other credit will default.

There could also be *negative* default correlation. Suppose that Credit A and Credit B are competitors. If Credit A defaults and goes out of business, it might be the case that Credit B will get Credit A's customers and be able to get price concessions from Credit A's suppliers. If this is true, the default of one credit makes it less likely the other credit will default. This would be an example of negative correlation.

Default correlation is not normally discussed with respect to the particular business relationship between one credit and another. And the existence of default correlation does not imply that one credit's default directly causes the change in another credit's default probability. It is a maxim of statistics that correlation does not imply causation. Nor do we think negative default correlation is very common. Primarily, we think positive default correlation generally exists among credits because the fortunes of individual companies are linked together via the health of the general economy or the health of broad subsets of the general economy.

Drivers of Default Correlation

The pattern of yearly default rates for U.S. corporations since 1920 is notable for the high concentrations of defaults around 1933, 1991, and 2001 (see Figure 13.1). A good number of firms in almost all industries defaulted on their credit obligations in these depressions and recessions. The boom years of the 1950s and 1960s, however, produced very few defaults in the high-yield space. As mentioned in Chapter 11, to varying degrees, all businesses tend to be affected by the health of the general economy. It's also worth noting that leverage was not as widely used in the 1950s–1960s as compared to later periods. The phenomena of companies tending to default together or not default together is indicative of positive default correlation.

FIGURE 13.1   Historical Default Rates Among High-Yield Issuers

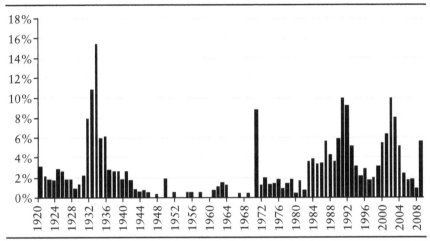

Data for this figure obtained from Moody's.

Defaults can also be caused by industry-specific events that only affect firms in those particular industries. Bad investments or perhaps bad regulation caused a number of thrifts to default in 1989 and 1990. More recently, the subprime mortgage meltdown and subsequent credit crisis beginning in 2007 put enormous pressure on the entire financial industry (see Figure 13.2), leading to 12 defaults of benchmark credits through December 2008 (including notable firms such as Lehman Brothers and Washington Mutual). Again, the phenomena of companies in a particular industry tending to default together or not default together is indicative of positive default correlation.

There are other default-risk relationships among businesses that do not become obvious until they occur. The effect of low oil prices in the 1980s rippled through the Texas economy affecting just about every industry and credit in the state. A spike in the price of silver once negatively affected both film manufacturers and silverware makers. The failure of the South American anchovy harvest in 1972 drove up the price of alternative sources of cattle feed and put both Peruvian fishermen and Midwest cattle ranchers under pressure. The U.S. subprime asset problem that emerged in early 2007 eventually forced the U.S. economy in to a recession. In that case, even the U.S. Federal Reserve did not recognize the default-risk relationship: "The

FIGURE 13.2   The Correlation of CDS Performance of Major Investment
Banks in 2008 Shows Various Periods of Industry Stress

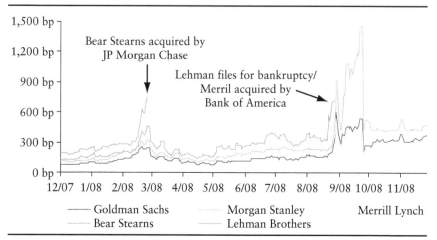

Data for this figure obtained from UBS.

impact on the broader economy and financial markets of the problems in the subprime market seems likely to be contained . . . ."[1] This
statement was made in March 2007, only nine months ahead of the
U.S. economy falling into a recession. These default-producing characteristics hide until, because of the defaults they cause, their presence becomes obvious.

Finally, there are truly company-specific default factors such as
the health of a company's founder or the chance an uninsured ware-
house will be destroyed by fire. These factors do not transfer default
contagion to other credits. Recent defaults brought on by corporate
fraud are also considered to be company-specific events. For example,
the default of Parmalat in December 2003 did not widen the credit
default swap premiums of other industrial companies.

Defaults are therefore the result of an unknown and unspecified
multifactor model of default that seems akin to a multifactor equity
pricing model. Default correlation occurs when, for example, econ-
omy-wide or industry-wide default-causing variables assume particular values and cause widespread havoc. Uncorrelated defaults occur

---

[1] Federal Reserve, *Economic Outlook*, March 28, 2007.

when company specific default-causing variables cause trouble for individual credits.

Why We Care About Default Correlation

Default correlation is critical in understanding and predicting the behavior of credit portfolios. It directly affects the risk return profile of investors in credit risky assets and is therefore important to the creditors and regulators of these investors. Default correlation also has implications for industrial companies that expose themselves to the credit risk of their suppliers and customers through the normal course of business. We support these assertions with an example.

Suppose we wish to understand the risk of a bond portfolio and we know that each of the 10 bonds in the portfolio has a 10% probability of default over the next five years. What does this tell us about the behavior of the portfolio as a whole? Not much, it turns out, unless we also understand the default correlation among credits in the portfolio.

It could be, for example, that all the bonds in the portfolio always default together. Or to put it another way, if one of the 10 bonds default, they all default. If so, this would be an example of "perfect" *positive* default correlation. Combined with the fact that each bond has a 10% probability of default, we can make a conclusion about how this portfolio will perform. There is a 10% probability that *all* the bonds in the portfolio will default. And there is a 90% probability that *none* of the bonds will default. Perfect positive default correlation, the fact that all the bonds will either default together or not default at all, combines with the 10% probability of default to produce this extreme distribution, is shown in Figure 13.3.

At the other extreme, it could be the case that bonds in the portfolio *always* default separately. Or to put it another way, if one of the 10 bonds defaults, no other bonds default. This would be an example of "perfect" *negative* default correlation. Combined with the fact that each bond has a 10% probability of default, we can make a conclusion about how this portfolio will perform: there is a 100% probability that *one* and only one bond in the portfolio will default. Perfect negative default correlation, the fact that when one bond defaults no other bonds default, combined with the 10% prob-

FIGURE 13.3   Extreme Positive Default Correlation

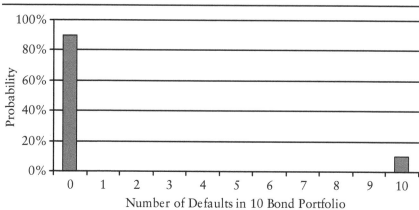

FIGURE 13.4   Extreme Negative Default Correlation

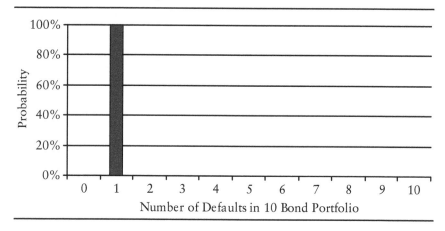

ability of default to produce this extreme distribution, as shown in Figure 13.4.

The difference in the distributions depicted in Figures 13.3 and 13.4 has profound implications for investors in these portfolios. Remember that in both cases, the default probability of bonds in the portfolio is 10% and the expected number of defaults is one. But one knows with *certainty* the result of the portfolio depicted in Figure 13.4: One and only one bond is going to default. This certainty would be of comfort to a lender to this investor. The lender knows with certainty that nine of the bonds are going to perform and that par and interest from those nine performing bonds will be available to repay the investor's indebtedness.

The investor in the portfolio depicted in Figure 13.3 has the greatest uncertainty. Ninety percent of the time the portfolio will have no defaults and 10% of the time every bond in the portfolio will default. A lender to an investor with this portfolio has a 10% risk that no bonds in the portfolio will perform.

A complete analysis of the risk of these two example portfolios would depend on the distribution of default recoveries. But it is obvious that the portfolio depicted in Figure 13.3 is much more risky than the portfolio depicted in Figure 13.4, even though the default probabilities of bonds in the portfolios are the same. The difference in risk profiles, which is due only to default correlation, has profound implications for investors, lenders, rating agencies, and regulators. Debt backed by the portfolio depicted in Figure 13.3 should bear a higher premium for credit risk and be rated lower. If this is a regulated entity, it should be required to have more capital.

DEFAULT PROBABILITY AND DEFAULT CORRELATION

In the sections to follow, we show default probability and default correlation pictorially (with the help of Venn diagrams), present the basic algebra of default correlation, and then delve into the deficiency of pairwise correlations in explaining default distributions.

Picturing Default Probability

Suppose we have two obligors, Credit A and Credit B, each with a 10% default probability. The circles A and B in Figure 13.5 represent the 10% probability that A and B will default, respectively. There are four possibilities depicted in the figure:

1. Both A and B default, as shown by the overlap of circles A and B.
2. Only A defaults, as shown by circle A that does not overlap with B.
3. Only B defaults, as shown by circle B that does not overlap with A.
4. Neither A or B default, as implied by the area outside both circles A and B.

FIGURE 13.5   Pictorial Representation of Credit A and Credit B Default Probability

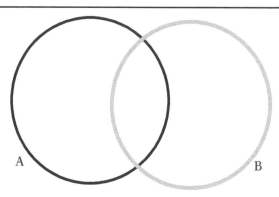

Recall that we defined positive and negative default correlation by how one revises their assessment of the default probability of one credit once one finds out whether another credit has defaulted. If, upon the default of one credit you revise the default probability of the second credit *upwards*, you implicitly think there is *positive* default correlation between the two credits. If upon the default of one credit you revise the default probability of the second credit *downwards*, you implicitly think there is negative default correlation between the two credits.

Figure 13.5 is purposely drawn so that knowing whether one credit defaults does not cause us to revise our estimation of the default probability of the other credit. The figure pictorially represents no or *zero default correlation* between Credits A and B, neither positive or negative default correlation. In other words, knowing that A has defaulted does not change our assessment of the probability that B will default.

Here is the explanation. Recall that the probability of A defaulting is 10% and the probability of B defaulting is 10%. Suppose A has defaulted. Now, pictorially, we are within the circle labeled A in Figure 13.5. No or zero correlation means that we do not change our estimation of Credit B's default probability just because Credit A has defaulted. We still think there is a 10% probability that B will default. Given that we are within circle A, and circle A represents 10% probability, the probability that B will default must be 10% of circle A or 10% of 10% or 1%. The intersection of circles A and B depicts this 1% probability. This leads to a very simple general formula for calculating the probability that both A and B will default when there is no or zero default correlation.

Recall the phrase in the above paragraph that the overlap of A and B, or the space where both A and B default is "10% of 10% or 1%." What this means mathematically is the probability of both Credits A and B defaulting (the joint probability of default for Credits A and B) is 10% × 10% or 1%. Working from the specific to the general (which we label equation (13.1)), our notation gives us the following:

$$10\% \times 10\% = 1\%$$

$$P(A) \times P(B) = P(A \text{ and } B) \tag{13.1}$$

where

$P(A)$ = the probability of Credit A defaulting (10% in our example)

$P(B)$ = the probability of Credit B defaulting (10% in our example)

$P(A \text{ and } B)$ = the probability of both Credits A and B defaulting

The $P(A \text{ and } B)$ is called the *joint probability* of default for Credit A and Credit B (1% in our example). This is the general expression for joint default probability assuming zero correlation.

Now that we have calculated the joint probability of A and B defaulting, we can assign probabilities to all the alternatives in Figure 13.5. We do this in Figure 13.6. We assumed that the default probability of Credit A was 10%, which we represent by the circle labeled A in Figure 13.6. We have already determined that the joint probability and Credit A and Credit B defaulting, as represented by the intersection of the circles labeled A and B, is 1%. Therefore, the probability that Credit A will default and Credit B will not default, represented by the area within circle A but also outside circle B, is 9%. Likewise, the probability that Credit B will default and Credit A will not default is 9%. The probabilities than either or both Credit A and Credit B will default, the area within circles A and B, adds up to

FIGURE 13.6   Pictorial Representation of Default Probabilities

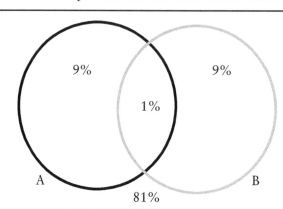

19%. Therefore, the probabilities that neither Credit A nor Credit B will default, represented by the area outside circles A and B, is 81%.

These results are also shown below throwing some "nots," "ors," and "neithers" into the notation:

$P(A) = 10\%$
$P(A \text{ and } B) = 1\%$
$P(A \text{ not } B) = P(A) - P(A \text{ and } B) = 10\% - 1\% = 9\%$
$P(A \text{ or } B) = P(A) + P(B) - P(A \text{ and } B) = 10\% + 10\% - 1\% = 19\%$
$P(\text{neither } A \text{ or } B) = 100\% - P(A \text{ or } B) = 100\% - 19\% = 81\%$

$P(A \text{ not } B)$ means that A defaults and B does not default. $P(A \text{ or } B)$ means that either A or B defaults and includes the possibility that both A and B default. "Neither" means neither A or B defaults.

Picturing Default Correlation

We have pictorially covered scenarios of joint-default, single-default, and no-default probabilities in our two credit world *assuming zero default correlation*. Figure 13.6, showing moderate overlap of the "default circles" has been our map to these scenarios. There are, of course, other possibilities. There could be no overlap, or 0% joint de-fault probability, between Credit A and Credit B, as depicted in Figure 13.7 Or there could be *complete* overlap as depicted in Figure 13.8.

FIGURE 13.7   No Joint Probability

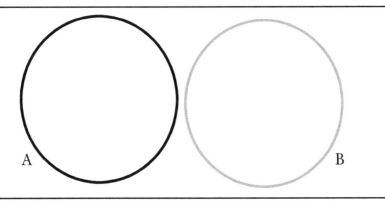

FIGURE 13.8   Maximum Joint Probability

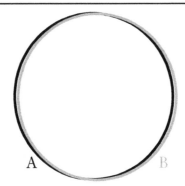

The joint default probability equals 10% because we assume that Credit A and B each have a 10% probability of default and in Figure 13.8 they are depicted as always defaulting together. (Note that we draw the circles in Figure 13.8 a little offset so you can see that there are two of them. Otherwise, they rest exactly on top of each other.)

Recall that Figure 13.7 depicts perfect *negative* default correlation since if one credit defaults we know the other will not. Figure 13.8 depicts perfect *positive* default correlation because if one credit defaults we know the other one will too. Unfortunately, equation (13.1) does not take into account the situations depicted in Figures 13.7 and 13.8. That formula does not help us calculate joint default probability in either of these circumstances or in any circumstance other than zero default correlation. Which leads us to the next part of this section.

Calculating Default Correlation Mathematically

With the Venn diagrams under our belt, we can become more precise in understanding default correlation with a little high school algebra. What we are going to do in this section is mathematically define default correlation. Once defined, the equation will allow us to compute default correlation between any two credits given their individual default probabilities and their joint default probability. Then we will solve the same equation for joint default probability. The reworked equation will allow us to calculate the joint default probability of any two credits given their individual default probabilities and the default correlation between the two credits.

What we would like to have is a mathematical way to express the degree of overlap in the Venn diagrams or the joint default probability of the credits depicted in the Venn diagrams. As shown earlier we have no overlap depicted in Figure 13.7, "moderate" overlap depicted back in Figure 13.6, and complete overlap depicted in Figure 13.8. One way is to refer to the joint probability of default. It's 0% in Figure 13.7, 1% in Figure 13.6, and 10% in Figure 13.8. All possible degrees of overlap could be described via the continuous scale of joint default probability running from 0% to 10%. However, this measure is tied up with the individual credit's probability of default. A 1% joint probability of default is a very high default correlation if both credits have only a 1% probability of default to begin with. A 1% joint probability of default is a very negative default correlation if both credits have a 50.5% probability of default to begin with. We would like a measure of overlap that does not depend on the default probabilities of the credits.

This is exactly what default correlation, a number running from −1 to +1, does. Default correlation is defined mathematically as

$$\text{Default correlation (A and B)} = \frac{\text{Covariance}(A, B)}{\text{Standard deviation}(A)\text{Standard deviation}(B)} \tag{13.2}$$

What we are going to do now is to delve more into the equation (13.2) and better define default correlation between Credits A and B.

The *standard deviation* in the formula is a measure of how much A can vary. A, in this case, is whether or not Credit A defaults. What this means intuitively is how certain or uncertain we are that A will default. We are very certain about whether A will default if A's default probability is 0% or 100%. Then we know with certainty whether or not A is going to default. At 50% default probability of default, we are most uncertain whether A is going to default.

The term for an event such as default, where either the event happens or does not happen, and there is no in between, is *binomial* and the probability is defined by a probability distribution called a binomial distribution. The standard deviation of a binomial distribution is

$$\text{Standard deviation}(A) = \{P(A) \times [1 - P(A)]\}^{1/2} \qquad (13.3)$$

In the example we have been working with, where the default probability of A is 10%, or $P(A) = 10\%$, the standard deviation of A is

$$\text{Standard deviation}(A) = (10\% \times 90\%)^{1/2} = 30\%$$

All the possible standard deviations of a binomial event, where the probability varies from 0% to 100%, are shown in Figure 13.9. Above 10% probability on the horizontal axis we can see that the

FIGURE 13.9 Standard Deviation and Default Probability

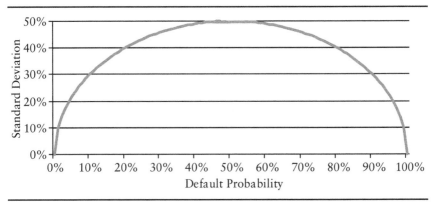

standard deviation is indeed 30%. The figure also illustrates the statements we made before likening standard deviation to the uncertainty of whether or not the credit is going to default. At 0% and 100% default probability, where we are completely certain what is going to happen, standard deviation is 0%. At 50% default probability, where we are least certain whether the credit is going to default, standard deviation is at its highest.

The *covariance* of A and B is a measure of how far the actual joint probability of A and B is from the joint probability that we would obtain if there was zero default correlation. Mathematically, this is simply *actual joint probability of A and B* minus the *joint probability of A and B assuming zero correlation*. Recall from equation (13.1) that the joint probability of A and B assuming zero correlation is $P(A) \times P(B)$. Therefore the covariance[2] between A and B is

$$\text{Covariance}(A, B) = P(A \text{ and } B) - P(A) \times P(B) \qquad (13.4)$$

In our earlier example, we worked out that the joint probability of default, assuming zero default correlation, is 1%. From Figure 13.7, we know that given perfect negative default correlation, the actual joint probability can be as small as 0%. From Figure 13.8, we know that given perfect positive default correlation, the actual joint probability can be as high as 10%. Figure 13.10 depicts the relationship between joint default probability and covariance graphically.

Substituting equations (13.3) and (13.4) into equation (13.2) we get

$$\text{Correlation}(A \text{ and } B)$$
$$= \frac{P(A \text{ and } B) - P(A) \times P(B)}{\{P(A) - [1 - P(A)]\}^{1/2} \times \{P(B) - [1 - P(B)]\}^{1/2}} \qquad (13.5)$$

Now, finally, we can define mathematically the default correlation we saw visually in Figures 13.6, 13.7, and 13.8. In Figure 13.6, the joint default probability of A and B, $P(A \text{ and } B)$ was 1% simply because we wanted to show the case where the default probability of

---

[2] Covariance is more formally defined as the Expectation(A × B) − Expectation(A) × Expectation(B). When we define default as 1 and no default as 0, equation (13.4) is the result.

FIGURE 13.10   Covariance and Joint Probability

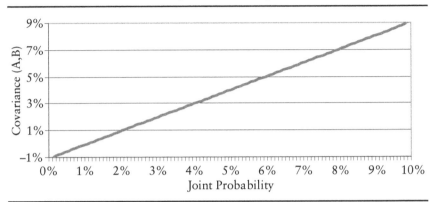

one credit does not depend on whether another credit had defaulted. The product of A's and B's default probabilities, $P(A) \times P(B)$, is 10% $\times$ 10%, or 1%. Moving to the denominator of equation (13.5), the product of A's and B's standard deviations, $\{P(A) \times [1 - P(A)]\}^{1/2} \times \{P(B) \times [1 - P(B)]\}^{1/2}$ is 9%. Putting this all together, we get

$$\text{Correlation}(A \text{ and } B) = \frac{1\% - 1\%}{9\%} = 0.00$$

Similarly, for Figure 13.7, where the joint default probability is 0%, default correlation is –0.11. In Figure 13.8, where joint default probability is 10%, default correlation is +1.00. In our example, as the joint default probability moves from 0% to 10%, default correlation increases linearly from –0.11 to +1.00, as shown in Figure 13.11.

Theoretically, correlation can range from –1.00 to +1.00. But for binomial events such as default, the range of possible default correlations is dictated by the default probabilities of the two credits. With 10% probability of default for both credits, the possible range of default correlation is reduced to the range from –0.11 to +1.00. If both credits do not have the same default probability, they cannot have +1.00 default correlation. Only if the default probability of both credits were 50% would it be mathematically possible for default correlation to range fully from –1.00 to +1.00.

FIGURE 13.11 Default Correlation and Joint Default Probability

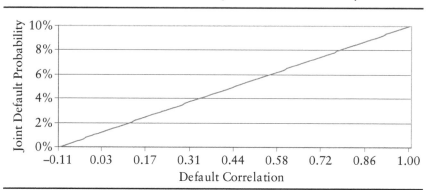

FIGURE 13.12 Default Correlation, Joint Default Probability, and Underlying Default Probability

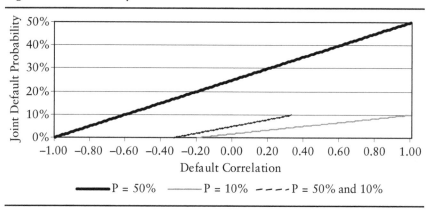

Figure 13.12 shows the relationship between default correlation and joint default probability when the individual default probability of both credits is 50%, when the individual default probability of both credits is 10%, and when the individual default probabilities of credits are 10% and 50%, respectively.

Note that as described, default correlation in the case where the default probability of both credits is 50% ranges from +1.00 to –1.00. Also, note the slope of the two lines. The same increase in default correlation has a bigger effect on the joint probability of default when individual default probabilities are 50% than when individual default probabilities are 10%.

Equation (13.5) allows us to calculate historic default correlations from empirical default data. Rearranging equation (13.5) to solve for the joint probability of default, we can calculate the joint default probability of A and B given their individual probabilities of default and their default correlation. From that, we arrive at equation (13.6):

$$P(\text{A and B}) = \text{Correlation}(\text{A and B}) \times \{P(\text{A}) \times [1 - P(\text{A})]\}^{1/2} \\ \times \{P(\text{B}) \times [1 - P(\text{B})]\}^{1/2} + P(\text{A}) \times P(\text{B}) \tag{13.6}$$

Default Correlation in a Triplet

We have already seen in Figure 13.11 how the range of default correlation can be restricted. Many people are used to looking at portfolio risk in the context of Markowitz's portfolio theory which relies on the variance-covariance matrices.[3] In that framework, armed with an estimate of the standard deviation of the return for each security, and the correlation of the return of each pair of securities, a portfolio manager can explain the behavior of the entire portfolio. Not so with a binomial variable such as default. We illustrate the difference in this section.

Instead of the two-credit world that we have focused on, suppose we have three credits, A, B, and C, each with a 10% probability of default. Also suppose that the default correlation between each pair of credits is zero. As we have discussed before, this means that the joint probability between each pair of credits is 1%. We illustrate this situation in Figure 13.13.

Now we are eager to understand the behavior of all three credits together. We seem to have a lot of information: each credit's default probability and the default correlation between each pair of credits. What does this tell us about how defaults will occur among all three credits? Not much, it turns out. One might jump to the conclusion that if the pairs AB, BC, and AC all are zero default correlated, the default correlations between the *pair* AB and the single credit, C, or the *pair* BC and the single credit A, or the *pair* AC and B must also all be zero default correlated. Since the zero default correlation joint

---

[3] Harry M. Markowitz, "Portfolio Selection," *Journal of Finance* 7, no. 1 (March 1952): 77–91.

FIGURE 13.13   Pairwise Joint Default Correlation

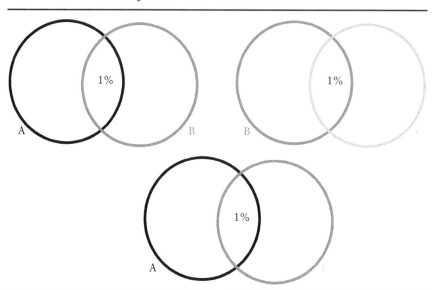

default probability of any pair is 10% × 10% or 1%, the zero default correlation triple joint probability of default is 1% × 10% or 0.1%. In general, the triple joint default probability assuming zero pairwise and zero triplet default correlation is

$$P(A \text{ and } B \text{ and } C) = P(A) \times P(B) \times P(C)$$
$$= 10\% \times 10\% \times 10\% = 0.1\%$$

Once we know that $P(A \text{ and } B \text{ and } C) = 0.1\%$, we can figure out that $P(A \text{ and } B \text{ not } C)$ is 0.9% and that $P(A \text{ not } B \text{ not } C)$ is 8.1%. This is illustrated pictorially in Figure 13.13. Table 13.1 shows the probabilities of all possible default outcomes under the heading "0.00 Triplet Default Correlation."

There is no reason why just because pairs of credits have zero default correlation that the default correlation between a *pair* and a *third* credit must also be zero. Figures 13.15 and 13.16 show the extremes of possible correlation. (Note the switch from circles to rectangles and ovals in these Venn diagrams to show the overlapping probabilities clearly.)

FIGURE 13.14   Zero Pairwise and Zero Triplet Default Correlation

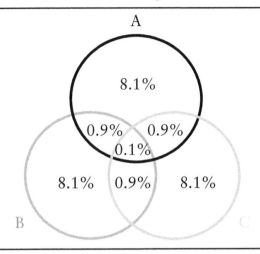

TABLE 13.1   Default Probabilities Under 0.00 Pairwise Default Correlation and Various Triplet Default Correlation

Number of Defaults	−0.03 Triplet Default Correlation	0.00 Triplet Default Correlation	0.30 Triplet Default Correlation
0	73.0%	72.9%	72.0%
1	24.0%	24.3%	27.0%
2	3.0%	2.7%	0.0%
3	0.0%	0.1%	1.0%

In Figure 13.15, whenever two credits default, the third credit joins them in default and there is no situation where only *two* credits default. Table 13.1 shows the probabilities of all possible default outcomes under the heading "0.30 Triplet Default Correlation." There is a 1% probability that all three credits default, 0% probability that two credits default, 27% probability that one credit will default and 72% probability that no credits will default.

This sounds like positive default correlation: If you know that any two credits have defaulted, your estimate of the default probability of the third credit increases from 10% to 100%. We can solve for the triplet default correlation by treating the default of A and B as *one* event

FIGURE 13.15   Zero Pairwise and Positive Triplet Default Correlation

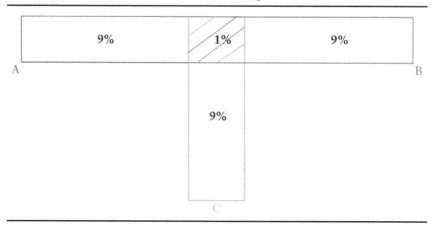

FIGURE 13.16   Zero Pairwise and Negative Triplet Default Correlation

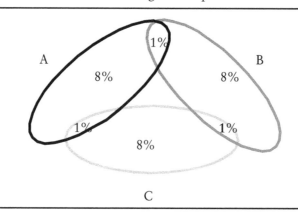

and comparing that event to the default of C. Using equation (13.5), and substitution in AB for A and C for B we have equation (13.7)

$$
\begin{aligned}
&\text{Correlation(AB and C)}\\
&= \frac{P(\text{AB and C}) - P(\text{AB}) \times P(\text{C})}{\{P(\text{AB}) \times [1 - P(\text{AB})]\}^{1/2} \times \{P(\text{C}) \times [1 - P(\text{C})]\}^{1/2}}\\
&= \frac{1\% - 1\% \times 10\%}{\{1\% \times [1 - 1\%]\}^{1/2} \times \{10\% \times [1 - 10\%]\}^{1/2}} = 0.30
\end{aligned}
\tag{13.7}
$$

But this triplet default correlation of 0.30 occurs while all pairwise default correlations are zero.

In Figure 13.16, in contrast, there is no situation where all three credits default. In this case, if you know that two credits have defaulted, your estimate of the default probability of the third credit decreases from 10% to 0%. This sounds like negative default correlation. In this situation, the triplet default correlation is –0.03. Table 13.1 shows the probabilities of all possible default outcomes under the heading "–0.03 Triplet Default Correlation." There is a 0% probability that all three credits default, 3% probability that two credits default, 24% probability that one credit will default and 73% probability that no credits will default.

Note that the expected number of defaults in each triplet correlation scenario is the same. In the zero triplet correlation scenario, the expected number of defaults is 24.3% × 1 + 2.7% × 2 + 0.1% × 3 or 0.3. In the positive triplet correlation scenario, the expected number of defaults in the portfolio is 27% × 1 + 1% × 3 or 0.3. In the negative triplet correlation scenario, the expected number of defaults in the portfolio is 24% × 1 + 3% × 2 or also 0.3.

Note also that the probability of any two credits defaulting at the same time in any of the triplet default scenarios is 1%. In the –0.03 triplet correlation scenario, the 3.0% probability of two defaults divides into a 1% probability of any pair of credits defaulting. In the positive triplet correlation scenario, the probability of *all* three credits defaulting at the same time is 1%. Which means that the probability of each possible pair of credits defaulting is also 1%. In the zero triplet correlation scenario, the 2.7% probability of two defaults divides into a 0.9% probability of any pair of credits defaulting. Also in the 0.00 triplet correlation scenario, the probability of *all* three credits defaulting at the same time is 0.1%. Which adds another 0.1% of probability and brings the total probability of any pair of credits defaulting to 1.0%.

So in all three triplet correlation scenarios, the defaults of pairs AB, BC, and AC each have a 1% chance of occurring. This is proof that pairwise default correlation is 0.00. But the sad truth is that knowing pairwise default correlations does not tell you everything you would like to know about the behavior of this three credit portfolio. This makes default correlation computationally very difficult.

Pairwise and Triplet Default Correlation

In Figure 13.17 we show the range of triplet default correlation for the whole range of pairwise default correlation, given that the default probability of each of the three credits is 10%. That is, for any point on the horizontal axis giving a possible pairwise default correlation, we show the *minimum* triplet default correlation can be and the *maximum* triplet default correlation can be.

The effects of varying triplet default correlation are shown in Figures 13.17 and 13.18. In Figure 13.17, we show the probabilities of one, two, and three defaults given triplet default correlation is as *low* as it can be (given pairwise default correlation). In Figure 13.19, we show the probabilities of one, two, and three defaults given triplet default correlation is as *high* as it can be (given pairwise default correlation).

Comparing Figures 13.18 and 13.19, the probability of extreme default results is greater with maximum triplet default correlation than it is in the minimum triplet default correlation case. In Figure 13.19, two defaults is the most probable outcome under a wide range of pairwise default correlations. In Figure 13.19, two defaults never occur. This harkens back to Figures 13.3 and 13.4, where there was

FIGURE 13.17   Range of Triplet Default Correlation

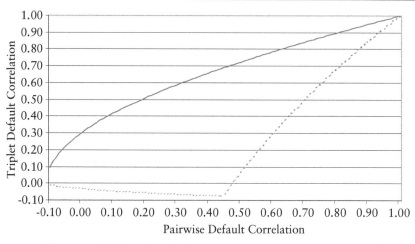

—— Maximum Triplet Correlation   ⋯⋯ Minimum Triplet Correlation

FIGURE 13.18 Default Probabilities with Minimum Triplet Default Correlation

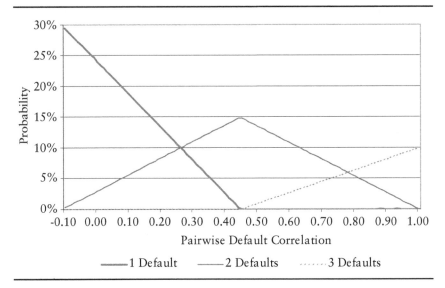

FIGURE 13.19 Default Probabilities with Maximum Triplet Default Correlation

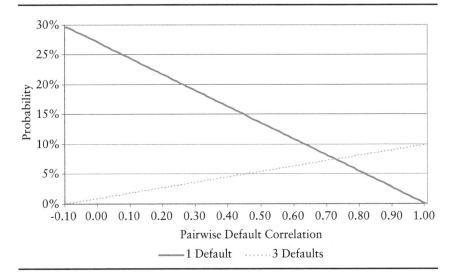

a wide range of default results with positive default correlation and a narrow range of default results with negative default correlation. Given pairwise default correlation, low triplet default correlation works to create a stable number of defaults and high triplet default correlation works to create a wide range in the number of defaults.

Group Default Correlation

We wanted to make sure that higher orders of default correlation were also important for large portfolios. So we consider a 100-credit portfolio where each credit has a 10% probability of default. We computed the probabilities of zero to 100 credits defaulting under three correlation scenarios:

- Zero pairwise default correlation and zero higher correlations.
- Zero pairwise default correlation and maximum negative higher correlations.
- Zero pairwise default correlation and maximum positive higher correlations.

The results are shown in Figure 13.20 and show the extreme distribution of the positive higher correlation portfolio and the very stable distribution of the negative higher correlation portfolio relative to the zero higher correlation portfolio. Again, our conclusion is

FIGURE 13.20   Default Probabilities in a 100-Credit Portfolio

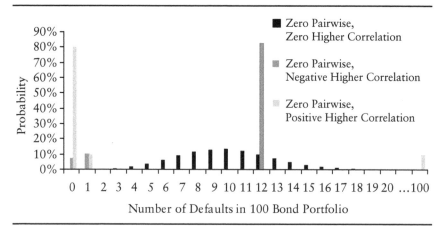

that pairwise default correlations do not give us all the information we need to understand the behavior of a portfolio.

Intuitively, increasing higher-level default correlation seems logical. Assuming that positive pairwise default correlation exists, the first default in the portfolio will cause us to revise our estimation of the default probability of remaining credits in the portfolio upwards. It seems logical that if a *second* credit defaults, we would want to again revise our estimation of the default probabilities of remaining credits upwards. This is the effect of higher-order positive default correlation. As more and more credits default, we think it more likely that remaining credits will also default.

SUMMARY

In this chapter, we provide a not overly mathematical guide to default correlation. We defined default correlation and discussed its causes in the context of systematic and unsystematic drivers of default. We used Venn diagrams to picture default probability and default correlation; and provide mathematical formulas for default correlation, joint probability of default, and the calculation of empirical default correlation. We emphasized higher orders of default correlation and the insufficiency of pairwise default correlation to define default probabilities in a portfolio comprised of more than two credits.

14

Empirical Default Correlations

Problems and Solutions

In the previous chapter, we provided the basic foundation for understanding default correlation. In this chapter, we explore the determination of historical default correlations and the problems inherent in empirical default correlation. We then compare different approaches of incorporating default correlation into portfolio credit analysis. Finally, we recommend the approach that makes the most direct use of historical data and is easiest to understand.

EMPIRICAL RESULTS

With enough data—and one very strong assumption that we discuss in detail later—we can calculate *historic default correlations*. The default correlation formula was given in Chapter 13 (as equation (13.5)) and is reproduced below as equation (14.1):

$$\text{Correlation(A and B)} = \frac{P(A \text{ and } B) - P(A) \times P(B)}{\{P(A) \times [1 - P(A)]\}^{1/2} \times \{P(B) \times [1 - P(B)]\}^{1/2}} \quad (14.1)$$

To compute, say, the default correlation of two B-rated companies over one year, we set $P(A)$ and $P(B)$ in equation (14.1) for the default correlation equal to the historic average 1-year default rate for B-rated companies. The remaining variable in equation (14.1) is the joint probability of default, $P(A \text{ and } B)$. We compute $P(A \text{ and } B)$ by first counting the number of companies rated B at the beginning of a year that subsequently defaulted over that particular year. We then calculate all possible *pairs* of such defaulting B-rated companies. If X is the number of B-rated companies defaulting in a year, the possible pairs are

$$\frac{X \times (X-1)}{2}$$

We next calculate all possible pairs of B-rated companies, whether or not they defaulted, using the same formula, $[Y \times (Y-1)]/2$, where Y is the number of B-rated companies *available* to default. The joint default probability of B-rated companies in a particular year is

$$\frac{[X \times (X-1)]/2}{[Y \times (Y-1)]/2}$$

The average of this statistic is taken over available years in the dataset to determine $P(A \text{ and } B)$.

Now, having all the terms in equation (14.1), we can solve for the default correlation between two B-rated credits, A and B. In a similar manner, it is possible to calculate default correlations over longer periods and between groups of credits of different ratings, for example the default correlation between double-A and double-B credits over five years.

Default correlations between all combinations of Moody's rating categories for time periods from 1 to 10 years were computed elsewhere.[1] The data used included 24 years of default data covering the years 1970 through 1993, including industrial companies, utilities, financial institutions, and sovereign issuers. We reproduce the results for historic default correlations in Table 14.1.

We conclude the following from the results reported in Table 14.1:

- Default correlations increase as ratings decrease.
- Default correlations initially increase with time and then decrease with time.

---

[1] Douglas Lucas, "Default Correlation and Credit Analysis," *Journal of Fixed Income* 4, no. 4 (March 1995): 76–87.

TABLE 14.1   Historic Default Correlations

	Aaa	Aa	A	Baa	Ba	B
1-Year Default Correlations × 100						
Aaa	0					
Aa	0	0				
A	0	0	0			
Baa	0	0	0	0		
Ba	0	0	0	0	2	
B	0	1	0	1	4	7
2-Year Default Correlations × 100						
Aaa	0					
Aa	0	0				
A	0	0	0			
Baa	0	0	0	0		
Ba	0	1	1	1	6	
B	0	1	1	2	10	16
Three-Year Default Correlations × 100						
Aaa	0					
Aa	0	0				
A	0	1	1			
Baa	0	0	0	0		
Ba	0	2	2	1	9	
B	0	2	3	3	17	22
Four-Year Default Correlations × 100						
Aaa	0					
Aa	0	0				
A	0	1	1			
Baa	0	1	1	0		
Ba	0	2	3	3	13	
B	0	2	4	5	22	27
Five-Year Default Correlations × 100						
Aaa	0					
Aa	0	0				
A	0	1	1			
Baa	0	1	1	0		
Ba	0	3	4	3	15	
B	0	4	6	7	25	29

TABLE 14.1 (continued)

	Aaa	Aa	A	Baa	Ba	B
6-Year Default Correlations × 100						
Aaa	0					
Aa	1	1				
A	1	1	1			
Baa	0	1	1	0		
Ba	1	3	4	3	15	
B	1	4	7	7	25	29
7-Year Default Correlations × 100						
Aaa	0					
Aa	1	0				
A	1	1	2			
Baa	0	1	1	0		
Ba	2	2	4	3	13	
B	3	3	9	8	24	30
8-Year Default Correlations × 100						
Aaa	1					
Aa	1	0				
A	1	1	2			
Baa	1	1	1	0		
Ba	3	3	5	2	10	
B	6	5	11	7	23	37
9-Year Default Correlations × 100						
Aaa	1					
Aa	1	0				
A	2	1	2			
Baa	2	1	1	0		
Ba	4	3	5	2	8	
B	8	6	12	6	20	39
10-Year Default Correlations × 100						
Aaa	1					
Aa	2	1				
A	2	2	2			
Baa	2	1	1	0		
Ba	4	3	4	2	8	
B	9	8	9	6	17	38

Data for this table obtained from Exhibit 6 in Douglas Lucas, "Default Correlation and Credit Analysis," *Journal of Fixed Income* 4, no. 4 (March 1995): 76–87.

We believe that default correlations increase as ratings decrease because lower-rated companies are relatively more susceptible to problems in the *general economy* while higher-rated companies are relatively more susceptible to *company-specific* problems. Low-rated companies, being closer to default already, are more likely to be pushed into default because of an economic downturn. As economic conditions affect all low-rated credits simultaneously, defaults among these credits are likely to be correlated. In contrast, defaults of highly rated companies, besides being rare, are typically the result of company-specific problems. As these problems are by definition isolated to individual credits, they do not produce default correlation.

With respect to default correlation increasing and then decreasing with the time period analyzed, we note that default correlations peak at five- and six-year periods for rating pairs Baa/Ba, Baa/B, Ba/Ba, and Ba/B. However, default correlations peak at nine years for rating pairs A/B and B/B.

The decrease in default correlation that occurs in most rating categories over longer time periods may be caused by the relationship of the time period being studied to the average business cycle. If the time period studied covers the entire ebb and flow of the business cycle, defaults caused by general economic conditions average out over the period, thus lowering default correlation. We think that default correlation is maximized when the time period tested most closely approximates the length of an economic recession or expansion.

Just as the pairwise default correlations in Table 14.1 can be calculated, so too can higher-order default correlations. Rather than demonstrate this, we instead turn to a discussion of the reliability of empirically observed default correlations.

PROBLEMS WITH HISTORICAL DEFAULT CORRELATIONS

Implicit in our discussion on empirical default correlation is the idea that wide swings in default rates are indicative of positive default correlation while small swings or steady default rates are indicative of low or even negative default correlation. We illustrate this concept explicitly in Figure 14.1.

The figure depicts annual default rates for three 100-credit portfolios assuming 10% default probability per year for each credit and

FIGURE 14.1 Simulated Annual Default Rates Under Different Default Correlations

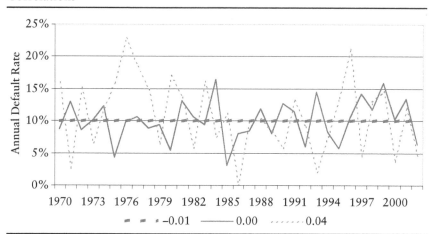

pairwise default correlations of –0.01, 0.00, and 0.04, respectively. The dashed line, steady at exactly 10%, is produced with perfect negative default correlation, in this case –0.01. The solid line that ranges between 3% and 16% was produced with 0.00 default correlation. Finally, the most volatile series, the dotted line, which varies between 0% and 23%, was produced with default correlation of 0.04. This shows that a little bit of default correlation can cause substantial swings in experienced defaults.

However, the default rates of the most volatile series in Figure 14.1 could have been produced by *varying default probability* instead of default correlation. Suppose that over the time period shown in Figure 14.1, annual default probability averaged 10%, but varied from year to year. For example, maybe in 1976 the default probability of credits in the portfolio was 22% and in 1986 it was 1%. In this case, high and low experienced default rates are caused by varying default probability, not positive default correlation. In any particular year, given that year's specific default probability, default correlation could be zero.

For another perspective on our inability to distinguish varying default probability from default correlation, consider our discussion at the outset of Chapter 13. We said that the variability in annual corporate default rates since 1920 was evidence of default correlation. Our implicit assumption was that the long-term average of the series, 1%, was the year-in and year-out annual default probability. Of course, we do not directly observe default probability, we only observe default results. But it seems logical that credit analysts in 1934 and 1952 would have had vastly different expectations of future defaults.

The assumption in calculating default correlation is that default probability is constant for each rating class. This turns out to be unsupportable. Varying default probability, a simple and plausible alternative explanation of fluctuating default rates, puts into question all our work deriving empirical default correlations in the previous part of this section. It puts into question all consideration of default correlation. We cannot be sure whether the variability in default rates from year to year or over longer periods is due to default correlation or changing default probability.

Pragmatic scrutiny of credit ratings and the credit rating process suggests to us instead that ratings are more *relative* than *absolute* measures of default probability and that default probabilities for different rating categories change year-to-year. It is a hard enough job to arrange credits in an industry in relative order of credit quality. It seems to us very difficult to assess credit quality against an absolute measure like default probability and then calibrate this measure across different industries. In fact, the rating agencies themselves say that ratings are relative measures of credit quality.[2]

If ratings are relative measures of credit quality, or if for any reason the probabilities of default for different rating categories change over time, this would mean that the historically derived default correlations presented in Table 14.1 are based on an inaccurate assumption and overstate true default correlation. But more importantly, default correlation is just not the right way to look at or think about experienced default rates.

Another perspective on the idea of varying default rates is shown in Figure 14.2. Here we have rearranged the annual default rates of the positively correlated series in Figure 14.1 so that the default rates are in strict order from lowest to highest. In the calculation of default

---

[2] Jerome Fons, Richard Cantor, and Christopher Mahoney, *Understanding Moody's Corporate Bond Ratings and Rating Process*, Moody's Investors Service, May 2002.

FIGURE 14.2 Time-Correlated Default Rates

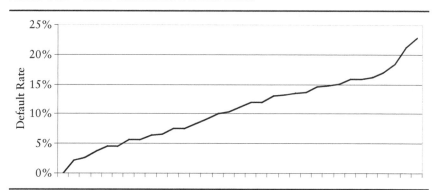

correlation, assuming a constant 10% annual default probability, the *order* of default rates does not make a difference. This series would still have default correlation of 0.04.

On average, it is true that the annual default rate is 10%. But looking at this time series, some simple rules to explain and predict default rates present themselves. First, "defaults this year will be what they were last year." Second, "defaults this year will be what they were last year *plus* the change in default rate between last year and the previous year." Yet our method of calculating default correlation would not pick up the "memory," or *time series correlation*, of default rates. This suggests another type of correlation, along the dimension of time, which also seems important to our understanding of defaults.

The indistinctiveness of default correlation and changing default probability will drive our conclusions as we assess different default correlation methodologies in the next section.

PROPOSED SOLUTIONS

Given the importance of default correlation in evaluating credit portfolios, it is not surprising that a lot of effort has been given to incorporating default correlation into the analysis of credit risky portfolios. The goal of various approaches is to create default probability distributions that accurately depict the effect of default correlation upon a credit portfolio. From the default distribution and assumptions about loss in the event of default, one can determine required economic capital against a credit portfolio or the credit risk of a portfolio.

The default correlation solutions we highlight in this chapter take very different approaches to the problem. We find no single approach completely satisfying, but certain solutions have strengths in certain applications. We present this survey of default correlation methodologies to help understand the comparative advantages and disadvantages of different methodologies and develop an appreciative, but skeptical, view to them all.

Single-Name and Industry Limits

The effect of default correlation is not a new discovery, despite the new technologies brought to bear on the challenge. Often, the issue of default correlation is discussed and expressed in terms of portfolio diversity. Banks and other fixed income investors have an incentive to create low default correlated, or diverse, portfolios. Investors want loss distributions that are more stable rather than distributions that experience wide swings. This is because the potential for large credit losses is lower in a less positively default-correlated portfolio. Ideally, a bank would prefer the stable default distribution of the extremely negatively default correlated portfolio (as we reviewed in Chapter 13). With that portfolio, future defaults and required capital are known with certainty.

One tool that has been used through the ages to manage default correlation and create less volatile default losses is *exposure limits* or *concentration limits*. In the previous chapter, we discussed industry-specific factors as a cause of defaults and default correlation and cited examples in the oil and thrift industries. The rationale behind industry exposure limits in credit portfolios is that credits within a particular industry are more default-correlated than credits in different industries. Besides industry limits, credit portfolios might have risk limits on obligors from specific countries.

Credit portfolios also have *single-name limits*. Technically, this has nothing to do with default correlation but with *portfolio diversity* or the "law of large numbers." Simply put, the more individual credits there are in the portfolio, the more likely it is that the port-

FIGURE 14.3 Illustration of Law of Large Numbers

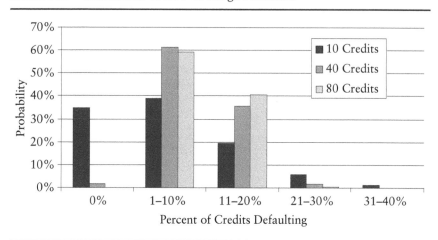

folio's actual credit results will equal the theoretical expectation.[3] Figure 14.3 shows the probability of defaults in three portfolios comprised of 10, 40, and 80 credits, respectively. We assume a 10% default probability for each credit in their respective portfolios and zero default correlation. Figure 14.3 shows the probability of 0% of the credits defaulting, as well as the probability of defaults in the ranges of 1% to 10%, 11% to 20%, 21% to 30%, and 31% to 40% of credits in the respective portfolios. In the 10-credit portfolio, the range of defaults is from 0% to 40% of credits in that portfolio. In the 40-credit portfolio, the range of portfolio defaults is from 0% to 30%. Finally, in the 80-credit portfolio, almost all probability is encompassed between 1% and 20% of the portfolio defaulting. This demonstrates that the more credits added to a portfolio, the more stable its potential outcomes become.

The problem with single-name and industry limits is that there is no way to determine optimum levels. Diversity is good, but how much is enough? This is a relevant question because diversity is not free. Single-name and industry limits require that more individual credits in more industries be included in the portfolio. The cost of reviewing and monitoring credits is expensive. Also, the search for a

---

[3] This is true as long as the portfolio does not have complete positive correlation, which is to say it is almost always true.

more diverse portfolio might lead to one that has lower credit quality, resulting in more defaults and greater default severity. Meanwhile, as more and more credits are added to the portfolio, the diversification benefit of adding still more credits diminishes (i.e., the benefit of going from 50 to 60 credits is far less than the benefit of going from 10 to 20). At some point, the cost of diversity exceeds the benefits of diversity. Also, the trade off between single-name, industry, and other limits is not quantified. Is it better to have relatively low single-name limits and relatively high industry limits or the opposite?

Rating agencies began to consider portfolio diversity explicitly when they rated collateralized debt obligations in the mid-1980s. Back then, the rating agencies controlled default correlation risk in CDO portfolios by setting strict limits on industry and single-name concentrations. The rating agencies simply refused to rate any CDO that did not comply with their standards. However, the rating agencies also did not give credit to a CDO for having additional industry or single-name diversity. The issue of the costs and benefits of industry and single-name limits took on more prominence as the CDO market grew in the late 1980s.

In 1989, Moody's struggled to handle default correlation and diversity in the rating of CDOs and developed some simple ad hoc rules.[4] To handle nondiversifiable default correlation due to general economic conditions, Moody's stressed historic default rates. For example, Moody's first corporate bond default study, also completed in 1989, had just calculated the historic 10-year B2 default rate to be 29.3%. However, when assessing B2 bonds in a CDO portfolio, the rating agency assumed a 37.9% 10-year default rate, reflecting the average historic default rate plus two standard deviations based on the historic volatility of the 10-year default rate.

To assess single-name and industry concentrations in a CDO portfolio, Moody's developed a single index measurement it christened *Diversity Score*. The measure explicitly quantified the trade-off between industry diversity and single-name diversity in CDO portfolios.

Moody's divided the economy into 32 industries. As shown in Table 14.2, the first name in any industry earned a CDO one diversity point, the next two in the same industry earned the CDO one-half a point

---

[4] Douglas Lucas, *Rating Cash Flow Transactions Backed by Corporate Debt*, Moody's Investors Service, September 1989.

TABLE 14.2 Moody's Diversity Score Calculation

Number of Credits in Same Industry	Diversity Points
1	1.0
2	1.5
3	2.0
4	2.33
5	2.67
6	3.0
7	3.25
8	3.50
9	3.75
10	4.0
11	4.2
12	4.4
13	4.6
14	4.8
15	5.0

each, the next three one-third a point each, the next four one-fourth a point each, and finally the next five after that, one-fifth a diversity point each. The CDO's Diversity Score was the sum of all the points accumulated in each of the industries represented in the CDO portfolio. So, if a CDO had three credits in each of 10 industries, by Table 14.2 the CDO earned 2.0 diversity points in each of the 10 industries for a Diversity Score of 20. Another ad hoc formulaic adjustment was made to adjust for uneven par amounts in the CDO portfolio.

The idea behind the Diversity Score was that a large number of default-correlated credits behave like a smaller number of uncorrelated credits. In modeling the default distribution of a CDO collateral portfolio, a portfolio with 80 correlated credits with a Diversity Score of 40 would be evaluated as if it contained only 40 uncorrelated credits. Intuitively, this is the same as saying that credits in the portfolio always default in pairs. Instead of the relatively narrow default distribution of the 80-credit portfolio, the CDO collateral portfolio would be considered to have the wider default distribution of the 40-credit portfolio in that table. The wider distribution of defaults would require the CDO to have more credit enhancement to issue its debts, all other things being equal.

Moody's Diversity Score became an obligatory concept in CDOs because it was part of Moody's CDO rating methodology. However, the Diversity Score also obtained recognition outside the area of CDOs when applied to other credit risk portfolios. Its appeal was that it explicitly quantified trade-offs between default correlation caused by the general economy, default correlation caused by industry factors, and the effects of single-name diversity. But while these trade-offs were explicitly quantified, they lacked any theoretical or empirical justification. Their appropriateness relied on an intuitive grasp of very unintuitive questions—for example, is a portfolio of 30 names in 30 industries as diversified as a portfolio of 60 names in 10 industries? Should CDOs of these portfolios be required to have the same credit enhancement, all other things being equal? For these reasons, some quantification of default correlation was required.

Credit Suisse's Changing Default Probability Model

Analysts at Credit Suisse made good use of the insight discussed early in this chapter regarding empirical default correlations and the associated problems with its estimation that there is no objective distinction between changing default probability and default correlation. Their method of incorporating default correlation into credit modeling was to change default probabilities and assume zero default correlation.[5] An illustration will help make their approach clearer.

Let us assume we have a 10-credit portfolio comprised of high risk loans that we believe have a 10% annual probability of default. Our belief in the loan's default probability springs from the fact that over the last 20 years, loans like these have defaulted at an average annual rate of 10%. However, it turns out that there is great variability in their annual default rate, as shown in Figure 14.4.

As we state, we do not know whether volatility of annual default rates stems from default correlation or from changes in default probability from one year to the next. The Credit Suisse approach assumes

---

[5] The widely distributed and annotated approach was first documented in Tom Wilde, *CreditRisk+: A Credit Risk Management Framework*, Credit Suisse First Boston, 1997, available at www.csfb.com/creditrisk/.

FIGURE 14.4 Hypothetical Annual Default Rates of High-Risk Loans

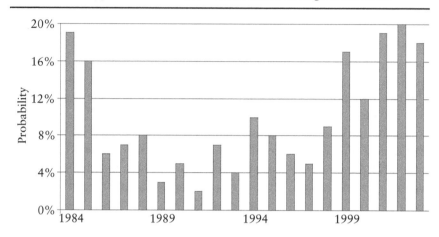

Source: Douglas Lucas, *Rating Cash Flow Transactions Backed by Corporate Debt*, Moody's Investors Service, September 1989.

that each annual default rate reflects that year's default probability for these types of loans. Given that assumption, what are the "probabilities of annual loan default probabilities?" Figure 14.5 reassembles the default rates of Figure 14.4 into a graph showing the historic likelihood of any specific annual default rate. For example, as shown in Figure 14.5, there is a 5% chance of a 2% default probability, a 5% chance of a 3% default probability, and so on.

We would like to determine the default probability distribution of a 10-credit loan portfolio. From year to year, we believe the default probability of these credits ranges from 2% to 20%. When the probability of default is 2%, the probability of different numbers of loan defaults is as shown in Figure 14.6. The default probability distribution in the exhibit is the result of the 2% default probability, 10 credits in the portfolio, and the assumption of zero default correlation among the credits. As we pointed out in discussing Figure 14.3, if there were more credits in the portfolio, the distribution would be tighter. In contrast to the assumption in Figure 14.6, Figure 14.7 shows the default probability distribution given that annual loan default probability is 20%. Naturally, the probability of more defaults in the 10-credit loan portfolio is higher.

FIGURE 14.5 Historic Probability of Annual Default Rates

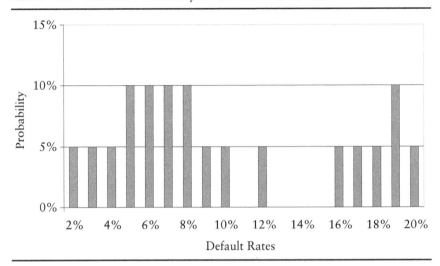

FIGURE 14.6 Historic Probability of Annual Default Rates

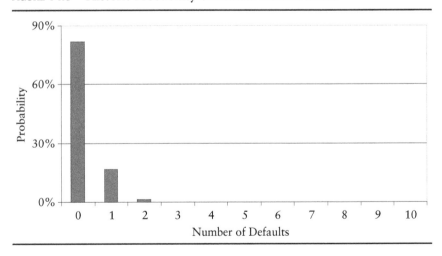

Given that annual default probability is distributed as shown in Figure 14.5, what is the default probability distribution allowing annual default probability to vary? This is shown in Figure 14.8. For comparison, we show the default probability distribution assuming a constant 10% annual default rate. Varying default probability cre-

FIGURE 14.7   Defaults Given 20% Default Probability

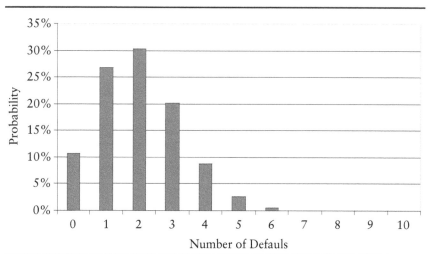

FIGURE 14.8   Static vs. Varying Default Probability

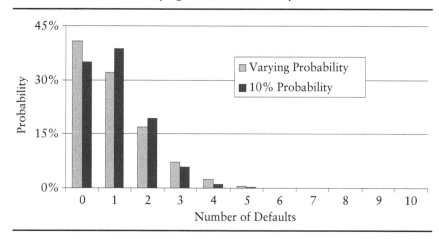

ates a wider default distribution than assuming a static 10% default probability. This is exactly what we said was the effect of default correlation.

The analysts at Credit Suisse confronted the problem of default probability and default correlation in a unique manner. They avoided altogether the calculation problems associated with default correlation. However, their method is best suited for credits of homogenous quality where a long default history of similar credits is available. The method is ill suited to heterogeneous credits or credits where a long history of default behavior is not available. Likewise, it does not differentiate between individual credits in a portfolio. All credits in the portfolio are assumed to have the same probability of default and the same default correlation with other credits. To take into account a portfolio comprised of debt with different default probabilities and different default correlations, another approach is necessary.

Merton-KMV Default Probability Model

To explain the Merton-KMV approach to estimating default probability, consider the following three quantities:

1. The market value of the firm
2. The volatility of the market value of the firm
3. The liabilities of the firm

A firm is insolvent when its market value is less than its liabilities. Creditors will refuse to refinance its debt or advance working capital, the company will run out of cash, and it will default. A credit is less apt to experience this dire scenario (1) the greater its market value, (2) the less volatile its market value, and (3) the smaller its liabilities.

Implementing Robert Merton's theoretical framework,[6] the partners of KMV (now Moody's KMV) developed a model that estimates the default probabilities of corporate credits. In essence, the model employs the following formula:

$$\frac{\text{Market value of the firm} - \text{Liabilities of the firm}}{\text{Volatility of the market value of the firm}}$$

In this formula, the numerator is the difference in the market value of the firm and the amount of the firm's liabilities. Dividing this dollar amount by the volatility (i.e., standard deviation) of market value standardizes the formula into a number that is comparable between firms. Assuming normal distributions, the probability of one credit

---

[6] Robert C. Merton, "On the Pricing of Corporate Debt: The Risk Structure of Interest Rates," *Journal of Finance* 29, no. 2 (1974): 449–470.

experiencing a two standard deviation decline in market value is the same as any other credit experiencing a two standard deviation decline in market value.

There are a myriad of practical obstacles to building this model to estimate relative default probability. For example, how does one quantify the three variables? How does one take into account that not only must the firm be technically insolvent, there must also be a *default trigger*, such as the need to refinance debt or the need for working capital, to precipitate an actual default? KMV made pragmatic decisions to increase the model's ability to rank the relative default probability of credits. For example, KMV research found that weighting long-term debt less than short-term debt in the calculation of a firm's liabilities increased the predictive accuracy of the model. It was also found that the size of the firm affected the probability of default (larger firms default less often) and chose to include this variable as an adjustment to the volatility of the firm's market value. KMV made other adjustments to calibrate modeled default probabilities to historical default rates. In the end, the practical implementation of the theoretical model lost some of the latter's mechanistic and objective beauty, but produced useful means of assessing relative credit quality.

A bonus of KMV's default prediction model is its insight into default correlation.[7] Recall that the default of a firm occurs when its market value sinks below the level of its liabilities. (The firm's liabilities are assumed to remain static in the model.) If one can correlate the volatility of one firm's market value to the volatility of another firm's market value, one discovers something about their default correlation.

For example, suppose the market value of Credit A and Credit B always move in the same direction; that is, both firms' market values increase or both firms' market values decrease. This means that as the market value of the two firms change, those market values either both fall closer to the level of each firm's liabilities or both rise above the level of each firm's liabilities. If the relationship between the market value of the two firms is understood, one can calculate the prob-

---

[7] Peter Crosbie and Jeffrey Bohn, *Modeling Default Risk*, Moody's KMV, 2002.

ability that the market values of both firms will decline below the level of their liabilities causing both credits to default.

This approach to default correlation has several wonderful properties. First, since a firm's market value is a continuous variable, it does not have all the problems referred to in the previous change of handling the binomial default variable. Just as for stock returns, pairwise correlations of firm market values are sufficient to calculate a portfolio's default distribution.

When market values are simulated, the KMV model keeps track of individual credits and when defaults occur. The default results of multiple simulations of firm market value can be used to create a default probability distribution. Finally, the KMV model is credit specific. Individual credits can have different default probabilities and pairwise market value correlations can be specific to each pair of credits in the portfolio.

The KMV approach to default correlation is so entrenched that when most practitioners speak of "default correlation" they are really referring to "market value correlation." But the relationship between the two is not straightforward. As Figure 14.9 shows, default correlation (on the vertical axis of the exhibit) is a function of both market value correlation and the individual default probabilities of the two firms. At any default probability, however, a particular market value

FIGURE 14.9 Asset Correlations vs. Default Correlations

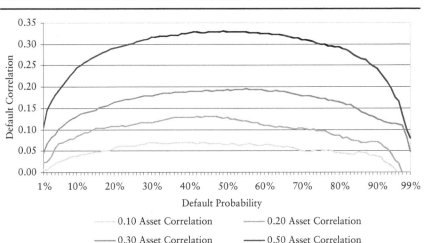

correlation produces a much smaller default correlation between the two credits. Given any particular market value correlation, default correlation is highest at 50% individual credit default probability and lowest at 1% or 99% individual credit default probability.

Of all the variables in the KMV Merton default model, the most critical in arriving at default probability distributions is the correlation of potential market values of firms.

Modeling Firm Market Values

There are at least three methods of predicting a firm's market value volatility and the correlation of one firm's market value to another's. KMV's first method, since discarded, used an econometric model of firm value. Each firm's market value was modeled as a unique function of 18 or so economic and financial variables, including gross disposable product (GDP), the level of interest rates, and industry health factors. The steps in determining correlated defaults were to:

1. Simulate a fluctuation in the econometric variables.
2. Calculate a new market value for each of the firms from the values of the econometric variables.
3. Determine which credits' market values had declined below their liabilities and thus defaulted.
4. Repeat many times to form a default probability distribution.

The problem with this approach was that it depended on how well the econometric model captured firms' potential market value changes. The variables in the econometric model itself limited how credits could be market value- and thus default-correlated. With 18 econometric variables, there are only 18 ways credits can be correlated. Surprising connections between credits cannot be captured in such a model.

For whatever reasons, KMV abandoned the econometric method and moved to a model of future firm market values that depends on *historic* relationships. KMV now simply looks at the correlation of two firms' *past* market values (which it determines as part of its default probability modeling) to predict a joint distribution of the two firm's *future* market values. This raises the question of whether these market values, which are optimized to help produce good default probability estimates in a statistical model, are also good at estimating default correlation. Competitors of KMV have argued that historic equity price correlations, which are much easier to obtain, are just as good as historic market value correlations in predicting future firm market value correlations. Equity price correlations are certainly more available.

But the larger question is whether the past relationship of the market value of two firms (as calculated by KMV) or equity prices of two firm, is so indicative of their future relationship that default correlations can be determined. It seems to us that the relationship between two firms' market values is unstable and might completely change in the future, especially if one or both of them become more at risk to default.

Judging Default Correlation Methodologies

Ultimately, there is no objective way to measure the goodness of a default correlation model. First, when comparing the model's estimated default probability distribution to actual default results, we never know whether the model is wrong or whether the actual result is wrong. By a "wrong" actual result, we mean an atypical result from nature (i.e., a 100-year flood or six-sigma event).

Second, if we could determine that a default probability distribution is wrong, we can never be sure why. The distribution could be off because either the default correlations or default probabilities were wrong. We covered the inability to separate the two factors earlier in this chapter. Without the ability to objectively measure the performance of default correlation models, one has to rely on an intuitive view of their reasonableness.

Moody's Diversity Score is a good way to express and enforce diversity requirements upon a CDO manager. It is convenient to have a single measurement that trades off industry diversity and single-name diversity. Our view is that the formula overrewards industry diversity relative to single-name diversity. We would rather have a portfolio of 10 firms in the same industry rather than four firms in four different industries. Moody's Diversity Score would rank these portfolios as equally diverse.

That raises the question of whether one needs default correlation modeling to compare diversified credit portfolios. Take two portfolios, each comprised of 50 or more credits pretty evenly dispersed among 15 industries. Given this diversity, how likely is it that one portfolio is much more default correlated than another? Or, if a correlation methodology suggests that one portfolio is more default correlated than another, how likely is it that analysis is correct? In comparing two diversified portfolios, we do not think it can be persuasively argued that one portfolio is better than the other because of its default correlation.

Yet, to analyze the risk of a credit portfolio, we see value in simulating default rates via the approach by Credit Suisse and creating a default probability distribution. To be most appropriate to the approach by Credit Suisse, credits in a portfolio must be homogenous, we must not be interested in tracking which individual credits default, and we must have a long default history of similar credits. Many credit portfolios generally fulfill these requirements.

On a theoretical level, we have a great deal of sympathy for the view that historical default rate fluctuations are caused by fluctuations in default probabilities rather than the workings of default correlation. Our view of rating agency ratings, internal bank rating systems, and statistical models of default probability is that they are all better indicators of *relative* default probability than *absolute* default probability. The theory behind the approach by Credit Suisse is in harmony with our experience.

We also think the approach by Credit Suisse is easy to grasp. For example, the difference between assuming that annual default probability is always 10% versus assuming that annual default probability varies according to a distribution like the one in Figure 14.5 is intuitive. One can look at various versions of that exhibit with narrower or wider distributions and easily understand what is being assumed about the volatility of default probability.

Finally, in preferring the approach by Credit Suisse over the KMV approach, we note that the efficacy of the approach could be improved by certain empirical studies. We now have a long time series of annual default rates by rating thanks to the rating agencies' default studies. We also have models that predict the *absolute* level of future default rates for speculative grade bonds and loans.[8] We also know that credits can be grouped into more harmonious credit risk buckets by looking not only at their current rating, but also at their past ratings history, their rating outlook status, and their yield relative to that of other similarly rated credits. Why could empirical studies not be conducted to determine historical default by *all* these default-predicting variables? Another avenue of study, helpful to this analysis, would be how default rates vary from one year to another and how one year's default rate is affected by the previous year's default rate. In other words, one should look at the time series autoregressive correlation of default rates.

If an analyst is faced with a heterogeneous portfolio or needs to keep track of which credits default or when they default, he has to consider the KMV approach. The approach is appropriate when looking at *n*th to default swaps and other basket swaps with a relatively small number of underlyings.

However, in recommending the KMV approach for this application, we are skeptical about using historic market values or historic equity prices to make fine distinctions in the relationships of particular credits. The volatility of these variables is itself volatile from measurement period to measurement period. Using historic asset or equity data at the firm or even the industry level may create distinctions that are not stable or predictive. And the number of correlation estimates that must be made, one for every pair of credits in the portfolio, increases the chances for errors to affect the predictive ability of the model.

People who see the Merton model of default as immutably true tend to go along with its extension into default correlation. People who see the KMV implementation of the Merton model as a statistically fitted model that provides insight into relative default probability are more skeptical. We are in the later camp.

SUMMARY

In this chapter, we explained the calculation and results of historic default correlation. We showed that default correlations among well-

---

[8] For example, Moody's prediction of speculative grade bond defaults and S&P LCD's prediction of speculative-grade loan defaults.

diversified portfolios vary by the ratings of the credits and also by the time period over which defaults are examined. We described two major problems in measuring default correlation and, therefore, implementing a default correlation solution: (1) There is no way to distinguish changing default probability from default correlation; and (2) the way default correlation is commonly looked at ignores time series correlation of default probability. We feel that these problems in applying default correlation to actual portfolios have not been adequately explored.

We discussed the various ways analysts have attempted to incorporate default correlation into their analysis of credit risky portfolios:

- The antiquated method of industry and single-name exposure limits.
- Moody's ad hoc method of assessing the trade-off between industry and single-name diversity in their Diversity Score.
- The changing default probability approach of Credit Suisse.
- The historical market value approach of KMV.

In comparing well-diversified portfolios, we wondered whether any default correlation modeling is necessary. Given a certain level of single-name and industry diversity, we doubt that typical portfolios have very different default correlations and we are skeptical of any measurement showing that they do. However, we saw value in creating default probability distributions. We appreciated the Credit Suisse method that focuses on observable default rates and were skeptical of making credit-by-credit distinctions in default correlation based on estimates of historical firm market value.

Index